Counseling
American Minorities

Donald R. Atkinson
University of California-Santa Barbara

George Morten
University of California-Santa Barbara

Derald Wing Sue
California State University-Hayward

Counseling American Minorities
A Cross-Cultural Perspective

wcb
Wm. C. Brown Company Publishers
Dubuque, Iowa

Contents

Preface

Counseling American Minorities: A Cross-Cultural Perspective is a text devoted to helping counselors and mental health practitioners maximize their effectiveness when working with a culturally diverse population. A major thesis of this book is that counselors can establish the necessary and sufficient conditions of a counseling relationship with clients who are culturally different. While similarity in race, ethnicity, and culture may be highly correlated with counseling success, we believe that other attributes (ability to share a similar world view, appropriate use of counseling strategies, awareness of own values, etc.) may be equally important factors in cross-cultural counseling.

The purposes of this book are twofold. First, as a collection of readings, it is intended to sensitize counselors (minority as well as non-minority) to the life experiences of culturally distinct populations. Minority observers have strongly criticized the counseling profession for its lack of attention to the unique needs and experiences of minority individuals. We hope this text can serve as a first step in sensitizing counselors to these needs and experiences. While direct exposure to the environment of the clientele population is perhaps best, reading relevant materials written by and about minority individuals is at least a starting point.

A second major purpose of the book is to examine the traditional counseling role, which has been heavily criticized by minority authors, and for the future to suggest new directions for the counseling profession when dealing with minorities. By combining the present empirical, theoretical, and conceptual work on counseling minorities, it is our purpose to offer direction for future counseling practice, counselor education, and counseling research.

The text is divided into six major sections. Parts 1 and 6 are devoted to counseling issues which cut across racial, ethnic and cultural lines. For example, the introductory chapter in Part 1 seeks to clarify concepts and terms related to minority group/cross-cultural counseling that have been a constant source of confusion in our field. The second chapter is a broad overview of the unfulfilled promise of counseling for minorities. The major criticisms leveled at counseling by minority group members and the major barriers to the traditional counseling process are discussed in this chapter. In Part 6, a Minority Identity Development model is proposed. Alternatives to the traditional counseling role are discussed for counselors who work with minority clients, and recommendations for training minority group/cross-cultural counselors, are summarized. The book concludes by pointing out the need to develop a body of research related to this area, with special attention to investigation which inquires how counselor credibility can be enhanced in cross-cultural situations.

Parts 2-5 include articles about four racial/ethnic minorities in the United States. Blacks, Latinos and Asian Americans were selected for inclusion since they represent numerically large racial/ethnic minorities in this country. Native Americans are included since they are, in many ways, the most oppressed of all minority groups. Furthermore, any book that purports to discuss American minorities would be remiss if it did not include the first Americans, a group which oppression has almost made extinct.

It is the editors' opinion that many of the concepts presented in Parts 1 and 6 of this book are applicable to other minority groups, including non-racial/ethnic minorities; it is only due to limitations of time, space, and our own sense of priorities that these groups are not included in this volume. Women and homosexuals, for example, are two other numerically large categories of persons who experience considerable physical, social, and economic oppression; the reader will find reference to these groups throughout Parts 1 and 6.

Less widely acknowledged is the minority status of groups like the handicapped, the aged, religious denominations, and others. A great deal has been written about the handicapped; indeed, an entire field of counseling has evolved which is devoted to fulfilling the psychological needs of this group. Little has been written, however, concerning the thesis that handicapped people are a minority *because they are oppressed;* rather, the accepted view is that they are a minority because they are an identifiable group and represent a numerical minority. The elderly represent a minority class whom we will all join sooner or later, barring premature death; in the past counseling has tended to ignore this group. Mandatory retirement, spiraling inflation, social ostracization, and numerous other forces all militate against the aged, rendering them in many ways the most powerless of all minorities. It is evident that the oppression of the aged in the United States has not received the attention it merits. Prison populations have their own unique vocabulary and well defined culture; they too constitute a minority group. Drug users, also, have an identifiable culture of which many counselors, even drug counselors, are quite ignorant. Religious groups like the Jews, Mormons, Amish, Hutterites and others are minorities about whom the average counselor knows little except what he or she learned from the pages of a high school history book. Certainly the economically disadvantaged (referred to by some writers as the "underclass"), a group encompassing other minority categories, constitute a minority group of their own.

The reader, we are sure, can think of other minorities that deserve attention in the counseling literature. We readily admit that the inclusion or exclusion of certain groups is almost indefensible. Our decisions reflect our own priorities and judgments. Nonetheless, we hope the reader will find many of the concepts presented in this book useful when working with any minority client. We also hope additional writing on minority groups not included in this book will be forthcoming.

Whenever possible, each of the sections includes at least one article written from a historical-social perspective and one article offering suggestions for counselors working with that particular minority. Also, whenever possible, discussions are included that were written by members of the minority group in question rather than by an outside observer.

This book of readings originated because each of us saw the need for a book in the counseling field that would treat a broad range of minority groups in a single volume. The books available on counseling minorities are, for the most part, limited in perspective to the problems of a single category. A few of these texts have demonstrated or at least implied that other minority groups experience similar concerns in an oppressive society. Although this approach has proven somewhat valuable, it runs the risk of glossing over minority differences. This book is designed to foster direct comparison and contrast of various racial/ethnic minority group experiences and concerns that may be similar or dissimilar.

We believe that a text with this approach and orientation will make a useful contribution to the profession. As a book of readings, it can be used to supplement other courses in this field: counseling techniques, theories of counseling, the counselor and urban problems, community counseling, changing roles of the counselor, outreach counseling, individual and group analysis. Its primary use, however, is likely to be in undergraduate and graduate courses designed specifically to facilitate understanding the minority experience as it relates to such objectives as counseling minority youth, cross-cultural counseling, multicultural counseling. To this end, it can serve as the principal text for such courses.

Parts 2 through 6 conclude with a number of hypothetical cases which require the reader to assume he or she is interacting with a minority client. Each case is followed by several questions designed to induce the reader to examine his/her own biases and stereotypes, and to explore potential obstacles to minority group/cross-cultural counseling. The most effective use of these cases and questions will probably occur when they serve to stimulate group discussion, preferably in settings where a number of racial/ethnic groups are represented.

We trust that this text, which places so much information at the counselor's fingertips, will serve as an important training tool in counselor education programs across the country. It is our belief that the sensitivities and skills prerequisite to effective counseling with culturally different clients can be acquired by individuals who are willing to discard preconceived biases and to learn from their clients. We are aware that some may challenge this assumption and others may vehemently disagree with it. Yet, as three culturally distinct individuals, our professional and personal experiences lead us to this conclusion.

D.R.A.
G.M.
D.W.S.

Part 1 Why a Cross-Cultural Perspective?

1 Introduction
Defining Terms

The late 1960's and early 1970's witnessed a sudden increase in the number of articles that related to minority group counseling appearing in the professional counseling literature. A number of these studies identified such diverse groups as the aged, Asian Americans, Blacks, Chicanos, drug users, gays, the handicapped, Native Americans, prison inmates, students, and women as minority groups; this led to some question about what the term *minority* means. To add to the confusion, a number of terms are often used interchangeably with *minority* and/or with each other when their applicability is questionable. Writers, researchers and practitioners have frequently failed to clearly distinguish between such important concepts as race, ethnic group, culture, and minority. The rhetoric and emotionalism surrounding the field of counseling minorities have distorted communications sufficiently without added confusion arising from undefined terms. Since counseling effectiveness relies so heavily on accurate and appropriate communication, especially in working with a culturally diverse client, it seems imperative that counselors clarify the meaning of these words. The following discussion is offered to define and elucidate certain basic terms and concepts related to minority group/cross-cultural counseling.

Race, Ethnicity and Culture

Two terms that are often used interchangeably in the counseling literature are race and ethnicity. According to the *Oxford Dictionary of Words,* the term "race" first appeared in the English language less than three hundred years ago. Yet in that brief time race has come to be one of the most misused and misunderstood terms in the American vernacular (Rose, 1964).

The term race, as it is most frequently used today, borrows much of its meaning from a biological conception. As such, race refers to a system by which both plants and animals are classified into sub-categories according to specific physical and structural characteristics. As it pertains to the human group, Krogman (1945) defines race as "...a sub-group of peoples possessing a definite combination of physical characters, of genetic origin, the combination of which to varying degrees distinguishes the sub-group from other sub-groups of mankind" (p. 49). Physical differences involving skin pigmentation, head form, facial features, stature, and the color distribution and texture of body hair, are among the most commonly recognized factors distinguishing races of people. But, as Anderson (1971) points out, this system is far from ideal, in that not all racial group members fit these criteria precisely. While we commonly recognize three basic racial types—Caucasoid, Mongoloid and Negroid—a great deal of overlapping occurs among these groups. In fact, when we look beneath the superficial characteristics, we find there are more similarities between groups than differences (owing to the fact that all humanoids originate from a single specie), and more differences within racial groups than between them. The apparent flexibility of this definition poses little difficulty for biologists, whose major intent is to create a schema for showing genetic relationships. Unfortunately, this same level of functional clarity is not shared by the social sciences.

Most of the confusion surrounding the term race occurs when it is used in social context. As Mack (1968) so adequately points out, race in the biological sense has no biological consequences, but what people *believe* about race has very profound social consequences. Through subtle yet effective socializing influences, group members are taught and come to accept as "social fact" a myriad of myths and stereotypes regarding skin color, stature, facial features and so forth. Thus, as Mack (1968) contends, "most of men's discussions about race are discussions about their beliefs, not about biological fact" (p. 103).

Ethnicity, on the other hand, refers to a group classification in which the members share a unique social and cultural heritage passed on from one generation to the next (Rose, 1964). Ethnicity is often erroneously assumed to have a biological or genetic foundation. For instance, Jews, as well as numerous other groups, are frequently identified as a racially distinct group. But, as Thompson and Hughes (1958) point out:

> . . .(Jews). . . .are not a biological race because the people known as Jews are not enough like each other and are too much like other people to be distinguished from them. But as people act with reference to Jews and to some extent connect the attitudes they have about them with real and imagined biological characteristics, they become a socially supposed race (p. 67).

If one accepts the view that ethnicity is the result of shared social and cultural heritage, it is apparent that Jews are an ethnic group. Hence, ethnic differences often involve differences in customs, language, religion and other cultural factors; racial differences may or may not be germane to ethnic differences.

Finally, there is common confusion over the relationship of the term "culture" with race and ethnicity. Moore (1974) hits at the heart of the confusion:

> Sometimes we tend to confuse race and ethnic groups with culture. Great races do have different cultures. Ethnic groups within races differ in cultural content. But, people of the same racial origin and of the same ethnic groups differ in their cultural matrices. All browns, or blacks, or whites, or yellows, or reds are not alike in the cultures in which they live and have their being. The understanding

of the culture of another, or of groups other than our own, demands a knowledge of varied elements within a culture or the variety of culture components within a larger cultural matrix (p. 41).

Numerous definitions of culture have been offered by anthropologists over the years, including Kroeber and Kluckhohn's (1952) attempt to synthesize many of them:

> Culture consists of patterns, explicit and implicit, of and for behavior acquired and transmitted by symbols, constituting the distinctive achievement of human groups, including their embodiments in artifacts; the essential core of culture consists of traditional (i.e., historically derived and selected) ideas and especially their attached values; culture systems may, on the other hand, be considered as products of action, on the other as conditioning elements of further action (p. 181).

Needless to say, the myriad of confusing definitions that Kroeber and Kluckhohn set out to eliminate was only augmented by their earnest efforts. The most succinct and useful definition, for our purposes, is that offered by Linton (1945), who sees culture as, "...the configuration of learned behavior and results of behavior whose components and elements are shared and transmitted by the members of a particular society" (p. 32). By virtue of this definition of culture and those concepts of race and ethnicity accepted earlier, it is clear that the various ethnic groups within racial and among racial categories have their own unique cultures. It should also be clear that even within ethnic groups, small groups of individuals may develop behavior patterns they share and transmit, which in essence constitute a form of culture.

Before leaving this discussion of culture, it is important to dismiss two terms that have been widely used in the past to describe minority groups: "culturally deprived" and "culturally disadvantaged." The term "culturally deprived" implies the absence of culture, a (perhaps hypothetical) situation which has no relationship to the groups addressed in this book. Notwithstanding the effects of the larger society's culture on minorities through the mass media, minority groups clearly possess and transmit a culture of their own.

The term "culturally disadvantaged" suggests the person to whom it is applied is at a disadvantage because she/he lacks the cultural background formed by the controlling social structure. The use of "disadvantaged" rather than "deprived" is intended to recognize that the individual possesses a cultural heritage, but also suggests it is not the *right* culture. While less noxious than "culturally deprived," "culturally disadvantaged" still implies a cultural deficiency, whereas the real issue is one of ethnocentrism, with the values of the majority culture viewed as more important than those of minority cultures. A person may be economically disadvantaged because he/she has less money than the average person, or educationally disadvantaged due to inferior formal education. We seriously object, however, to any inference that minority peoples have less culture.

Even the currently popular terms "culturally different" and "culturally distinct" can carry negative connotation when they are used to imply that a minority person's culture is at variance (out-of-step) with the dominant (accepted) culture. The inappropriate application of these two terms occurs in counseling when their usage is restricted to minority clients. Taken literally, it is grammatically and conceptually correct to refer to a majority client as "culturally different" or "culturally distinct" from the counselor if the counselor is a minority individual.

Minority and the Third World

The term *minority* is frequently used in counseling literature to refer to racial/ethnic minorities or the non-white populations. Other authors have defined minority groups as physically or behaviorally identifiable groups that make up less than 50 percent of the United States population. Included in this definition are racial/ethnic minorities, the aged, the poor, "gay" people and others of a non-straight sexual orientation, handicapped persons, drug users, and prison populations.

In common usage, however, numerical size alone does not determine minority status. Over 80 percent of the population of South Africa is nonwhite, yet this group is frequently referred to as a minority by individuals within and outside South Africa (Rose, 1964). In such cases, the term *minority* is used to imply political, economic, or some other form of oppression. A definition of minority preferred by the present authors and employed in this book has been offered by Wirth (1945) who defines minority as:

> . . .a group of people who, because of physical or cultural characteristics, are singled out from the others in society in which they live for differential and unequal treatment, and who therefore regard themselves as objects of collective discrimination (p. 347).

Since we have already established culture as characterized by shared and transmitted behavior, this definition allows us to accept all those groups included in the racial/ethnic and numerical definitions, plus other groups that are oppressed by society *primarily because of their group membership* as minorities. Most importantly, this definition allows us to include women as minorities, a group of oppressed individuals who constitute a numerical majority in this country.

Another term that is frequently used interchangeably with the word "minority" is "Third World." The term Third World is of French derivation (*tiers monde*), which enjoys international acceptance to describe the non-industrialized nations of the world that are neither Western nor Communist (Miller, 1967). Many of these countries are located in Africa, South America, and Asia, primarily non-white portions of the world. In the

United States, non-white individuals are frequently referred to as Third World persons. The term has certain political connotations, however, and to some degree has been used as a symbol of comradeship among all oppressed people. The misuse of the term occurs when it is used in this broader sense to apply to all oppressed people, since oppressed people live in First World (Capitalist societies), Second World (Socialist societies), and Third World nations, and are not necessarily distinguished by skin color.

Minority Group/Cross-Cultural Counseling

Minority group counseling, then, can be defined as any counseling relationship in which the client is a member of a minority group, regardless of the status of the counselor (who may be a member of the same minority group, a different minority group, or the majority group). To date much of the writing on minority group counseling has dealt exclusively with racial minorities and has examined the majority counselor-minority client relationship to the exclusion of other possibilities. This limited view of minority group counseling has fallen into some disfavor, perhaps because it ignores the special conditions of a counseling relationship in which the counselor is also a minority person. Further, there is concern that the term minority group counseling suggests a minority pathology; this is perceived as analogous to ''Black pathology,'' an attempt to explain Black behavior in terms of White norms.

Cross-cultural counseling, by way of contrast, refers to any counseling relationship in which two or more of the participants are culturally different. This definition of cross-cultural counseling includes situations in which both the counselor and client(s) are minority individuals but represent different racial/ethnic groups (Black-Chicano, Asian American-Native American, Puerto Rican-Black and so forth). It also includes the situation in which the counselor is a racial/ethnic minority person and the client is White (Black counselor-White client, Chicano counselor-White client, etc.). Additionally it includes the circumstance in which the counselor and client(s) are racially and ethnically similar but belong to different cultural groups because of other variables such as sex, sexual orientation, socioeconomic factors, and age (White male-White female, Black straight person-Black ''gay'', poor Asian American-wealthy Asian American).

This book is primarily concerned with counseling situations in which the client is a minority group member and culturally different than the counselor. Although the readings selected for inclusion in this volume relate specifically to racial/ethnic (Third World) minorities, the contributions here included are believed to be applicable to all oppressed people. Since the intention is to include counseling relationships defined as minority group counseling *and* cross-cultural counseling, the editors have elected to identify this focus as *minority group/cross-cultural counseling.*

References

Anderson, C.H. *Toward a new sociology: A critical view*. Homewood, Ill.: The Dorsey Press, 1971.

Kroeber, A.L., & Kluckhohn, C. *Culture: A critical review of concepts and definitions*. New York: Vintage Books, 1952.

Krogman, W.M. The concept of race. In R. Linton's (Ed.) *The science of man in world crisis*. New York: Columbia University Press, 1945, 38-62.

Linton, R. *The cultural background of personality*. New York: Appleton-Century Co., 1945.

Mack, R.W. *Race, Class, & Power*. New York: American Book Co., 1968.

Miller, J.D.B. *The politics of the third world*. London: Oxford University Press, 1967.

Moore, B.M. Cultural differences and counseling perspectives. *Texas Personnel and Guidance Association Journal*, 1974, *3*, 39-44.

Rose, P.I. *They and we: Racial and ethnic relations in the United States*. New York: Random House, 1964.

Thompson, E.T., & Hughes, E.C. Race: *Individual and collective behavior*. Glencoe, Ill.: Free Press, 1958.

Wirth, L. The problem of minority groups. In R. Linton (Ed.) *The science of man in the world crisis*. New York: Columbia University Press, 1945.

2 Minority Group Counseling
An Overview

Until the mid 1960's, the counseling profession demonstrated little interest in or concern for the status of racial, ethnic, or other minority groups. Counseling and Guidance, with its traditional focus on the needs of the "average" student, tended to overlook the special needs of students who, by virtue of their skin color, physical characteristics, socioeconomic status, etc., found themselves disadvantaged in a world designed for White, middle class, physically able, "straight" people. Psychotherapy, with its development and practice limited primarily to middle and upper class individuals, also overlooked the needs of minority populations. By the late 1960's, however, "The winds of the American Revolution II...(were)...howling to be heard" (Lewis, Lewis & Dworkin, 1971, p. 689). And as Aubrey (1977) points out, the view that counseling and guidance dealt with the normal developmental concerns of individuals to the exclusion of special groups' concerns could no longer be accepted.

> Events in the 1960's, however, would blur this simple dichotomy by suddenly expanding potential guidance and counseling audiences to include minority groups, dissenters to the war in Viet Nam, alienated hippie and youth movements, experimenters and advocates of the drug culture, disenchanted students in high schools and universities, victims of urban and rural poverty and disenfranchised women (p. 293).

The forces that led to this voluminous, and often emotional, outcry in the professional counseling literature go far beyond the condition of social unrest existing in the United States in the late 1960's early 1970's. The note of dissatisfaction was struck when the guidance movement first began and accepted, intentionally or unintentionally, the practically unfulfilled, idealistic promises of the Declaration of Independence as a guideline (Byrne, 1977). As Shertzer and Stone (1974) suggest, "The pervasive concept of individualism, the lack of rigid class lines, the incentive to exercise one's talents to the best of one's ability may have provided a philosophical base..." (p. 22) for the dramatic shift in emphasis the profession took almost 60 years after its inception. Fuel for the fire was added when the Civil Rights movement of the 1950's provided convincing evidence that the educational establishment had failed to make provision for equal educational opportunity to all and that the time had come to correct existing discrepancies. The fire of discontent was fanned into a bright flame as the political activism associated with the Viet Nam war touched almost all phases of American life.

Yet the promise of counseling and guidance for minority individuals remains, as yet, unfulfilled. Nor has counseling to date been able to bring much clarity to issues raised in the minority group literature. Central to all other considerations is the role of the profession itself vis a vis minorities. Should counselors work in the domain of "special" minority needs and experiences or should they continue to aim at serving the "middle American" population? While to some extent the question appears moot, one need only examine the curricula of major counselor training programs to determine that the profession continues to train counselors for working with White, middle class, straight, mainstream clientele. Indeed, this has been a serious bone of contention for many minority professionals.

The Unfulfilled Promise of Counseling for Minorities

Minority group authors, particularly those representing racial/ethnic minority groups, have been vociferous and unequivocal in their denunciations of the counseling profession since the mid 1960's. In a comprehensive review of counseling literature related to racial/ethnic minority groups, Pine (1972) found the following view of counseling to be representative of that held by most minority individuals:

> . . .that it is a waste of time; that counselors are deliberately shunting minority students into dead end non-academic programs regardless of student potential, preferences, or ambitions; that counselors discourage students from applying to college; that counselors are insensitive to the needs of students and the community; that counselors do not give the same amount of energy and time in working with minority as they do with White middle-class students; that counselors do not accept, respect, and understand cultural differences; that counselors are arrogant and contemptuous; and that counselors don't know themselves how to deal with their own hangups (p. 35).

Although Pine's article deals primarily with racial/ethnic minorities, similar views of counseling have been expressed by feminist, "gay", pacifist, and other activist minority groups (Counseling and the Social Revolution, 1971).

To some extent minority group unhappiness with counseling reflects disillusionment with all the organized social sciences because of their poor performance as instruments for correcting social ills (Sanford, 1969). Psychology in particular has been criticized for its role as the "handmaiden of the status quo" (Halleck, 1971, p. 30). Frequently minorities see psychology functioning to maintain and promote the status and power of the Establishment (Sue & Sue, 1972).

To a large degree, minority group dissatisfaction with the counseling profession can be explained as disenchantment with unfulfilled promises. As suggested earlier, counseling has at least covertly accepted such ideal rights as "equal access to opportunity," "pursuit of happiness," "fulfillment of personal destiny,'' and ''freedom'' as omnipresent, inherent goals in the counseling process (Adams, 1973; Belkin, 1975; Byrne, 1977). Although these lofty ideals may seem highly commendable and extremely appropriate goals for the counseling profession to promote, in reality they have often been translated in such a way as to justify support for the status quo (Adams, 1973).

While the validity of minority criticisms can and will be argued by professional counselors, there is little doubt that, for whatever reasons, counseling has failed to serve the needs of minorities, and in some cases, has proven counterproductive to their well-being. The fact that various minority groups are underrepresented in conventional counseling programs (Sue, 1973) suggests these groups see counseling as irrelevant to their needs. There is also substantial evidence that Asian Americans, Blacks, Chicanos and Native Americans terminate counseling after an initial counseling session, at a much higher rate than do Anglos (Sue, Allen, & Conaway, in press; Sue & McKinney, 1975; Sue, McKinney, Allen, & Hall 1974). Clearly, minorities see the counseling process, as currently implemented, contrary to their own life experiences and inappropriate or insufficient for their felt needs.

Perhaps the most insidious commentary on the failure of counseling for minorities is the evidence that minorities are diagnosed differently and receive ''less preferred'' forms of treatment than do majority clients. In the area of diagnosis, Lee and Temerlin (1968) found that psychiatric residents were more likely to arrive at a diagnosis of mental illness when the individual's history suggested lower-class origin than when a high socioeconomic class was indicated. Haase (1956) demonstrated that clinical psychologists given identical sets of Rorschach test records made more negative prognostic statements and judgments of greater maladjustment when the records were identified as the products of lower-class individuals than when associated with middle-class persons. Broverman, Broverman, Clarkson, Rosenkrantz, and Vogel (1970) found sex also to be a factor in diagnosis, with less favorable judgments by clinical psychologists with respect to female clients than for male clients. In a related study, Thomas and Stewart (1971) presented counselors with taped interviews of a high school girl in counseling and found the girl's career choice rated more appropriate when identified as traditional than when identified as deviant (traditionally male attitude). Similar results have been cited by Schlossberg and Pietrofesa (1973).

In the area of treatment, Garfield, Weiss, and Pollack (1973) gave two groups of counselors identical printed descriptions (except for social class) of a 9-year-old boy who engaged in maladaptive classroom behavior. The counselors indicated a greater willingness to become ego-involved when the child was identified as having upper-class status than when assigned lower-class status. Habermann and Thiry (1970) found that doctoral degree candidates in Counseling and Guidance more frequently programmed students from low-socioeconomic backgrounds into a non-college bound track than a college preparation track. Research documentation of the inferior quality of mental health services provided to racial/ethnic minorities are commonplace (Clark, 1965; Cowen, Gardner, & Zox, 1967; Guerney, 1969; Lerner, 1972; Thomas & Sillen, 1972; Torion, 1973; Yamamoto, James, Bloombaum, & Hattem, 1967; Yamamoto, James & Palley, 1968).

Criticism of the Traditional Counseling Role

Due in part to the unfulfilled promise of counseling for minorities, a great deal of criticism has been directed at the traditional counseling role in which an office-bound counselor engages the client in verbal interaction with the intention of resolving the client's psychological problems. For the most part, this criticism can be summarized as three interrelated concerns: criticism of the intrapsychic counseling model, criticism of how counseling approaches have developed, and criticism related to counseling process variables.

Criticism of Intrapsychic Counseling Model

Perhaps the strongest, most cogent indictment of the traditional counseling role has been criticism of the intrapsychic view of client problems inherent to some degree in all current counseling approaches. The intrapsychic model assumes client problems are the result of personal disorganization rather than institutional or societal dysfunctioning (Bryson & Bardo, 1975). Counselors, these critics argue, should view minority clients as victims of a repressive society and rather than intervene with the victim, counselors should attempt to change the offending portion of the client's environment (Banks, 1972; Williams & Kirkland, 1971).

The issue of whether one focuses on the *person* or *system* is an important one. Counseling in this country has grown out of a philosophy of "rugged individualism" in which people are assumed to be responsible for their own lot in life. Success in society is attributed to outstanding abilities or great effort. Likewise, failures or problems encountered by the person may be attributed to some inner deficiency (lack of effort, poor abilities, etc.). For the minority individual who is the victim of oppression, the person-blame approach tends to deny the existence of external injustices (racism, sexism, age, bias, etc.).

Pedersen (1976) has suggested that the counselor can help the minority client either adopt, or adapt to the dominant culture. Vexliard (1968) has coined the terms autoplastic and alloplastic to define two levels of adaption; the first, ". . .involves accommodating oneself to the givens of a social setting and structure and the latter involves shaping the external reality to suit one's needs" (Draguns, 1976, p. 6). Thus, critics of the traditional counseling role see cultural adoption and the autoplastic model of adaption as repressive but predictable outcomes of the intrapsychic counseling model. The counseling roles they advocate can be viewed as directed toward the alloplastic end of the auto-alloplastic adaption continuum, and will be discussed in some detail in the final chapter of this book.

Criticism of How Counseling Approaches Have Developed

Minority intellectuals have criticized contemporary counseling approaches which they contend have been developed by and for the White, middle class person (Bell, 1971; Gunnings, 1971; Mitchell, 1971). Little or no attention has been directed to the need to develop counseling procedures that are compatible with minority cultural values. Unimodal counseling approaches are perpetuated by graduate programs in counseling that give inadequate treatment to the mental health issues of minorities. Cultural influences affecting personality, identity formation, and behavior manifestations frequently are not a part of training programs. When minority group experiences are discussed, they are generally seen and analyzed from the "White, middle class perspective." As a result, counselors who deal with the mental health problems of minorities often lack understanding and knowledge about cultural differences and their consequent interaction with an oppressive society.

Majority counselors who do not have firsthand experience with the minority client's specific cultural milieu may overlook the fact that the client's behavior patterns have different interpretations in the two cultures represented. Behavior that is diagnosed as pathological in one culture may be viewed as adaptive in another (Wilson & Calhoun, 1974). Grier & Cobbs (1968) in their depiction of Black cultural paranoia as a "healthy" development make reference to the potential for inappropriate diagnoses. Thus, the determination of normality or abnormality tends to be intimately associated with a White, middle class standard.

Furthermore, counseling techniques which are a product of the White middle class culture are frequently applied indiscriminately to the minority population (Bell, 1971). In addition, counselors themselves are often culturally encapsulated (Wrenn, 1962), measuring reality against their own set of monocultural assumptions and values, and demonstrating insensitivity to cultural variations in clients (Pedersen, 1976). New counseling techniques and approaches are needed, it is argued, that take into account the minority experience (Gunnings, 1971).

The issue is perhaps best represented semantically by the emic-etic dichotomy, which was first presented by the linguist, Pike (1954). Draguns (1976) offers the following definition of these two terms:

> Emic refers to the viewing of data in terms indigenous or unique to the culture in question, and etic, to viewing them in light of categories and concepts external to the culture but universal in their applicability (p. 2).

The criticisms relevant to the current discussion, then, focus on what can be called the "pseudoetic" approach to cross-cultural counseling (Triandis, Malpass, & Davidson, 1973); culturally encapsulated counselors assume that their own approach and associated techniques can be culturally generalized and are robust enough to cope with cultural variations. In reality, minority critics argue, we have developed emic approaches to counseling that are designed by and for White, middle-class individuals.

Criticisms Related to Counseling Process Variables—Barriers to Minority Group/Cross-Cultural Counseling

Much of the criticism related to minority group counseling focuses upon the interactions that occur between counselor and client. Counseling is seen as a process of interpersonal interaction and communication which requires accurate sending and receiving of both verbal and nonverbal messages. When the counselor and client come from different cultural backgrounds, barriers to communication are likely to develop, leading to misunderstandings that destroy rapport and render counseling ineffective. Thus, process manifestations of cultural barriers pose a serious problem in minority group/cross-cultural counseling.

Most of the writing on barriers to minority group/cross-cultural counseling has focused on racial/ethnic minorities as clientele with a major portion of these studies examining the White counselor—Black client relationship. It is evident, however, that many of the concepts developed by these authors have relevance to any counseling situation involving an individual from a minority (i.e., oppressed) group. It is equally clear that although presented from a majority counselor-minority client perspective, many of the same barriers may exist between a counselor and client who represent two different minority groups (i.e., two different cultures).

In the present discussion, we make a distinction between cultural barriers that are unique to a minority group/cross-cultural counseling situation (e.g., language differences) and those that are process barriers present in every counseling relationship but are particularly thorny and more likely to occur in a cross-cultural situation (e.g., transference).

Barriers Indigenous to Cultural Differences

In discussing barriers and hazards in the counseling process, Johnson and Vestermark (1970) define barriers as, ''. . .real obstacles of varying degrees of seriousness . . .'' (p. 5). They go on to describe cultural encapsulation as one of the most serious barriers that can affect the counseling relationship. Padilla, Ruiz, and Alvarez (1975) have identified three major impediments to counseling that a non Latino counselor may encounter when working with a Latino client. Sue & Sue (1977) have generalized these barriers as relevant to all Third World people. We expand the concept further and attempt to relate the three barriers to all minority group/cross-cultural counseling situations. The three barriers are: (a) language differences; (b) class-bound values; and (c) culture-bound values. These three categories are used to facilitate the present discussion; it should be pointed out, however, that all three categories are recognized as functions of culture broadly defined.

Language Differences—Much of the criticism related to the traditional counseling role has focused on the central importance of verbal interaction and rapport in the counseling relationship. This heavy reliance by counselors on verbal interaction to build rapport presupposes that the participants in a counseling dialogue are capable of understanding each other. Yet many counselors fail to understand the client's language and its nuances sufficiently so as to make rapport building possible (Vontress, 1973). Furthermore, educationally and economically disadvantaged clients may lack the prerequisite verbal skills required to benefit from "talk therapy" (Calia, 1966; Tyler, 1964), especially when confronted by a counselor who relies on complex cognitive and conative concepts to generate client insight.

Sue & Sue (1977) have pointed out that the use of standard English with a lower-class or bilingual client may result in misperceptions of the client's strengths and weaknesses. Certainly the counselor who is unfamiliar with a client's dialect or language system will be unlikely to succeed in establishing rapport (Wilson & Calhoun, 1974). Furthermore, Vontress (1973) suggests that counselors need to be familiar with minority group body language lest they misinterpret the meaning of postures, gestures, and inflections. For example, differences in nonverbal behavior are frequently seen in the comparison of Blacks and Whites. When speaking to another person, Anglos tend to look away from the person (avoid eye contact) more often than do Black individuals. When listening to another person speak, however, Blacks tend to avoid eye contact while Anglos make eye contact. This may account for statements from teachers who feel that Black pupils are inattentive (they make less eye contact when spoken to) or feel that Blacks are more angry (intense stare) when speaking.

Similar observations can be made regarding cross-cultural counseling with other, non-racially-identified minority groups. For instance, prison inmates have developed a language system that tends to change over a period of time. The naive counselor who enters the prison environment for the first time may find that his/her use of standard English may elicit smiles or even guffaws from clients, to say nothing of what this does to the counselor's credibility. Gays, too, have developed a vocabulary that may be entirely foreign to a "straight" counselor. Anyone who doubts this statement need only visit a gay bar in San Francisco or elsewhere and listen to the public dialogue. Any counselor unfamiliar with gay vocabulary is likely to be perceived as too straight by a gay client to be of any help. Gays, like other minority groups, rely heavily upon their own vernacular to convey emotions and, understandably, they prefer a counselor who can grasp these emotions without further translation into standard English.

Unique language patterns can also be associated with poor Appalachian whites, drug users, the handicapped, and to some extent, almost any category which qualifies as a minority group as defined in this book. Often with political activism, minority groups will develop expressive language that is not common to, or has a different connotation than, standard English. Inability to communicate effectively in the client's language may contribute significantly to the poor acceptance which counseling has received from minorities.

Class-bound Values—Differences in values between counselor and client that are basically due to class differences are relevant to minority group/cross-cultural counseling since, almost by definition, many minority group members are also of a lower socioeconomic class. Furthermore, for the purposes of this book, differences in attitudes, behaviors, beliefs, and values among the various socioeconomic groups constitute cultural differences. The interaction of social class and behavior has been well documented by Hollingshead (1949). The importance of social class for school counseling has been discussed by Bernard (1963). Combining the results of several studies, Havighurst and Neugarten (1962) concluded that at least fifty percent of the American population falls into either the upper lower or lower lower socioeconomic classes, suggesting that a large portion of the counselor's potential clientele may be from these socioeconomic classes. The impact of social class differences on counseling in general acquires added significance if one accepts the statement presented earlier in this chapter, that existing counseling techniques are middle and upper class based.

One of the first and most obvious value differences encountered by the middle class counselor and the lower class client involves the willingness to make and keep counseling appointments. As Sue and Sue (1977) point out, "...lower-class clients who are concerned with 'survival' or making it through on a day-to-day basis expect advice and suggestions from the counselor...(and)...appointments made weeks in advance with short weekly 50 minute contacts are not consistent with the need to seek immediate solutions" (p. 424). Vontress (1973) states that Appalachian Whites refuse to be enslaved by the clock and not only do they refuse to adhere to values of promptness, planning, and protocol, but they suspect people who do adhere to these values.

Differences in attitudes toward sexual behavior often enter the counseling relationship between a counselor and client representing different socioeconomic classes. For the most part, open acceptance of sexual promiscuity differs from one socioeconomic level to another, although other factors (e.g., religious beliefs) play heavy roles. Middle class counselors, whether consciously or unconsciously, often attempt to impose middle class sexual mores on lower and upper class clients.

The fact that the clients' socioeconomic status affects the kind of therapeutic treatment clients receive has been well documented. Ryan & Gaier (1968), for instance, found that students from upper socioeconomic backgrounds have more exploratory interviews with counselors than do students representing other social classes. Middle class patients in a veterans administration clinic tend to remain in treatment longer than do lower class patients. And Hollingshead and Redlich (1958) found that the level of therapeutic intensiveness varies directly with socioeconomic background.

Culture-bound Values—Culture, as broadly defined for the purposes of this book, consists of behavior patterns shared and transmitted by a group of individuals. In addition to language and class-bound values already discussed, culture-bound values obviously involve such elements as attitudes, beliefs, customs, and institutions identified as integral parts, of a group's social structure.

Counselors frequently impose their own cultural values upon minority clients in ignorance, reflecting an insensitivity to the clients' values. Referring to clients from racial/ethnic minorities as "culturally deprived" is an example of this imposition. "Straight", male counselors sometimes make sexual remarks about females in front of a male client that may be repugnant to the client if he is gay (to say nothing about how it would affect females who overheard it). Nor is the experience reported by Granberg (1967) in which he found himself incorrectly assuming his homosexual client wanted to become "straight" an unusual example of the counselor's cultural values interfering with the counseling relationship. Drug and prison "counselors" often fulfill roles of instilling the values of the larger society upon their clientele without full awareness of their impact.

For some time the role of the counselor's values in the counseling relationship has been a thorny professional issue. The issue becomes even more poignant when a majority counselor and minority client are involved. In this case, "...the values inherent in (the) two different sub-cultures may be realistically as diverse as those of two countries" (Wilson & Calhoun, 1974). While the major concern with this issue, in the broader context, centers on the counselor's influence upon the client, class- and culture-bound value differences can impede further rapport building.

For example, one of the most highly valued aspects of counseling entails self-disclosure, a client's willingness to let the counselor know what he or she thinks or feels. Many professionals argue that self-disclosure is a necessary condition for effective counseling. Jourard (1964) suggests that people are more likely to disclose themselves to others who will react as they do, implying that cultural similarity is an important factor in self-disclosure. Furthermore, self-disclosure may be contrary to basic cultural values for some minorities. Sue and Sue (1972) have pointed out that Chinese American clients, who are taught at an early age to restrain from emotional expression, find the direct and subtle demands by the counselor to self-disclosure very threatening. Similar conflicts have been reported for Chicano (Cross & Maldonado, 1971) and Native American (Trimble, 1976) clients. Poor clients, of whatever racial or ethnic background, frequently resist attempts by the counselor to encourage client self-exploration and prefer to ascribe their problems, often justifiably, to forces beyond their control (Calia, 1966). In addition, many racial minorities have learned to distrust Whites in general and may "shine on" a majority counselor, since this has proven to be adaptive behavior with Whites in the past. Sue and Sue (1977) suggest that self-disclosure is itself a cultural value and counselors who, "...value verbal, emotional and behavioral expressiveness as goals in counseling are transmitting their own cultural values" (p. 425).

Related to this last point is the lack of structure frequently provided by the counselor in the counseling relationship. Often, in order to encourage self-disclosure, the counseling situation is intentionally designed to be an ambiguous one, one in which the counselor listens empathically and responds only to encourage the client to continue talking (Sue & Sue, 1972). Minority clients frequently find the lack of structure confusing, frustrating, and even threatening (Haettenschwiller, 1971). Atkinson, Maruyama, and Matsui (1978) found that Asian Americans prefer a directive counseling style to a non-directive one, suggesting the directive approach is more compatible with their cultural values. Black students also were found to prefer a more active counseling role over a passive one (Peoples & Dell, 1975).

Process Manifestations of Cultural Differences

Many of the problems encountered in minority group/cross-cultural counseling which have been identified as cultural barriers might better be conceived of as process manifestations of cultural differences, since they may be present to some extent in any counseling relationship but are aggravated by cultural differences. We will briefly discuss five of them: stereotyping, resistance, transference, countertransference and client expectations.

Stereotyping—Stereotyping is a major problem for all forms of counseling. It may broadly be defined as rigid preconceptions which are applied to all members of a group or to an individual over a period of time, regardless of individual variations. The key word in this definition is *rigidity,* an inflexibility to change. Thus, a counselor who believes that Blacks are "lazy," "musical," "rhythmic," and "unintelligent"; Asians are "sneaky," "sly," "good with numbers," and "poor with words"; or that Jews are "stingy," "shrewd," and "intellectual" will behave toward representatives of these groups as if they possessed these traits. The detrimental effects of stereotyping have been well documented in professional literature (Rosenthal & Jacobsen, 1968; Smith, 1977; Sue, 1973). First, counselors who have preconceived notions about minority group members may unwittingly act upon these beliefs. If Black students are seen as possessing limited intellectual potential, they may be counseled into terminal vocational trade schools. Likewise, if Asian Americans are perceived as being only good in the physical sciences but poor in verbal-people professions, counselors may direct them toward a predominance of science courses. The second and even more damaging effect is that many minorities may eventually come to believe these stereotypes about themselves. Thus, since the majority of stereotypes about minorities are negative, an inferior sense of self-esteem may develop.

Due to stereotyping or attempts to avoid stereotyping by the counselor, majority counselors frequently have difficulty adjusting to a relationship with a minority client. The most obvious difficulty in this area occurs when the counselor fails to recognize the client as an individual and assigns to the client culturally stereotypic characteristics that are totally invalid for this individual (Smith, 1977). In an effort to treat the client as just another client, on the other hand, the counselor may demonstrate "color or culture blindness" (Wilson & Calhoun, 1974). In this case the counselor may avoid altogether discussing the differences between the two participants, thus implying that the client's attitudes and behaviors will be assessed against majority norms. The content of the counseling dialogue may also be restricted by the preoccupation of the majority counselor with fear that the client will detect conscious or unconscious stereotyping on the part of the counselor (Gardner, 1971).

Resistance—Resistance is usually defined as client opposition to the goals of counseling and may manifest itself as self-devaluation, intellectualization, and overt hostility (Vontress, 1976). While it is a potential difficulty in any counseling encounter, the problem becomes particularly acute when the counselor and client are culturally different, since the counselor may misinterpret the resistance as a dynamic of the client's culture.

Transference—Transference occurs when the client responds to the counselor in a manner similar to the way he or she responded to someone else in the past (Greenson, 1964, pp. 151-152), and this may manifest itself as either a liking or disliking of the counselor. Clients may or may not be aware of the transference effect themselves. This phenomena is particularly problematic in the majority counselor-minority client dyad, "...because minority group members bring to the relationship intense emotions derived from experiences with and feelings toward the majority group" (Vontress, 1976, p. 49). Minority clients for instance, due to their experiences with an oppressive, majority-controlled society are likely to anticipate authoritarian behavior from the counselor.

Countertransference—Countertransference occurs when the counselor responds to a client as he or she responded to someone in the past (Wilson & Calhoun, 1974, p. 318). Countertransference is particularly difficult for the counselor to recognize and accept since counselors typically view themselves as objective, although empathic, participants in the counseling relationship. It seems highly unlikely, however, that majority counselors in this society are entirely free of the stereotypic attitudes toward minority peoples (Jackson, 1973). An argument can be made that counselors, like everyone else, carry with them conscious and unconscious attitudes, feelings, and beliefs about culturally different people, and that these will manifest themselves as countertransference (Vontress, 1976).

Client Expectations—Closely related to transference, client expectations for success in the counseling relationship can directly affect counseling outcome. When the minority client finds him/herself assigned to a majority counselor, the client's prognostic expectations may be reduced (Wilson & Calhoun, 1974). Prior to the initial counseling session the client may experience feelings of distrust, futility, and anger which generate an expectation that counseling will not succeed. Such an expectation usually dooms the counseling relationship to failure.

Barriers to Minority Counselor-Minority or Majority Client Counseling

As used in the counseling literature, minority group counseling frequently implies that the counselor is a member of the dominant culture and the client a minority group member, suggesting that this combination is of greatest threat to effective counseling. A few authors have referred to the problems encountered in counseling when the client and counselor are from the same minority group. Virtually none have discussed the difficulties experienced when the counselor is from a different minority group than the client. Lest the impression be given that culturally related barriers only exist for the majority counselor-minority client dyad, we now turn briefly to difficulties experienced by minority counselors and their clients.

Intra-Minority Group Counseling

Several authors have identified problems that the minority counselor may encounter when working with a client from a cultural background similar to that of the counselor. Jackson (1973) points out that the minority client may respond with anger when confronted by a minority counselor. The anger may result from finding a minority person associated with a majority controlled institution. Some clients may experience anger, on the other hand, because they feel a majority counselor would be more competent, thus enhancing the probability of problem resolution. Or the client's anger may reflect jealousy that the counselor has succeeded through personal efforts in breaking out of a repressive environment. In the case of a Third World counselor, the counselor may also be seen as:

> . . .too white in orientation to be interested in helping, as less competent than his colleagues, as too far removed from problems that face the patient, or as intolerant and impatient with the patient's lack of success in dealing with problems (Jackson, 1973, p. 277).

The minority counselor may respond to minority client anger by becoming defensive (Jackson, 1973), thus impeding the counseling process. Minority counselors may also either deny identification with or over-identify with the client (Gardner, 1971). Sattler (1970) has suggested that minority counselors may have less tolerance and understanding of minority clients and view the contact as low status work compared to counseling a majority client.

Calnek (1970) points out the danger that Third World counselors too often adopt stereotypes which Whites have developed, concerning how minority clients think, feel, and act. The counselor may deny that the client is also a minority person, for fear the common identification will result in a loss of professional image for the counselor. Over-identification, on the other hand, may cause the counseling experience to degenerate into a gripe session. Calnek also refers to the danger of the counselor projecting his/her own self image onto the client because they are culturally similar.

While the foregoing comments are, for the most part, directed at the Black counselor-Black client dyad, it is easy to see that the problem could be generalized to include other intra-minority group situations.

Inter-Minority Group Counseling

Counselors representing one minority group who find themselves working with a client representing a different minority group often face the problems associated with both the majority counselor-minority client and the intra-minority group counseling situations. Although the camaraderie of Third World peoples that results from awareness of shared oppression helps to bridge cultural differences on college and university campuses, in the non-academic world these differences are often as intense or more intense than those between the dominant and minority cultures. One need only observe Chicano students and parents in East Los Angeles or Black students and parents in Bedford-Stuyvesant to gain an appreciation of ethnocentrism and the difficulty which culturally different-minority counselors can perceive in these situations. Furthermore, the counselor representing a different minority than the client may be suspect to the client, for the same reasons counselors of similar minority backgrounds would be suspect.

Potential Benefits in Cross-Cultural Counseling

Almost no attention has been given in the counseling literature to identifying the benefits of cross-cultural counseling. In reference to the minority counselor-majority client dyad, Jackson (1973) suggests that the client may find it easier to, "...share information that is looked on as socially unacceptable without censor from the therapist" (p. 275), suggesting self-disclosure, at least of some materials, may be enhanced. Students who are rebelling against the Establishment, for instance, may prefer a minority counselor, feeling that the counselor's experience with oppression qualifies him/her to acquire empathy with the client (Gardner, 1971). Gardner (1971) also suggests majority clients may prefer minority counselors if they are dealing with material that would be embarrassing to share with a majority counselor. Jackson (1973) points out that there is a tendency in this situation to perceive the counselor more as another person than as a superhuman, notwithstanding those cases where the counselor is perceived as a "super-minority." In the latter case, the client may view the minority counselor as more capable than his/her majority counterpart, owing to the obstacles the counselor had to overcome. The net effect in this case may be a positive expectation. The possibility that minority counselors are less likely to let secrets filter back into the client's community is also cited by Gardner (1971) as a positive variable in cross-cultural counseling.

Several authors (Draguns, 1975, 1976; Trimble, 1976), while referring in part to national cultures, have suggested that cross-cultural counseling is a learning experience to be valued in and of itself. The counseling process, with its intentional provision for self-disclosure of attitudes, values and intense emotional feelings, can help the counselor and client gain a perspective on each other's culture, frequently in a way never experienced outside of counseling.

Again it seems apparent that much of the foregoing can be generalized to apply to non-racially or ethnically identified minorities. It also seems evident that further research and discussion are needed regarding both the barriers and benefits of cross-cultural counseling. Those discussed above, along with several proposed by the current authors, are outlined in Figure 1. In addition to citing positive and negative aspects of cross-cultural situations, the authors have attempted, as shown in Figure 1, to identify their counterparts when counselor and client are culturally similar.

Editors' View

The editors of this book of readings are in agreement with those earlier writers who have suggested that cross-cultural counseling can not only be effective for resolving client difficulties, but can also serve as a forum for a unique learning experience. That barriers to cross-cultural counseling exist is not at issue here. Clearly, cultural differences between counselor and client

Figure 1 Culturally Relevant Barriers
and Benefits in Inter- and
Intra-Cultural Counseling

Inter-Cultural Counseling

Barriers	*Benefits*
—client resistance	—client's willingness to self-disclose some material
—client transference	
—client cultural restraints on self-disclosure	—client less likely to view counselor as omniscient
—client expectations	—client expectation for success may be enhanced
—counselor countertransference	
—counselor maladjustment to the relationship	—potential for considerable cultural learning by both client and counselor
—counselor misdirected diagnosis	—increased need for counselor and client to focus on their own processing
—counselor patronization of client's culture	
—counselor denial of culturally dissonant component of client problem	—potential for dealing with culturally dissonant component of client problem
—counselor "missionary zeal"	
—language differences	
—value conflicts	

Intra-Cultural Counseling

Barriers	*Benefits*
—unjustified assumption of shared feelings	—shared experience may enhance rapport
—client transference	—client willingness to self-disclose some materials
—counselor countertransference	
	—common mode of communication may enhance process

can result in barriers that are, in some instances, insurmountable. As suggested earlier, however, cross-cultural counseling can involve benefits to both client and counselor that may not be possible in intra-cultural counseling.

Furthermore, it is our contention that the primary barrier to effective counseling and one which underlies many other barriers is the traditional counseling role itself. No one has yet offered conclusive evidence that differences in status variables (e.g., race, ethnicity, sex, sexual orientation) alone create barriers to counseling. The fact that one person in a counseling dyad is born Black and one White, for instance, should not negate the possibility of their working together effectively. From our perspective, it is how we perceive and experience our and our client's Blackness and Whiteness which creates barriers to constructive communication. For the most part, our perceptions and experiences are shaped by a socialization process that begins at birth. We feel that the traditional counseling role (nonequalitarian, intrapsychic model, office bound, etc.) often helps to perpetuate the very socialization process which creates a barrier between culturally different individuals.

Some critics will argue that differences in experiences are paramount, that a counselor who experiences being Black will understand the Black client's perspective better than any White counselor ever can. We agree to a point. There is simply no conclusive evidence, however, that a counselor must experience everything his/her client does. Carried to the extreme, the similarity of experience argument suggests that all counseling is doomed to failure since no two individuals can ever fully share the same life experiences. Furthermore, while cultural differences do result in unique experiences for both the client and the counselor, our experiences as human beings are remarkably similar. This view—that we are more alike than different—is perhaps best expressed by the sociobiologist De Vore (1977):

> Anthropologists always talk about crosscultural diversity, but that's icing on the cake. The cake itself is remarkably panhuman. Different cultures turn out only minor variations on the theme of the species—human courtship, our mating systems, child care, fatherhood, the treatment of the sexes, love, jealousy, sharing. Almost everything that's importantly human—including behavior flexibility—is universal, and developed in the context of our shared genetic background. (p. 88)

We hope this book will serve as a starting point for counselors who want to learn about the American minorities and about themselves. In the chapters that follow, the reader will detect threads of similarities among the experiences of the various minorities presented as well as obvious dissimilarities of experience. In Chapter 15, we present a model of Minority Identity Development which we suggest applies to members of all minority groups by virtue of their common experience of oppression. In Chapter 16, we suggest some new directions for counseling practice, counselor education, and for counselor research. We hope the final section of this book will assist the readers in bridging the existing barriers to minority group/cross-cultural counseling.

References

Adams, H.J. The progressive heritage of guidance: A view from the left. *Personnel and Guidance Journal,* 1973, *51,* 531-538.

Atkinson, D.R., Maruyama, M., & Matsui, S. The effects of counselor race and counseling approach on Asian Americans' perceptions of counselor credibility and utility. *Journal of Counseling Psychology,* 1978, *25* (1), 76-83.

Aubrey, R.F. Historical development of guidance and counseling and implications for the future. *Personnel and Guidance Journal,* 1977, *55,* 288-295.

Banks, W. The Black client and the helping professionals. In R.I. Jones (Ed.) *Black Psychology.* New York: Harper & Row, 1972.

Belkin, G.S. *Practical Counseling in the Schools,* Dubuque, Iowa: William C. Brown, 1975.

Bell, R.L. The culturally deprived psychologist. *Counseling Psychologist,* 1971, *2,* 104-107

Bernard, H.W. Socioeconomic class and the school counselor. *Theory into practice,* 1963, *2,* 17-23.

Broverman, I., Broverman, D.M., Clarkson, F.E., Rosenkrantz, P.S., & Vogel, S. Sex role stereotype and clinical judgments of mental health. *Journal of Consulting and Clinical Psychology,* 1970, *34,* 1-7.

Bryson, S., & Bardo, H. Race and the counseling process: An overview. *Journal of Non-White Concerns in Personnel and Guidance,* 1975, *4,* 5-15.

Bryne, R.H. *Guidance: A behavioral approach.* Englewood Cliffs, N.J.: Prentice-Hall, 1977.

Calia, V.F. The culturally deprived client: A re-formulation of the counselor's role. *Journal of Counseling Psychology,* 1966, *13,* 100-105.

Calnek, M. Racial factors in the countertransference: The Black therapist and the Black client. *American Journal of Orthopsychiatry,* 1970, *40,* 39-46.

Clark, K.B. *Dark Ghetto: Dilemmas of Social Power.* New York: Harper and Row, 1965.

Counseling and the Social Revolution. *Personnel and Guidance Journal,* 1971, *49* (9).

Cowen, E.L., Gardner, E.A., & Zox, M. (Eds.) *Emergent approaches to mental health problems.* New York: Appleton-Century-Crofts, 1967.

Cross, W.C., & Maldonado, B. The counselor, the Mexican American, and the stereotype. *Elementary School Guidance and Counseling,* 1971, *6,* 27-31.

De Vore, I. The new science of genetic self-interest. *Psychology Today,* 1977, *10* (9), 42-51, 84-88.

Draguns, J.G. Resocialization into culture: The complexities of taking a worldwide view of psychotherapy. In R.W. Brislin, S. Bochner, & W.J. Lonner (Eds.), *Cross-cultural perspectives in learning.* New York: John Wiley & Sons, Halsted, 1975.

Draguns, J.G. Counseling across cultures: Common themes and distinct approaches. In P. Pedersen, W.J. Lonner, & J.G. Draguns (Eds.), *Counseling across cultures.* Honolulu: The University of Hawaii Press, 1976.

Gardner, L.H. The therapeutic relationship under varying conditions of race. *Psychotherapy: Theory, Research and Practice,* 1971, *8* (1), 78-87.

Garfield, J.C., Weiss, S.L., & Pollack, E.A. Effects of the child's social class on school counselor's decision making. *Journal of Counseling Psychology,* 1973, *20,* 166-168.

Granberg, L.I. What I've learned in counseling. *Christianity Today,* 1967, *2,* 891-894.

Greenson, R.R. *The technique and practice of psychoanalysis* (Vol. 1). New York: International Universities Press, 1964.

Grier, W.H. & Cobbs, P.M. *Black Rage.* New York: Bantam Books, Inc., 1968.

Guerney, B.G. (Ed.) *Psychotherapeutic agents: New roles for nonprofessionals, parents, and teachers.* New York: Holt, Rinehart & Winston, 1969.

Gunnings, T.S. Preparing the new counselor. *The Counseling Psychologist,* 1971, *2* (4), 100-101.

Haase, W. *Rorschach diagnosis, socio-economic class and examiner bias.* Unpublished doctoral dissertation, New York University, 1956.

Habermann, L., & Thiry, S. *The effect of socio-economic status variables on counselor perception and behavior.* Unpublished master's thesis, University of Wisconsin, 1970.

Haettenschwiller, D.L. Counseling black college students in special programs. *Personnel and Guidance Journal,* 1971, *50,* 29-35.

Halleck, S.L. Therapy is the handmaiden of the status quo. *Psychology Today,* 1971, *4,* 30-34, 98-100.

Havighurst, R.J., & Neugarten, B.L. *Society and Education* (Second edition). Boston: Allyn and Bacon, Inc., 1962.

Hollingshead, A.B. *Elmtown's youth: The impact of social classes on adolescents.* New York: John Wiley and Sons, Inc., 1949.

Hollingshead, A.B. & Redlich, F.C. *Social class and mental health.* New York: John Wiley & Sons, Inc., 1958.

Jackson, A.M. Psychotherapy: Factors associated with the race of the therapist. *Psychotherapy: Theory, Research and Practice,* 1973, *10* (3), 273-277.

Johnson, D.E., & Vestermark, M.J. *Barriers and hazards in counseling.* Boston: Houghton Mifflin Co., 1970.

Jourard, S.M. *The transparent self.* Princeton, N.J.: D. Van Nostrand Co., 1964.

Lee, S., & Temerlin, M.K. *Social class status and mental illness.* Unpublished doctoral dissertation, University of Oklahoma, 1968.

Lerner, B. *Therapy in the ghetto: Political impotence and personal disintegration.* Baltimore: Johns Hopkins University Press, 1972.

Lewis, M.D., Lewis, J.A., & Dworkin, E.P. Editorial: Counseling and the social revolution. *The Personnel and Guidance Journal,* 1971, *49,* 689.

Mitchell, H. Counseling black students: A model in response to the need for relevant counselor training programs. *The Counseling Psychologist,* 1971, *2* (4), 117-122.

Padilla, A.M., Ruiz, R.A., & Alvarez, R. Community mental health services for the Spanish-speaking/surnamed population. *American Psychologist,* 1975, *30,* 892-905.

Pedersen, P.B. The field of intercultural counseling. In P.B. Pedersen, W.J. Lonner, & J.G. Draguns (Eds.) *Counseling across cultures.* Honolulu: The University of Hawaii Press, 1976.

Peoples, V.Y., & Dell, D.M. Black and white student preferences for counselor roles. *Journal of Counseling Psychology,* 1975, *22,* 529-534.

Pike, K.L. *Language in relation to a unified theory of the structure of human behavior.* Part 1: Preliminary edition. Summer Institute of Linguistics, 1954.

Pine, G.J. Counseling minority groups: A review of the literature. *Counseling and Values,* 1972, *17,* 35-44.

Rosenthal, R., & Jacobson, L. *Pygmalion in the classroom: Teacher expectation and pupils' intellectual development.* New York: Holt, Rinehart, & Winston, 1968.

Ryan, D.W., & Gaier, E.L. Student socio-economic status and counselor contact in junior high school. *Personnel and Guidance Journal,* 1968, *46,* 466-472.

Sanford, N. Research with students as action and education. *American Psychologist,* 1969, *24,* 544-546.

Sattler, J.M. Racial "Experimenter Effects" in experimentation, testing, interviewing and psychotherapy. *Psychological Bulletin,* 1970, *73,* 137-160.

Schlossberg, N.K. & Pietrofesa, J.J. Perspectives on counseling bias: Implications for counselor education. *The Counseling Psychologist,* 1973, *4,* 44-54.

Shertzer, B., & Stone, S.C. *Fundamentals of Counseling* (2nd ed.) Boston: Houghton Mifflin, 1974.

Smith, E.J. Counseling Black individuals: Some stereotypes. *Personnel and Guidance Journal,* 1977, *55,* 390-396.

Sue, D.W. Ethnic identity: The impact of two cultures on the psychological development of Asians in America. In S. Sue & Wagner (Eds.) *Asian Americans: Psychological perspectives.* Ben Lomand, California: Science and Behavior Books, Inc., 1973, 140-149.

Sue, D.W., & Sue, S. Counseling Chinese-Americans. *Personnel and Guidance Journal,* 1972, *50,* 637-644.

Sue, D.W. & Sue, D. Barriers to effective cross-cultural counseling. *Journal of Counseling Psychology,* 1977, *24,* 420-429.

Sue, S., Allen, D., & Conaway, L. The responsiveness and equality of mental health care to Chicanos and Native Americans. *American Journal of Community Psychology,* in press.

Sue, S., & McKinney, H. Asian Americans in the community mental health care system. *American Journal of Orthopsychiatry,* 1975, *45,* 111-118.

Sue, S., McKinney, H., Allen, D., & Hall, J. Delivery of community health services to Black and White clients. *Journal of Consulting Psychology,* 1974, *42,* 794-801.

Thomas, A., & Sillen, S. *Racism and psychiatry.* New York: Brunney Mazel, 1972.

Thomas, A.H., & Stewart, N.R. Counselor response to female clients with deviate and conforming career goals. *Journal of Counseling Psychology,* 1971, *18,* 352-357.

Torion, R.P. Socioeconomic status and traditional treatment approaches reconsidered. *Psychological Bulletin,* 1973, *79,* 263-270.

Triandis, H.C., Malpass, R.S., & Davidson, A.R. Psychology and Culture. *Annual Review of Psychology,* 1973, *24,* 355-378.

Trimble, J.E. Value differences among American Indians: Concern for the concerned counselor. In P. Pedersen, W.J. Lonner, & J.G. Draguns (Eds.), *Counseling across cultures.* Honolulu: The University of Hawaii Press, 1976.

Tyler, L. The methods & processes of appraisal & counseling. In A.S. Thompson & D.E. Super (Eds.) *The professional preparation of counseling psychologists.* New York: Bureau of Publications, Teachers College, Columbia University, 1964.

Vexliard, A. Tempérament et modalités d'adaptation. *Bulletin de Psychologie,* 1968. *21,* 1-15.

Vontress, C.E. Counseling: Racial and ethnic factors. *Focus on Guidance,* 1973, *5,* 1-10.

Vontress, C.E. Racial and ethnic barriers in counseling. In P. Pedersen, W.J. Lonner, & J.G. Draguns (Eds.), *Counseling across cultures.* Honolulu: The University of Hawaii Press, 1976.

Williams, R.L., & Kirkland, J. The white counselor and the black client. *Counseling Psychologist,* 1971, *2,* 114-117.

Wilson, W. & Calhoun, J.F. Behavior therapy and the minority client. *Psychotherapy: Theory, Research and Practice,* 1974, *11* (4), 317-325.

Wrenn, C.G. The culturally encapsulated counselor. *Harvard Educational Review,* 1962, *32* (4), 444-449.

Yamamoto, J., James, Q.C., Bloombaum, M., & Hatten, J. Racial factors in patient selection. *American Journal of Psychiatry,* 1967, *124,* 630-636.

Yamamoto, J., James, Q.C., & Palley, N. Cultural problems in psychiatric therapy. *Archives of General Psychiatry,* 1968, *19,* 45-49.

Part 2 The American Indian Client

We are not free. We do not make choices. Our choices are made for us; we are the poor. For those of us who live on reservations these choices are made by federal administrators, bureaucrats, and their 'yes men,' euphemistically called tribal governments. Those of us who live in non-reservation areas have our lives controlled by local white power elites. We have many rulers. They are called social workers, 'cops,' school teachers, churches, etc., . . .(Warrior, 1967, p. 72).

For nearly 500 years, Native Americans have been fighting a defensive war for their right to freedom, their lands, their organizations, their traditions and beliefs, their way of life, and their very lives. American Indians have experienced massacres by the United States Army, have seen the Bureau of Indian Affairs systematically destroy their leadership and way of life, have known promises broken, have had their land taken from them, and have watched their children die because of inadequate health care, poverty, and suicide. By almost every measure of impoverishment and deprivation, the Native American is the poorest of the poor (Farb, 1968). Their population has decreased from a high of 3,000,000 to about 600,000. While historically Indians were killed in massacres, cultural genocide continues to operate through institutional racism. The following statistics are provided by Josephy (1971):

- The average annual income of Native Americans ($1,500) is 75% below that of the national average, and $1,000 less than that of Blacks;
- Unemployment rate for American Indians is nearly 40% (10 times the average);
- Infant mortality for Native Americans after the first month of life is three times the national average;
- Fifty percent of Indian school children (double the national average) fail to complete high school;
- Suicide rate of Indian teenagers is 100 times that of Whites.

It is ironic that many of the Whites who created these problems refer to them as "Indian problems," and have tried a variety of White-imposed methods to solve them. Deloria, in "Indians Today, the Real and the Unreal," discusses this point at length. In essence, the attempts to solve the problems consisted of imposing White solutions onto the Indian;—turn the Indian into a White and the problem will go away! Such attempts were not only manifestations of cultural oppression; they marked a failure on the part of Whites to understand that the 2500 years of Indian histories and cultures had little in common with European-based cultures.

The fact that the helping professions (counseling, psychotherapy, social work) as practiced in the United States may be instruments of cultural oppression is indirectly discussed by Lewis and Ho in their article "Social Work with Native Americans." They point out how social work and other mental health approaches and strategies arise from the milieu of direct intervention. Native American cultural concepts of noninterference are at odds with such a therapeutic orientation. In addition, certain Native-American values revolving around sharing, time perspectives, patience, and nonverbal communication may also cause problems for the prospective, well-meaning counselor. Youngman & Sadongei in "Counseling the American Indian Child" discuss how misunderstandings can occur when different cultural interpretations of certain behaviors are made. For the young Indian child in a Western school system, the problems are immense.

Counselors must not only recognize the historical Native American experience of oppression and exploitation, but be alert to how their conventional training in mental health practices may be inappropriate to the life styles and values of Native Americans. To impose them blindly is to perpetuate oppression of the most damaging kind.

Farb, P. The American Indian: A portrait in limbo. *Saturday Review*, October 12, 1967, 26-29.

Josephy, Jr., Alvin M. *Red power,* New York: McGraw-Hill Book Co., 1971.

Warrior, C. We are not free. In Josephy, Jr., A. (Ed.) *Red power,* New York: McGraw-Hill, 1971.

3 Indians Today, the Real and the Unreal

Deloria, V.

Indians are like the weather. Everyone knows all about the weather, but none can change it. When storms are predicted, the sun shines. When picnic weather is announced, the rain begins. Likewise, if you count on the unpredictability of Indian people, you will never be sorry.

One of the finest things about being an Indian is that people are always interested in you and your "plight." Other groups have difficulties, predicaments, quandaries, problems, or troubles. Traditionally we Indians have had a "plight."

Our foremost plight is our transparency. People can tell just by looking at us what we want, what should be done to help us, how we feel, and what a "real" Indian is really like. Indian life, as it relates to the real world, is a continuous attempt not to disappoint people who know us. Unfulfilled expectations cause grief and we have already had our share.

Because people can see right through us, it becomes impossible to tell truth from fiction or fact from mythology. Experts paint us as they would like us to be. Often we paint ourselves as we wish we were or as we might have been.

The more we try to be ourselves the more we are forced to defend what we have never been. The American public feels most comfortable with the mythical Indians of stereotype-land who were always THERE. These Indians are fierce, they wear feathers and grunt. Most of us don't fit this idealized figure since we grunt only when overeating, which is seldom.

To be an Indian in modern American society is in a very real sense to be unreal and ahistorical. In this book we will discuss the other side—the unrealities that face *us* as Indian people. It is this unreal feeling that has been welling up inside us and threatens to make this decade the most decisive in history for Indian people. In so many ways, Indian people are re-examining themselves in an effort to redefine a new social structure for their people. Tribes are reordering their priorities to account for the obvious discrepancies between their goals and the goals whites have defined for them.

Indian reactions are sudden and surprising. One day at a conference we were singing "My Country 'Tis of Thee" and we came across the part that goes:

> *Land where our fathers died*
> *Land of the Pilgrims' pride . . .*

Some of us broke out laughing when we realized that our fathers undoubtedly died trying to keep those Pilgrims from stealing our land. In fact, many of our fathers died because the Pilgrims killed them as witches. We didn't feel much kinship with those Pilgrims, regardless of who they did in.

We often hear "give it back to the Indians" when a gadget fails to work. It's a terrible thing for a people to realize that society has set aside all non-working gadgets for their exclusive use.

During my three years as Executive Director of the National Congress of American Indians it was a rare day when some white didn't visit my office and proudly proclaim that he or she was of Indian descent.

Cherokee was the most popular tribe of their choice and many people placed the Cherokees anywhere from Maine to Washington State. Mohawk, Sioux, and Chippewa were next in popularity. Occasionally I would be told about some mythical tribe from lower Pennsylvania, Virginia, or Massachusetts which had spawned the white standing before me.

At times I became quite defensive about being a Sioux when these white people had a pedigree that was so much more respectable than mine. But eventually I came to understand their need to identify as partially Indian and did not resent them. I would confirm their wildest stories about their Indian ancestry and would add a few tales of my own hoping that they would be able to accept themselves someday and leave us alone.

Whites claiming Indian blood generally tend to reinforce mythical beliefs about Indians. All but one person I met who claimed Indian blood claimed it on their grandmother's side. I once did a projection backward and discovered that evidently most tribes were entirely female for the first three hundred years of white occupation. No one, it seemed, wanted to claim a male Indian as a forebear.

It doesn't take much insight into racial attitudes to understand the real meaning of the Indian-grandmother complex that plagues certain whites. A male ancestor has too much of the aura of the savage warrior, the unknown primitive, the instinctive animal, to make him a respectable member of the family tree. But a young Indian princess? Ah, there was royalty for the taking. Somehow the white was linked with a noble house of gentility and culture if his grandmother was an Indian princess who ran away with an intrepid pioneer. And royalty has always been an unconscious but all-consuming goal of the European immigrant.

The early colonists, accustomed to life under benevolent despots, projected their understanding of the European political structure onto the Indian tribe in trying to explain its political and social structure. European royal houses were closed to ex-convicts and indentured servants, so the colonists made all Indian maidens princesses, then proceeded to climb a social ladder of their own creation. Within the next generation, if the trend continues, a large portion of the American population will eventually be related to Powhattan.

While a real Indian grandmother is probably the nicest thing that could happen to a child, why is a remote Indian princess grandmother so necessary for many whites? Is it because they are afraid of being classed as foreigners? Do they need some blood tie with the frontier and its dangers in order to experience what it means to be an American? Or is it an attempt to avoid facing the guilt they bear for the treatment of the Indian?

The phenomenon seems to be universal. Only among the Jewish community, which has a long tribal-religious tradition of its own, does the mysterious Indian grandmother, the primeval princess, fail to dominate the family tree. Otherwise, there's not much to be gained by claiming Indian blood or publicly identifying as an Indian. The white believes that there is a great danger the lazy Indian will eventually corrupt God's hard working people. He is still suspicious that the Indian way of life is dreadfully wrong. There is, in fact, something *un-American* about Indians for most whites.

I ran across a classic statement of this attitude one day in a history book which was published shortly after the turn of the century. Often have I wondered how many Senators, Congressmen, and clergymen of the day accepted the attitudes of that book as a basic fact of life in America. In no uncertain terms did the book praise God that the Indian had not yet been able to corrupt North America as he had South America:

> It was perhaps fortunate for the future of America that the Indians of the North rejected civilization. Had they accepted it the whites and Indians might have intermarried to some extent as they did in Mexico. That would have given us a population made up in a measure of shiftless half-breeds.

I never dared to show this passage to my white friends who had claimed Indian blood, but I often wondered why they were so energetic if they did have some of the bad seed in them.

Those whites who dare not claim Indian blood have an asset of their own. They *understand* Indians.

Understanding Indians is not an esoteric art. All it takes is a trip through Arizona or New Mexico, watching a documentary on TV, having known *one* in the service, or having read a popular book on *them*.

There appears to be some secret osmosis about Indian people by which they can magically and instantaneously communicate complete knowledge about themselves to these interested whites. Rarely is physical contact required. Anyone and everyone who knows an Indian or who is *interested,* immediately and thoroughly understands them.

You can verify this great truth at your next party. Mention Indians and you will find a person who saw some in a gas station in Utah, or who attended the Gallup ceremonial celebration, or whose Uncle Jim hired one to cut logs in Oregon, or whose church had a missionary come to speak last Sunday on the plight of Indians and the mission of the church.

There is no subject on earth so easily understood as that of the American Indian. Each summer, work camps disgorge teenagers on various reservations. Within one month's time the youngsters acquire a knowledge of Indians that would astound a college professor.

Easy knowledge about Indians is a historical tradition. After Columbus "discovered" America he brought back news of a great new world which he assumed to be India and, therefore, filled with Indians. Almost at once European folklore devised a complete explanation of the new land and its inhabitants which featured the Fountain of Youth, the Seven Cities of Gold, and other exotic attractions. The absence of elephants apparently did not tip off the explorers that they weren't in India. By the time they realized their mistake, instant knowledge of Indians was a cherished tradition.

Missionaries, after learning some of the religious myths of tribes they encountered, solemnly declared that the inhabitants of the new continent were the Ten Lost Tribes of Israel. Indians thus received a religious-historical identity far greater than they wanted or deserved. But it was an impossible identity. Their failure to measure up to Old Testament standards doomed them to a fall from grace and they were soon relegated to the status of a picturesque species of wildlife.

Like the deer and the antelope, Indians seemed to play rather than get down to the serious business of piling up treasures upon the earth where thieves break through and steal. Scalping, introduced prior to the French and Indian War by the English,* confirmed the suspicion that Indians were wild animals to be hunted and skinned. Bounties were set and an Indian scalp became more valuable than beaver, otter, marten, and other animal pelts.

---

*Notice, for example the following proclamation:
> Given at the Council Chamber in Boston this third day of November 1755 in the twenty-ninth year of the Reign of our Sovereign Lord George the Second by the Grace of God of Great Britain, France, and Ireland, King Defender of the Faith.

> By His Honour's command
> J. Willard, Secry.
> God Save the King

> Whereas the tribe of Penobscot Indians have repeatedly in a perfidious manner acted contrary to their solemn submission unto his Majesty long since made and frequently renewed.

> I have, therefore, at the desire of the House of Representatives . . .thought fit to issue this Proclamation and to declare the Penobscot Tribe of Indians to be enemies, rebels and traitors to his Majesty. . . .And I do hereby require his Majesty's subjects of the Province to embrace all opportunities of pursuing, captivating, killing and destroy—all and every of the aforesaid Indians.

> And whereas the General Court of this Province have voted that a bounty . . .be granted and allowed to be paid out of the Province Treasury . . .the premiums of bounty following viz:

> For every scalp of a male Indian brought in as evidence of their being killed as aforesaid, forty pounds.

> For every scalp of such female Indian or male Indian under the age of twelve years that shall be killed and brought in as evidence of their being killed as aforesaid, twenty pounds.

American blacks had become recognized as a species of human being by amendments to the Constitution shortly after the Civil War. Prior to emancipation they had been counted as three-fifths of a person in determining population for representation in the House of Representatives. Early Civil Rights bills nebulously state that other people shall have the same rights as "white people," indicating there *were* "other people." But Civil Rights bills passed during and after the Civil War systematically excluded Indian people. For a long time an Indian was not presumed capable of initiating an action in a court of law, of owning property, or of giving testimony against whites in court. Nor could an Indian vote or leave his reservation. Indians were America's captive people without any defined rights whatsoever.

Then one day the white man discovered that the Indian tribes still owned some 135 million acres of land. To his horror he learned that much of it was very valuable. Some was good grazing land, some was farm land, some mining land, and some covered with timber.

Animals could be herded together on a piece of land, but they could not sell it. Therefore it took no time at all to discover that Indians were really people and should have the right to sell their lands. Land was the means of recognizing the Indian as a human being. It was the method whereby land could be stolen legally and not blatantly.

Once the Indian was thus acknowledged, it was fairly simple to determine what his goals were. If, thinking went, the Indian was just like the white, he must have the same outlook as the white. So the future was planned for the Indian people in public and private life. First in order was allotting them reservations so that they could sell their lands. God's foreordained plan to repopulate the continent fit exactly with the goals of the tribes as they were defined by their white friends.

It is fortunate that we were never slaves. We gave up land instead of life and labor. Because the Negro labored, he was considered a draft animal. Because the Indian occupied large areas of land, he was considered a wild animal. Had we given up anything else, or had anything else to give up, it is certain that we would have been considered some other thing.

Whites have had different attitudes toward the Indians and the blacks since the Republic was founded. Whites have always refused to give non-whites the respect which they have been found to legally possess. Instead there has always been a contemptuous attitude that although the law says one thing, "we all know better."

Thus whites steadfastly refused to allow blacks to enjoy the fruits of full citizenship. They systematically closed schools, churches, stores, restaurants, and public places to blacks or made insulting provisions for them. For one hundred years every program of public and private white America was devoted to the exclusion of the black. It was, perhaps, embarrassing to be rubbing shoulders with one who had not so long before been defined as a field animal.

The Indian suffered the reverse treatment. Law after law was passed requiring him to conform to white institutions. Indian children were kidnapped and forced into boarding schools thousands of miles from their homes to learn the white man's ways. Reservations were turned over to different Christian denominations for governing. Reservations were for a long time church operated. Everything possible was done to ensure that Indians were forced into American life. The wild animal was made into a household pet whether or not he wanted to be one.

Policies for both black and Indian failed completely. Blacks eventually began the Civil Rights movement. In doing so they assured themselves some rights in white society. Indians continued to withdraw from the overtures of white society and tried to maintain their own communities and activities.

Actually both groups had little choice. Blacks, trapped in a world of white symbols, retreated into themselves. And people thought comparable Indian withdrawal unnatural because they expected Indians to behave like whites.

The white world of abstract symbols became a nightmare for Indian people. The words of the treaties, clearly stating that Indians should have "free and undisturbed" use of their lands under the protection of the federal government, were case aside by the whites as if they didn't exist. The Sioux once had a treaty plainly stating that it would take the signatures or marks of three-fourths of the adult males to amend it. Yet through force the government obtained only 10 percent of the required signatures and declared the new agreement valid.

Indian solutions to problems which had been defined by the white society were rejected out of hand and obvious solutions discarded when they called for courses of action that were not proper in white society. When Crow Dog assassinated Spotted Tail the matter was solved under traditional Sioux customs. Yet an outraged public, furious because Crow Dog had not been executed, pressured for the Seven Major Crimes Act for the federal government to assume nearly total criminal jurisdiction over the reservations. Thus foreign laws and customs using the basic concepts of justice came to dominate Indian life. If, Indians reasoned, justice is for society's benefit, why isn't our justice accepted? Indians became convinced they were the world's stupidest people.

Words and situations never seemed to fit together. Always, it seemed, the white man chose a course of action that did not work. The white man preached that it was good to help the poor, yet he did nothing to assist the poor in his society. Instead he put constant pressure on the Indian people to hoard their worldly goods, and when they failed to accumulate capital but freely gave to the poor, the white man reacted violently.

The failure of communication created a void into which poured the white do-gooder, the missionary, the promoter, the scholar, and every conceivable type of person who believed he could help. White society failed to understand the situation because this conglomerate of assistance blurred the real issues beyond recognition.

The legend of the Indian was embellished or tarnished according to the need of the intermediates to gain leverage in their struggle to solve problems that never existed outside of their own minds. The classic example, of course, is the old-time missionary box. People were horrified that Indians continued to dress in their traditional garb. Since whites did not wear buckskin and beads, they equated such dress with savagery. So do-gooders in the East held fantastic clothing drives to supply the Indians with civilized clothes. Soon boxes of discarded evening gowns, tuxedos, tennis shoes, and uniforms flooded the reservations. Indians were made to dress in these remnants so they could be civilized. Then, realizing the ridiculous picture presented by the reservation people, neighboring whites made fun of the Indian people for having the presumption to dress like whites.

But in the East, whites were making great reputations as "Indian experts," as people who devoted their lives to helping the savages. Whenever Indian land was needed, the whites pictured the tribes as wasteful people who refused to develop their natural resources. Because the Indians did not "use" their lands, argued many land promoters, the lands should be taken away and given to people who knew what to do with them.

White society concentrated on the individual Indian to the exclusion of his group, forgetting that any society is merely a composite of individuals. Generalizations by experts universalized "Indianness" to the detriment of unique Indian values. Indians with a common cultural base shared behavior patterns. But they were expected to behave like a similar group of whites and rarely did. Whites, on the other hand, generally came from a multitude of backgrounds and shared only the need for economic subsistence. There was no way, therefore, to combine white values and Indian behavior into a workable program or intelligible subject of discussion.

One of the foremost differences separating white and Indian was simply one of origin. Whites derived predominantly from western Europe. The earliest settlers on the Atlantic seaboard came from England and the low countries. For the most part they shared the common experiences of their peoples and dwelt within the world view which had dominated western Europe for over a millenium.

Conversely Indians had always been in the western hemisphere. Life on this continent and views concerning it were not shaped in a post-Roman atmosphere. The entire outlook of the people was one of simplicity and mystery, not scientific or abstract. The western hemisphere produced wisdom, western Europe produced knowledge.

Perhaps this distinction seems too simple to mention. It is not. Many is the time I have sat in Congressional hearings and heard the chairman of the committee crow about "our" great Anglo-Saxon heritage of law and order. Looking about the hearing room I saw row after row of full-blood Indians with blank expressions on their faces. As far as they were concerned, Sir Walter Raleigh was a brand of pipe tobacco that you got at the trading post.

When we talk about European background, we are talking about feudalism, kings, queens, their divine right to rule their subjects, the Reformation, Christianity, the Magna Charta and all of the events that went to make up European history.

American Indians do not share that heritage. They do not look wistfully back across the seas to the old country. The Apache were not at Runymede to make King John sign the Magna Charta. The Cherokee did not create English common law. The Pima had no experience with the rise of capitalism and industrialism. The Blackfeet had no monasteries. No tribe has an emotional, historical, or political relationship to events of another continent and age.

Indians have had their own political history which has shaped the outlook of the tribes. There were great confederacies throughout the country before the time of the white invader. The eastern Iroquois formed a strong league because as single tribes they had been weak and powerless against larger tribes. The Deep South was controlled by three confederacies: the Creeks with their town system, the Natchez, and the Powhattan confederation which extended into tidelands Virginia. The Pequots and their cousins the Mohicans controlled the area of Connecticut, Massachusetts, Rhode Island, and Long Island.

True democracy was more prevalent among Indian tribes in pre-Columbian days than it has been since. Despotic power was abhorred by tribes that were loose combinations of hunting parties rather than political entities.

Conforming their absolute freedom to fit rigid European political forms has been very difficult for most tribes, but on the whole they have managed extremely well. Under the Indian Reorganization Act Indian people have generally created a modern version of the old tribal political structure and yet have been able to develop comprehensive reservation programs which compare favorably with governmental structures anywhere.

The deep impression made upon American minds by the Indian struggle against the white man in the last century has made the contemporary Indian somewhat invisible compared with his ancestors. Today Indians are not conspicuous by their absence from view. Yet they should be.

In *The Other America,* the classic study of poverty by Michael Harrington, the thesis is developed that the poor are conspicuous by their invisibility. There is no mention of Indians in the book. A century ago, Indians would have dominated such a work.

Indians are probably invisible because of the tremendous amount of misinformation about them. Most books about Indians cover some abstract and esoteric topic of the last century. Contemporary books are predominantly by whites trying to solve the "Indian problem." Between the two extremes lives a dynamic people in a social structure of their own, asking only to be freed from cultural oppression. The future does not look bright for the attainment of such freedom because the white does not understand the Indian and the Indian does not wish to understand the white.

Understanding Indians means understanding so-called Indian Affairs. Indian Affairs, like Gaul, is divided into three parts: the government, the private organizations, and the tribes themselves. Mythological theories about the three sectors are as follows: paternalism exists in the governmental area, assistance is always available in the private sector, and the tribes dwell in primitive splendor. All three myths are false.

The government has responsibility for the Indian estate because of treaty commitments and voluntary assumption of such responsibility. It allegedly cares for Indian lands and resources. Education, health services, and technical assistance are provided to the major tribes by the Bureau of Indian Affairs, which is in the Department of the Interior.

But the smaller tribes get little or nothing from the Interior Department. Since there are some 315 distinct tribal communities and only about 30 get any kind of federal services, there is always a Crisis in Indian Affairs. Interior could solve the problems of 250 small tribes in one year if it wanted to. It doesn't want to.

The name of the game in the government sector is TASK FORCE REPORT. Every two years some reporter causes a great uproar about how Indians are treated by the Bureau of Indian Affairs. This, in turn, causes great consternation among Senators and Congressmen who have to answer mail from citizens concerned about Indians. So a TASK FORCE REPORT is demanded on Indian problems.

The conclusion of every TASK FORCE REPORT is that Congress is not appropriating enough money to do an adequate job of helping Indians. Additionally, these reports find that while Indians are making some progress, the fluctuating policy of Congress is stifling Indian progress. The reports advise that a consistent policy of self-help with adequate loan funds for reservation development be initiated.

Since Congress is not about to appropriate any more money than possible for Indian Affairs, the TASK FORCE REPORT is filed away for future reference. Rumor has it that there is a large government building set aside as a storage bin for TASK FORCE REPORTS.

This last year saw the results of a number of TASK FORCE REPORTS. In 1960, when the New Frontier burst upon the scene, a TASK FORCE REPORT was prepared. It made the recommendations listed above. In 1966 two additional TASK FORCES went abroad in search of the solution to the ''Indian problem.'' One was a secret Presidential TASK FORCE. One was a semi-secret Interior TASK FORCE. In March of 1968 the President asked for a 10 percent increase in funds for Indian programs and after eight years of Democratic rule, a TASK FORCE recommendation was actually carried out.

Government agencies always believe that their TASK FORCES are secret. They believe that anonymous experts can ferret out the esoteric answers to an otherwise insoluble problem. Hence they generally keep secret the names of people serving on their TASK FORCES until after the report is issued. Only they make one mistake. They always have the same people on the TASK FORCE. So when Indians learn there is a TASK FORCE abroad they automatically know who are on it and what they are thinking.

Paternalism is always a favorite subject of the TASK FORCES. They make it one of the basic statements of their preambles. It has therefore become an accepted tenet that paternalism dominates government-Indian relationships.

Congress always wants to do away with paternalism. So it has a policy designed to do away with Indians. If there are no Indians, there cannot be any paternalism.

But governmental paternalism is not a very serious problem. If an employee of the Bureau of Indian Affairs gives any tribe any static the problem is quickly resolved. The tribal chairman gets on the next plane to Washington. The next morning he walks into the Secretary of the Interior's office and raises hell. Soon a number of bureaucrats are working on the problem. The tribal chairman has a good dinner, goes to a movie, and takes the late plane back to his reservation. Paternalism by field men is not very popular in the Department of the Interior in Washington. Consequently, there is very little paternalism in the governmental sector if the tribe knows what it is doing. And most tribes know what they are doing.

In the private sector, however, paternalism is a fact of life. Nay, it is the standard operating procedure. Churches, white interest organizations, universities, and private firms come out to the reservations asking only to be of service IN THEIR OWN INIMITABLE WAY. No one asks them to come out. It is very difficult, therefore, to get them to leave.

Because no chairman has the time to fly into New York weekly and ask the national churches to stop the paternalistic programs of their missionaries, the field is ripe for paternalism. Most of them are not doing much anyway.

But, people in the private area are working very hard to keep Indians happy. When Indians get unhappy they begin to think about kicking out the white do-gooders, paternalism or not. And if the private organizations were kicked out of a reservation, where would they work? What would they claim as their accomplishments at fund-raising time?

Churches, for example, invest great amounts to train white men for Indian missions. If there were ever too great a number of Indian missionaries, Indians might think they should have their own churches. Then there would be no opportunity to convert the pagans. Where, then, would clergy misfits go if not to Indian missions?

So paternalism is very sophisticated in the private sector. It is disguised by a board of "Indian advisors," selected from among the Indians themselves on the reservation. These "advisors" are put to use to make it appear as if all is well. Pronouncements by Indian advisory boards generally commend the private organization for its work. They ask it to do even more work, for only in that way, they declare, can justice be done to their people.

To hear some people talk, Indians are simultaneously rich from oil royalties and poor as church mice. To hear others, Indians have none of the pleasures of the mainstream, like riots, air pollution, snipers, ulcers, and traffic. Consequently, they class Indians among the "underprivileged" in our society.

Primitive purity is sometimes attributed to tribes. Some tribes keep their rituals and others don't. The best characterization of tribes is that they stubbornly hold on to what they feel is important to them and discard what they feel is irrelevant to their current needs. Traditions die hard and innovation comes hard. Indians have survived for thousands of years in all kinds of conditions. They do not fly from fad to fad seeking novelty. That is what makes them Indian.

Three books, to my way of thinking, give a good idea of the intangible sense of reality that pervades the Indian people. *When the Legends Die* by Hal Borland gives a good picture of Indian youth. *Little Big Man* by Thomas Berger gives a good idea of Indian attitudes toward life. *Stay Away, Joe,* by Dan Cushman, the favorite of Indian people, gives a humorous but accurate idea of the problems caused by the intersection of two ways of life. Anyone who can read, appreciate, and understand the spiritual forces brought out in these books will have a good idea of what Indians are all about.

Other books may be nice, accurate, and historical but they are not really about Indians. In general, they twist Indian reality into a picture which is hard to understand and consequently greatly in error.

Statistical information on Indians can easily be found in other books. What is important, for understanding the present state of Indian Affairs, is to know how tribes are organized today, how they work together, and what they anticipate for the future. And there is no easy way to broach the subject. So let us begin.

In 1934 the Indian Reorganization Act was passed. Under the provisions of this act reservation people were enabled to organize for purposes of self-government. Nearly three-quarters of the reservations organized. These reservations are not known as tribes. Often the remnants of larger historical tribal groups that were located on different pieces of land, they became under IRA officially recognized as "tribes."

There are nineteen different Chippewa tribes, fifteen Sioux tribes, four Potawatomi tribes, a number of Paiute tribes, and several consolidated tribes which encompass two different groups that happened to land on the same reservation.

Examples of consolidated tribes are the Salish and Kootenai of Montana, the Cheyenne-Arapaho of Oklahoma, the Kiowa-Comanche-Apache of Oklahoma, and the Mandan, Hidatsa, and Arikara of the Fort Berthold reservation in North Dakota.

Over the past generation tribes have discovered that they must band together to make themselves heard. Consequently most states have inter-tribal councils, composed of the tribes in that state, that meet regularly and exchange ideas. In some areas, particularly in the Northwest, tribal representation is on a regional basis. The Northwest Affiliated Tribes is an organization made up of tribes from Montana, Idaho, Washington, and Oregon. Its counterpart, the Western Washington Inter-tribal Coordinating Council consists of tribes that live in the Puget Sound area.

Rarely do tribes overlap across state boundaries. While there are fifteen Sioux tribes, the United Sioux is an organization of only South Dakota tribes. Sioux groups in North Dakota, Nebraska, or Minnesota are not invited.

Indians have two "mainstream" organizations, the National Congress of American Indians and the National Indian Youth Council. The NCAI is open to tribes, organizations, and individuals, both red and white. Its major emphasis is on strong tribal membership because it works primarily with legislation and legislation is handled on an individual tribal basis.

The NIYC is the SNCC of Indian Affairs. Organized in 1962, it has been active among the post-college group just entering Indian Affairs. Although NIYC has a short history, it has been able to achieve recognition as a force to be reckoned with in national Indian Affairs. Generally more liberal and more excitable than the NCAI, the NIYC inclines to the spectacular short-term project rather than the extended program. The rivalry between the two groups is intense.

Lesser known but with great potential for the future are the traditional organizations. Primary among these is the oldest continuous Indian-run organization: the League of Nations, Pan American Indians. Its President, Alfred Gagne, incorporates the best of traditional Indian life and national problems into a coherent working philosophy. Should this group ever receive sufficient funding to have field workers, it could very well overturn established government procedures in Indian Affairs. It has long fought the Bureau of Indian Affairs and seeks a return to traditional Indian customs.

From the work of the League of Nations has come the alliance of the traditional Indians of each tribe. In June of 1968 they met in Oklahoma to form the National Aborigine Conference. Discussions ranging from religious prophecies to practical politics were held. From this conference is expected to come a strong nationalistic push on the reservations in the next several years.

Another group well worthy of mention is the American Indian Historical Society of San Francisco. Begun by Rupert Costo, a Cauhilla man, the society has become the publishers of the finest contemporary material on Indians. Excellent research and wide knowledge of Indian people makes it an influential voice in Indian Affairs.

Recently, during the Poor People's March, Indian participants formed the Coalition of American Indian Citizens. A loose and perhaps temporary alliance of disgruntled young people, the Coalition brought to Indian Affairs a sense of urgency. Whether it will continue to function depends on the commitment of its members to goals which they originally stated.

Regional groups are occasionally formed around a specific issue. In the Northwest the Survivors of American Indians, Inc., works exclusively on the issue of fishing rights. In Oklahoma the Original Cherokee Community Organization has been formed to defend hunting and treaty rights of the Cherokees.

Most urban areas have urban centers or clubs composed of Indian people. For the most part these centers provide a place where urban Indians can meet and socialize. The best-known centers are in Los Angeles, Oakland, Chicago, and Minneapolis. New centers are always springing up in different cities. There are probably in excess of thirty functioning centers or clubs at any one time. The urban areas show the most potential for strong lasting organizations, however, and once the urban Indians stabilize themselves they will experience phenomenal growth.

All of these groups are primarily interested in issues and policies. The Indian Council Fire of Chicago works primarily in the field of public relations and Indian culture. The American Indian Development, Inc., works in the field of youth work and economic development of Indian communities.

There are a number of white organizations that attempt to help Indian people. Since we would be better off without them I will not mention them, except to comment that they do exist.

Movement occurs easily in Indian Affairs. Tribes are generally quite alert to issues and policies advocated by red and white alike. It is a rare event that goes unnoticed. Careful observation of the effects of the moccasin telegraph indicates a tendency by the Indian people to organize and coalesce around certain issues rather than according to any set pattern.

The National Congress of American Indians is the best example of this tendency. Membership fluctuates in the NCAI according to the urgency of national issues affecting member tribes. The NCAI attracts only those tribes that are interested in its programs. Unity for unity's sake is not yet a concept that has been accepted by the tribes. Nor has unity for future action been understood.

Within the NCAI personal leadership determines policies and programs. In 1954 Congress began the great push to abrogate Indian rights in a series of "termination bills" by which federal services and protections would be denied to tribes. Fortunately the northwestern tribes under the leadership of Joseph Garry, Chairman of the Coeur d'Alenes of Idaho, were then in control of the NCAI. Garry succeeded in uniting enough tribes under his leadership to bring the policy to a stalemate. It has remained in a deadlock ever since, with Congress waiting for the tribes to lose interest and the tribes remaining on the alert against any termination move by Congress.

Garry served as President of the NCAI from 1953-1959. He established a tradition in the Northwest of political cooperation between the tribes. National Indian Affairs has ever since been haunted by the memory of the powerful coalition of that era. Since Garry's days few decisions are made in Indian Affairs without first checking with northwestern tribal leadership. The recent alliance of the Northwest with the Alaskan natives will shortly result in a total takeover of the NCAI by the northwestern tribes as the Indian political balance is once again achieved.

The power of the Northwest has been balanced by the leadership and political ability of the Sioux. During twenty-five years of NCAI existence the Sioux have held the Executive Directorship for fourteen years. The Sioux reign is nearly at an end, however, as other tribes achieve more political sophistication and begin to exert more influence on the total national scene. The rise of the Wisconsin-Minnesota groups of Chippewas as a potent force was noted at the NCAI convention in Omaha in 1968. Since the Chippewa and the Sioux are traditional enemies and the Chippewa are now allied with the northwestern tribes, the Chippewa should be able to take over the entire field of Indian Affairs within a period of three years. They now lack only that charismatic leader who can articulate critical issues to other tribes.

The tribes from California, Kansas, and Nevada have traditionally been slow to rise to the challenge of national Indian political combat. Yet they could unite and take over the organization completely if they were to join it en masse. With the current inroads being made into national Indian Affairs by the Coalition of Indian Citizens and the National Indian Youth Council, California and Nevada may yet exert tremendous influence over other tribes by attending an NCAI convention with full voting power.

The NCAI is important to the Indian people only when it provides a forum in which issues can be discussed. Occasionally it has come to be dominated by a few tribes and then it has rapidly gone downhill. At the Omaha convention of 1968 non-tribal groups attended the meeting hoping to be allowed to participate. Instead they were rebuffed, and during the convention all non-tribal forces became allied outside the normal channels of Indian Affairs. This tragic blunder by the NCAI could cause a great conflict between reservation and non-reservation groups in the future. There is little doubt that urban Indians have more sophistication than do reservation people, and now urban Indians and the National Indian Youth Council have formed together as cooperating organizations to work for urban and young Indian people. It will probably take several years for Indian tribes to absorb the meaning of this new coalition. By then it may be too late for them to survive.

Individual tribes show incredible differences. No single aspect seems to be as important as tribal solidarity. Tribes that can handle their reservation conflicts in traditional Indian fashion generally make more progress and have better programs than do tribes that continually make adaptations to the white value system. The Pueblos of New Mexico have a solid community life and are just now, with the influx of college-educated Pueblos, beginning large development projects. In spite of the vast differences between the generations, the Pueblos have been able to maintain a sense of tribal purpose and solidarity, and developments are undertaken by the consensus of all the people of the community.

Even more spectacular are the Apaches of the Southwest—the Mescalero, San Carlos, White Mountain, and Jicarilla tribes. Numbering probably less than a dozen college graduates among them, the four tribes have remained close to their traditions, holding ancient ceremonies to be of utmost importance to the future of the tribe. Without the benefit of the white man's vaunted education, these four Apache groups have developed their reservations with amazing skill and foresight. Mescalero Apache owns a ski resort worth over one million dollars. Jicarilla has a modern shopping center. White Mountain has a tremendous tourism development of some twenty-six artificial lakes stocked with trout. San Carlos has a fine cattle industry and is presently developing an industrial park.

Contrast the Chippewas with the Apaches and the picture is not as bright. The Chippewas are located in Minnesota, Wisconsin, and Michigan. They have access to the large cities of Chicago, Minneapolis, Milwaukee, and Detroit. The brain drain of leadership from the Chippewa reservations to the cities has been enormous over the years. Migration to the cities has meant an emphasis on land sales, little development of existing resources, and abandonment of tribal traditions. Only among the Red Lake Chippewa has much progress been made. And Red Lake is probably the most traditional of the Chippewa tribes.

The Sioux, my own people, have a great tradition of conflict. We were the only nation ever to annihilate the United States Cavalry three times in succession. And when we find no one else to quarrel with, we often fight each other. The Sioux problem is excessive leadership. During one twenty-year period in the last century the Sioux fought over an area from LaCrosse, Wisconsin, to Sheridan, Wyoming, against the Crow, Arapaho, Cheyenne, Mandan, Arikara, Hidatsa, Ponca, Iowa, Pawnee, Otoe, Omaha, Winnebago, Chippewa, Cree, Assiniboine, Sac and Fox, Potawatomi, Ute, and Gros Ventre. This was, of course, in addition to fighting the U.S. Cavalry continually throughout that period. The United States government had to call a special treaty session merely to settle the argument among the tribes in the eastern half of that vast territory. It was the only treaty between tribes supervised by the federal government.

But the Sioux never quit fighting. Reservation programs are continually disrupted by bickering within the reservations. Each election on a Sioux reservation is generally a fight to the finish. A ten-vote margin of some 1,500 votes cast is a landslide victory in Sioux country. Fortunately strong chairmen have come to have a long tenure on several Sioux reservations and some of the tribes have made a great deal of progress. But the tendency is always present to slug it out at a moment's notice.

The northwestern tribes also have their fierce and gentle side. Over the past two decades there has been continual conflict between the western tribes and the Fish and Game commissions in Oregon and Washington. Violations of treaty fishing rights by the state can bring Yakimas to the riverbanks with guns so quick as to frighten an unsuspecting bystander.

Before anyone conceived of statehood for either state, Isaac Stevens, on behalf of the United States, traveled up the coast signing treaties with all of the Pacific tribes. These treaties promised perpetual hunting and fishing rights for the tribes if they would agree to remain on restricted reservations. After World War II, when the sportsmen began to have leisure time, the states sought to abrogate the treaties. But in the case of Washington there was a specific disclaimer clause in the act admitting Washington into the Union by which the state promised never to disturb the Indian tribes within its borders.

In recent years there have been a number of "fish-ins" by the smaller tribes in Washington in sporadic attempts to raise the fishing-rights issue. Unfortunately the larger tribes have not supported these people. The larger tribes cannot seem to understand that a precedent of law set against a small tribe means one for the larger tribes as well. It may well be that all Indian fishing will eventually be regulated by the states of the Northwest. This would be quite tragic as there is a fundamental difference between Indian and sports fishing. Indian people are fishing for food for their families. Sportsmen are fishing for relaxation and recreation. Indians may have to starve so that whites can have a good time on the weekends if present trends continue.

But the northwestern tribes have taken the lead in pursuing their rights in court in this century. In the last century the Cherokees went to the Supreme Court over and over again and set forth most of Indian law in its developing years. Similarly in this century the tribes of Oregon, Washington, and Idaho have won the more significant cases which have been taken to court. Such landmark cases as *Squire v. Capoeman,* a taxation case which spelled out exemption of individual allotments from income tax, *United States v. Winans,* which defined water rights and fishing rights, *Mason v. Sams,* another fishing-rights case, and *Seymour v. Superintendent,* a jurisdiction case which gave the modern definition of "Indian country"—a concept important for preservation of treaty rights—were all cases initiated by tribes of that area.

In 1967 ABC television began its ill-fated series on Custer. The Tribal Indians Land Rights Association began the national fight to get the series banned. Eventually the NCAI and other groups protested to ABC over the series and a great Indian war was on. Custer, who had never been a very bright character, was tabbed by the NCAI as the "Adolph Eichmann" of the nineteenth century. But not one could figure out the correct strategy by which ABC could be forced to negotiate.

Finally the Yakima tribal lawyer, James Hovis, devised the tactic of getting every tribe to file for equal time against ABC's local affiliate (ABC itself was not subject to FCC regulations). As tribes in the different areas began to move, ABC, through its affiliate board, arranged a trip to California to discuss the program with the NCAI. Several tribes filed against the local affiliates of ABC and did receive some air time to present the Indian side of the Custer story during the brief run of the show. Later we heard that it would have cost ABC some three thousand dollars per complaint if every tribe had gone ahead and demanded FCC hearings on the controversy. Whether this was true or not we never learned, but once again the northwestern Indians had devised a legal strategy by which Indians as a national ethnic group could air their complaints. The series was canceled after nine episodes.

The greatest potential, as yet untapped, lies in Nevada. With a small total population concentrated in Las Vegas and Reno, Nevada is presently on the threshold of development. Some twenty-six tribes, mainly Paiutes and Shoshones, live in Nevada. If these tribes were ever to form a strong political or economic alliance, they would exert tremendous influence within the state. The Nevadan Indian population is fairly young and the possibility of its developing a strong Indian swing vote as it comes of age is excellent.

Perhaps even more spectacular is the pattern by which Indian land is held in that state. In the closing years of the last century there were no large reservations set up in Nevada. Instead, because the groups were so small and scattered, Indians were given public-domain allotments adjoining the larger towns and cities in Nevada. These groups were called colonies and they were simply unorganized groups of Indians living, like the Lone Ranger and Tonto used to do, ''not far from town.'' Today the Nevada tribes have extremely valuable land in areas where development will have to move if the towns in Nevada are going to continue to grow. With few exceptions old desert lands of the last century are now prime prospects for industrial parks and residential subdivisions. If the Nevada tribes were to pursue a careful policy of land exchange, they would soon own great amounts of land and have a respectable bank account as well.

Indian tribes are rapidly becoming accustomed to the manner in which the modern world works. A generation ago most Indians would not have known which way Washington, D.C., lay. Today it is a rare tribe that does not make a visit once a year to talk with its Congressional delegation, tour the government agencies, and bring home a new program or project from the many existing programs being funded by the federal government. Many tribes receive the Congressional Record and a number subscribe to leading national publications such as *The Wall Street Journal, Life, Time,* and *Newsweek.* Few events of much importance pass the eyes of watchful tribal groups without comment.

Tribes are also becoming very skilled at grantsmanship. Among the larger, more experienced tribes, million-dollar programs are commonplace. Some tribes sharpened their teeth on the old Area Redevelopment Administration of the early sixties. When the Office of Economic Opportunity was created they jumped into the competition with incredibly complex programs and got them funded. One housing program on the Rosebud Sioux reservation is a combination of programs offered by some five different government agencies. The Sioux there have melded a winning hand by making each government agency fund a component of the total housing program for the reservation.

Some tribes take home upward of ten million dollars a year in government programs and private grants for their reservation people. Many tribes, combining a variety of sources, have their own development officer to plan and project future programs. The White Mountain Apaches are the first tribe to have their own public relations firm to keep tribal relations with the surrounding towns and cities on an even keel.

With a change in Congressional policy away from termination toward support of tribal self-sufficiency, it is conceivable that Indian tribes will be able to become economically independent of the federal government in the next generation. Most tribes operate under the provisions of their Indian Reorganization Act constitutions and are probably better operated than most towns, certainly more honestly operated than the larger cities.

Tribes lost some ten years during the 1950's when all progress was halted by the drive toward termination. Arbitrary and unreasonable harassment of tribal programs, denial of credit funds for program development, and pressure on tribes to liquidate assets all contributed to waste a decade during which tribes could have continued to develop their resources.

Today the Indian people are in a good position to demonstrate to the nation what can be done in community development in the rural areas. With the overcrowding of the urban areas, rural development should be the coming thing and understanding of tribal programs could indicate methods of resettling the vast spaces of rural America.

With so much happening on reservations and the possibility of a brighter future in store, Indians have started to become livid when they realize the contagious trap the mythology of white America has caught them in. The descendant of Pocahontas is a remote and incomprehensible mystery to us. We are no longer a wild species of animal loping freely across the prairie. We have little in common with the last of the Mohicans. We are TASK FORCED to death.

Some years ago at a Congressional hearing someone asked Alex Chasing Hawk, a council member of the Cheyenne River Sioux for thirty years, "Just what do you Indians want?" Alex replied, "A leave-us-alone law!!"

The primary goal and need of Indians today is not for someone to feel sorry for us and claim descent from Pocahontas to make us feel better. Nor do we need to be classified as semi-white and have programs and policies made to bleach us further. Nor do we need further studies to see if we are feasible. We need a new policy by Congress acknowledging our right to live in peace, free from arbitrary harassment. We need the public at large to drop the myths in which it has clothed us for so long. We need fewer and fewer "experts" on Indians.

What we need is a cultural leave-us-alone agreement, in spirit and in fact.

4 Social Work with Native Americans

Lewis, Ronald G.
Ho, Man Keung

*If social workers are to serve Native
Americans effectively, they must
understand their distinctive
characteristics and vary their
techniques accordingly.*

In the past, the social work profession has failed to serve effectively an
important segment of the population—the Native Americans. Although social
workers are in sympathy with the social problems and injustices long
associated with the Native American people, they have been unable to assist
them with their problems. This lack of success on the part of social workers
can be attributed to a multitude of reasons but it stems, in general, from the
following: (1) lack of understanding of the Native American culture,
(2) retention of stereotyped images of Native Americans, (3) use of standard
techniques and approaches.

Currently, the majority of social workers attempting to treat Native
Americans are whites who have never been exposed to their clients' culture.
Even when the social worker is a Native American, if his education and
training have been in an environment that has completely neglected the Native
American culture, there is still the possibility that he has drifted away from
his people's thinking. Social workers with no understanding of the culture
may have little or no sympathy for their Native American clients who fail to
respond quickly to treatment.

Furthermore, Native Americans continue to be stereotyped by the current
news media and often by the educational system. In all likelihood, the social
worker will rely on these mistaken stereotypes rather than on facts. As
Deloria explained, ''People can tell just by looking at us what we want, what
should be done to help us, how we feel, and what a 'real' Indian is like.''[1] If
a worker wishes to make progress in helping a Native American, he must
begin by learning the facts and discarding stereotypes.

The ineffectiveness of social workers in dealing with Native Americans
can often be attributed directly to the methods and techniques they use.
Naturally, social workers must work with the tools they have acquired, but
these may have a detrimental effect on a Native American. For example, the

concept of "social work intervention" may be consistent with much of the white man's culture, but it diametrically opposes the Native American's cultural concept of noninterference.[2] There is a great need for social workers to examine carefully those techniques they plan to use in treating their Native American clients. If the worker discovers any that might be in conflict with the cultural concepts of the Native American, he should search carefully for an alternative approach. To do this, of course, the social worker must be aware of common Native American cultural traits.

Although there is no monolithic Native American culture—because each tribe's culture is unique to that individual tribe, and no social worker could be expected to be familiar with the cultures of some two hundred tribes—the worker should familiarize himself with those customs that are generally characteristic of all Native Americans. Only after a worker has gained at least an elementary knowledge of Native American customs and culture can he proceed to evaluate the various approaches and techniques and choose the most effective ones.

Native American Traits

The concept of sharing is deeply ingrained among Native Americans who hold it in greater esteem than the white American ethic of saving. Since one's worth is measured by one's willingness and ability to share, the accumulation of material goods for social status is alien to the Native American. Sharing, therefore, is neither a superimposed nor an artificial value, but a genuine and routine way of life.

In contrast to the general belief that they have no concept of time, Native Americans are indeed time conscious. They deal, however, with natural phenomena—mornings, days, nights, months (in terms of moons), and years (in terms of seasons or winters).[3] If a Native American is on his way to a meeting or appointment and meets a friend, that conversation will naturally take precedence over being punctual for the appointment. In his culture, sharing is more important than punctuality.

Nature is the Native American's school, and he is taught to endure all natural happenings that he will encounter during his life. He learns as well to be an independent individual who respects others. The Native American believes that to attain maturity—which is learning to live with life, its evil as well as its good—one must face genuine suffering. The resilience of the Native American way of life is attested to by the fact that the culture has survived and continues to flourish despite the intense onslaught of the white man.

One of the strongest criticisms of the Native American has been that he is pessimistic; he is presented as downtrodden, low-spirited, unhappy, and without hope for the future. However, as one looks deeper into his personality, another perspective is visible. In the midst of abject poverty comes "the courage to be"—to face life as it is, while maintaining a tremendous sense of humor.[4] There exists a thin line between pathos and humor.

The Native American realizes that the world is made up of both good and bad. There are always some people or things that are bad and deceitful. He believes, however, that in the end good people will triumph just because they are good. This belief is seen repeatedly in Native American folktales about Iktomi the spider. He is the tricky fellow who is out to fool, cheat, and take advantage of good people. But Iktomi usually loses in the end, reflecting the Native American view that the good person succeeds while the bad person loses.[5] Therefore, the pessimism of Native Americans should instead be regarded as "optimistic toughness."

Those who are unfamiliar with the culture might mistakenly interpret the quiet Native American as being stoical, unemotional, and vulnerable. He is alone, not only to others but also to himself. He controls his emotions, allowing himself no passionate outbursts over small matters. His habitual mien is one of poise, self-containment, and aloofness, which may result from a fear and mistrust of non-Native Americans. Another facet of Native American thought is the belief that no matter where any individual stands, he is an integral part of the universe. Because every person is fulfilling a purpose, no one should have the power to impose values. For this reason, each man is to be respected, and he can expect the same respect and reverence from others. Hence, the security of this inner fulfillment provides him with an essential serenity that is often mistaken for stoicism.

Native American patience, however, can easily be mistaken for inactivity. For instance, the Kiowa, like other Native American tribes, teach their young people to be patient. Today, when the young Native American has to go out and compete in another society, this quality is often interpreted as laziness. The white man's world is a competitive, aggressive society that bypasses the patient man who stands back and lets the next person go first.

The foregoing are only a few of the cultural traits that are common to most Native American tribes, but they represent important characteristics about which the effective social worker must be informed. The concepts of sharing, of time, acceptance of suffering, and optimism differ significantly from the white man's concepts. In dealing with a Native American client, the social worker must realize this and proceed accordingly. He must be familiar with the Native American view that good will triumph over evil and must recognize that Native Americans are taught to be patient and respectful. If the worker fails to do this, he is liable to make false assumptions, thus weakening his ability to serve his client effectively.

Client-Worker Relations

A social worker's ability to establish a working relationship with a Native American will depend on his genuine respect for his client's cultural background and attributes. A worker should never think that the Native American is primitive or that his culture and background are inferior.

In the beginning, the Native American client might distrust the worker who is from a different race and culture. He might even view the worker as a figure of authority, and as such, the representative of a coercive institution. It is unlikely that he will be impressed with the worker's educational degrees or his professional title. However, this uncompromising attitude should not be interpreted as pugnacity. On the contrary, the Native American is gregarious and benevolent. His willingness and capacity to share depend on mutual consideration, respect, and noncoercion.

Because their culture strongly opposes and precludes interference with another's affairs, Native Americans have tended to regard social work intervention with disfavor. Social workers usually are forced to use culturally biased techniques and skills that are insensitive to the Native American culture and, therefore, are either detrimental to these clients or, at best, ineffective.

In an effort to communicate more fully, a social worker is likely to seat himself facing the client, look him straight in the eye, and insist that the client do likewise. A Native American considers such behavior—covert or overt—to be rude and intimidating; contrary to the white man, he shows respect by not staring directly at others. Similarly, a worker who is excessively concerned with facilitating the display of inner feelings on the part of the client should be aware of another trait. A Native American client will not immediately wish to discuss other members of his family or talk about topics that he finds sensitive or distressing. Before arriving at his immediate concern (the real reason he came to the worker in the first place), the client—particularly the Native American—will test the worker by bringing up peripheral matters. He does this in the hope of getting a better picture of how sincere, interested, and trustworthy the worker actually is. If the worker impatiently confronts the client with accusations, the client will be "turned off."

Techniques of communication that focus on the client—that is, techniques based on restating, clarifying, summarizing, reflecting, and empathizing—may help a worker relate to the client who sometimes needs a new perspective to resolve his problem. It is important that the worker provide him with such information but not coerce him to accept it. The worker's advice should be objective and flexible enough so that its adoption does not become the central issue of a particular interview.

For the Native American, personal matters and emotional breakdown are traditionally handled within the family or extended family system. For this reason, the client will not wish to "burden" the worker with detailed personal information. If the client is estranged from his family and cultural group, he may indirectly share such personal information with the worker. To determine the appropriate techniques for helping a Native American client deal with personal and psychological problems, the worker should carefully observe the client's cultural framework and his degree of defensiveness. The techniques of confrontation traditionally associated with the psychoanalytic approach and the introspective and integrative techniques used by the transactional analysts tend to disregard differences in culture and background between a client and worker.

Family Counseling

In view of the close-knit family structure of Native Americans, along with the cultural emphasis to keep family matters inside the family, it is doubtful that many social workers will have the opportunity to render family counseling services. In the event that a Native American family does seek the worker's help, the family worker should be reminded that his traditional role of active and manipulative go-between must be tempered so that family members can deal with their problems at their own pace.[6] Equally important is the worker's awareness of and respect for the resilience of Native American families, bolstered in crisis by the extended family system. The example of the Redthunder family serves as illustration.

> The Redthunder family was brought to the school social worker's attention when teachers reported that both children had been tardy and absent frequently in the past weeks. Since the worker lived near Mr. Redthunder's neighborhood, she volunteered to transport the children back and forth to school. Through this regular but informal arrangement, the worker became acquainted with the entire family, especially with Mrs. Redthunder who expressed her gratitude to the worker by sharing her homegrown vegetables.
>
> The worker sensed that there was much family discomfort and that a tumultuous relationship existed between Mr. and Mrs. Redthunder. Instead of probing into their personal and marital affairs, the worker let Mrs. Redthunder know that she was willing to listen should the woman need someone to talk to. After a few gifts of homegrown vegetables and Native American handicrafts, Mrs. Redthunder broke into tears one day and told the worker about her husband's problem of alcoholism and their deteriorating marital relationship.
>
> Realizing Mr. Redthunder's position of respect in the family and his resistance to outside interference, the social worker advised Mrs. Redthunder to take her family to visit the minister, a man whom Mr. Redthunder admired. The Littleaxe family, who were mutual friends of the worker and the Redthunder family, agreed to take the initiative in visiting the Redthunders more often. Through such frequent but informal family visits, Mr. Redthunder finally obtained a job, with the recommendation of Mr. Littleaxe, as recordkeeper in a storeroom. Mr. Redthunder enjoyed his work so much that he drank less and spent more time with his family.

Obviously, treating a family more pathogenic than the Redthunders might necessitate that the social worker go beyond the role of mediator. Nevertheless, since Native Americans traditionally favor noninterference, the social worker will not find it feasible to assume the active manipulative role that he might in working with white middle-class families. The social work profession needs new and innovative approaches to family counseling that take into account social and family networks and are sensitive and responsive to the cultural orientation of Native American families.[7]

Group Work

Groups should be a natural and effective medium for Native Americans who esteem the concept of sharing and apply it in their daily lives. Through the group process, members can share their joy, intimacy, problems, and sorrows, and find a means of improving their lives. Today's society tends to foster alienation, anomie, disenfranchisement, dissociation, loneliness, and schizoid coolness.[8] People wish for intimacy but at the same time fear it.[9] The new humanistic approaches to counseling and psychotherapy have developed a wide variety of powerful techniques for facilitating human growth, self-discovery, and interpersonal relations.[10] The effectiveness of these approaches in cutting through resistance, breaking down defenses, releasing creative forces, and promoting the healing process has been amply demonstrated. However, such approaches are highly insensitive to the cultural orientation of Native Americans. These people consider such group behavior to be false; it looks and sounds real but lacks genuineness, depth, and real commitment.

As the worker uses his skills in forming the group, diagnosing the problems, and facilitating group goals, he may inevitably retain certain elements of manipulation. However, if he is committed to recognizing individual potential and to capitalizing on the group model of mutual assistance, he should come close to meeting the needs of Native Americans who value respect and consideration for oneself as well as for others.[11]

To avoid manipulation and coercion, a group worker needs to utilize indirect and extra-group means of influence that will in turn influence the members. Thus the worker may act upon and through the group as a mediating structure, or through program activities, for the benefit of his clients.[12] The success of the worker's influences and activities is related to his knowledge and acceptance of Native American culture, its formal and informal systems and norms.

Regardless of whether the purpose of the group is for effecting interpersonal change or social action, such Native American virtues as mutual respect and consideration should be the essential components of the group process. Using the group to pressure members who are late or silent will not only jeopardize and shorten the group's existence, but will cause alienation and withdrawal from future group activities.

In view of the vast cultural difference between Native Americans and other ethnic groups, especially whites, it is doubtful that a heterogeneous grouping of members will produce good results. Similarly, group activities that are action oriented may be contradictory to Native Americans who view the compulsion to reduce or ignore suffering as immaturity.

Community Work

Because of the Native Americans' experience of oppression and exploitation—along with their emphasis on noninterference and resolute acceptance of suffering—it is doubtful that a social worker, regardless of his racial identity, could bring about any major change in community policies and programs. The only exception might be the social worker who is accepted and ''adopted'' by the community and who agrees to confine himself to the existing system and norms. A worker's adoption by the Native American community will depend on his sincerity, respect, and genuine concern for the people. This concern can best be displayed through patience in daily contact with the community as well as through his efforts to find positive solutions to problems.

A worker who uses the strategy of trying to resolve conflict as a means of bringing about social change will undoubtedly encounter native resistance and rejection. On the other hand, a worker who shows respect for the system, values, and norms of the Native American eventually places himself in a position of trust and credibility. Only through mutual respect, and not through his professional title and academic degree, can the worker produce meaningful social change.

Obviously, social work with Native Americans requires a new orientation and focus on attitudes and approaches. The term Native American encompasses many tribes, and within these there are intratribal differences; furthermore, individuals within each subtribe may react differently to problems or crises. Therefore, it is impossible for a social worker always to know precisely how to respond to a Native American client or group. The worker must be willing to admit his limitations, to listen carefully, to be less ready to draw conclusions, and to anticipate that his presuppositions will be corrected by the client. The worker must genuinely want to know what the problem or the situation is and be receptive to being taught. Such an unassuming and unobtrusive humanistic attitude is the key to working with Native American people.

The social worker who can deal most effectively with Native Americans will be genuine, respectful of their culture, and empathic with the welfare of the people. By no means does the Native American social worker have a monopoly on this type of attitude. In fact, the Native American social worker who has assimilated the white man's culture to the extent that he no longer values his own culture could do more harm than good.

Recognizing the distinct cultural differences of the Native American people, those who plan social work curricula and training programs must expand them to include specific preparation for workers who will be dealing with Native American clients. Literature on the subject is almost nonexistent, and researchers and educators would do well to devote more study to how social workers can serve Native Americans. More Native Americans should be recruited as students, faculty, and practitioners in the field of social work. All persons, regardless of race, should be encouraged to develop a sensitivity toward Native Americans whom they may have the opportunity to serve. Social work agencies that deal primarily with Native American clients should intensify and refocus their in-service training programs.

A worker has the responsibility of acquiring knowledge that is relevant to the Native American culture so that he is capable of providing this effective treatment. A joint effort on the part of all those involved is required to give the service to Native Americans that they justly deserve.

Notes and References

1. Vine Deloria, Jr., *Custer Died for Your Sins: An Indian Manifesto* (New York: Macmillan Co., 1969), p. 45.
2. For a detailed discussion of noninterference, *see* Rosalie H. Wax and Robert K. Thomas, "Anglo Intervention vs. Native Noninterference," *Phylon,* 22 (Winter 1961), pp. 53-56; and Jimm G. Good Tracks, "Native American Noninterference," *Social Work,* 18 (November 1973), pp. 30-34.
3. Good Tracks, op. cit., p. 33.
4. Clair Huffaker, *Nobody Loves a Drunken Indian* (New York: David McKay Co., 1967).
5. *See* John F. Bryde, *Modern Indian Psychology* (Vermillion, S. Dak.: Institute of Indian Studies, University of South Dakota, 1971), p. 15.
6. *See* Gerald Suk, "The Go-Between Process in Family Therapy," *Family Process,* 6 (April 1966), pp. 162-178.
7. Ross V. Speck and Carolyn L. Attneave, "Social Network Intervention," in Jay Haley, ed., *Changing Families* (New York: Grune & Stratton, 1971), pp. 17-34.
8. Rollo May, "Love and Will," *Psychology Today,* 3 (1969), pp. 17-24.
9. Edward A. Dreyfus, "The Search for Intimacy," *Adolescence,* 2 (March 1967), pp. 25-40.
10. *See* Bernard Gunther, *Sense Relaxation: Below Your Mind* (New York: Macmillan Co., 1968); Abraham Maslow, "Self-Actualization and Beyond," in James F. Bugental, ed., *Challenges of Humanistic Psychology* (New York: McGraw-Hill Book Co., 1967); H. Oho, *Explorations in Human Potentialities* (Springfield, Ill.: Charles C. Thomas, 1966); Carl Rogers, "Process of the Basic Encounter Group," in James F. Bugental, ed., op. cit.
11. For further discussion of a reciprocal model, *see* William Schwartz. "Toward a Strategy of Group Work Practice," *Social Service Review,* 36 (September 1962), pp. 268-279.
12. For further discussion of indirect and extra-group means, *see* Robert Vinter, *Readings in Group Work Practice* (Ann Arbor: Campus Publishers, 1967), pp. 8-38.

5 Counseling the American Indian Child

Youngman, Geraldine
Sadongei, Margaret

"The Indians are coming!" Or so it might be said by those who live in large metropolitan areas. The Indians are moving to the urban areas of the country and are sitting in the classrooms from kindergarten through college. Not all have descriptive last names. There are Browns, Smiths, Gutierrizes, and Johnsons, and they come in various sizes and colors. They come from various tribes—Apache, Pima, Sioux, Hopi, Navajo, Kiowa, Papago, and Pueblo. There are approximately 400 recognized tribes in the United States. Some children are bi-lingual and, depending on tribal background, some speak only English. Contrary to popular belief, there are many different tribal languages. This is why sign language was developed and is still used by the older members of the various tribes, particularly the Plains Indians.

Approximately 400,000 Indians are under 21 years of age today. Of these, 75 to 80 percent will obtain their education on reservations or in the federal boarding schools off reservations. To meet that need, many school systems can be found on one reservation. There are schools operated by the tribe, by churches, by public school districts, or by the Bureau of Indian Affairs. Five percent receive their education from both areas because of moving from reservations to urban areas and back. Another five percent who are handicapped, deaf, or blind receive their education through special institutions.

It is now shown that 10 percent of school-age Indian children are born and reared in cities. These children have never lived on a reservation but they too bring their cultural differences to the school systems, where many counselors are not fully aware of their needs. Many times it is assumed that the urban influence has made the Indian child like all other urban children but in reality they tend to have stronger ties to their own tribe, customs, and languages.

Differences exist in languages—a Papago cannot understand a Kiowa—and in customs: Southwest tribes strive to develop a reserved nature while the Plains Indians strive to develop openness and instant acquaintanceship. There are general characteristics among all Indians that are known as "Indian ways." Some of these are tribal loyalty, respect for elders, reticence, humility, avoidance of personal glory and gain, giving and sharing with as many as three generations of relatives, an abiding love for their own land, attribution of human characteristics to animals and nature, and strong spiritual beliefs. These characteristics are often in direct contrast to a school system based on competitiveness not humbleness, scientific research not social acceptance, verbosity not reticence.

Consequently, we often hear the comment, "Well, we don't have any problems with our Indian children. We get along fine." These "good Indians," as they are dubbed by some educators, are those who fit the concept held by the non-Indian society: All Indian children are slow learners, shy, lack positive identification, are thieves by nature, are undependable, and are potential alcoholics. Indian children who do not care to fit in the mold are labeled incorrigible, hyperactive, brain damaged, and rude.

The Indian child who has been reared with a tribal cultural background faces a difficult task in a non-Indian school, especially if he has no inkling as to what the dominant society expects. He must first learn what is expected and meet those expectations before he can be fully accepted.

One of the most common incidents involving Indian children that confronts teachers and counselors is the taking of things off the teacher's desk. Pencils, markers, tape, etc. from the teacher's desk are often found in an Indian child's desk. When confronted by the teacher, the child will usually admit to taking the objects. In the teacher's eyes the child is a thief, and the child is whisked off to the office.

The Indian child is surprised and hurt when such an act is called stealing, because Indian children know that any person of rank and importance *shares!* The child feels that it is his classroom (actually, it is a compliment to the teacher), and, since he has a sense of belonging, he also has the right to use things off the teacher's desk.

Another incident might involve eye contact, which is considered important and necessary in the non-Indian society. But, in the Indian culture it is (depending on the tribe) an act of rudeness. Indian children are taught to see without looking directly at someone.

In the first incident, a counselor can say to the child, "Sharing with mother and other family members is wonderful, but sharing with teacher in school is not possible because she is not family. There are too many other children in the room to allow taking things without asking permission first." Or, "I know that you did not steal; I know that you really needed the pencil, and I will try to help you get your own."

In the second incident, the counselor might say to a concerned teacher, "These children are taught that to stare or look directly is rude. Try to accept it, but check periodically on attention as you would with any other child. You know, there are many non-Indian children who look but never hear."

In most Indian cultures it is considered ill-mannered to speak of one's accomplishments. Praise is welcome when earned but is always given by someone else. Yet, in classrooms teachers use "self-disclosure" procedures that encourage children to talk about their strengths in front of their classmates. Therefore, most Indian children attempting to meet the teacher's request suffer extreme embarrassment. The child may stand but not talk at all or tell unbelievable stories. Teachers might suggest a general subject rather than talk about self. The Indian child is often aware of his own capabilities and if he sees the need to excel, he does. Last year in the sixth grade Richard sat in class, not doing anything, just sitting. When the reading specialist tested him, she found him capable of reading on the eighth-grade level. Richard knew he could do the work but he didn't see any pressing reason why he should put forth the effort. This year Richard is in the seventh grade, and, through a game, the reading teacher learned how "sharp" he was. The game was fun. Why such an attitude? Perhaps during his first three grades, Richard was told either verbally or nonverbally that he was not teachable or that because he was an Indian he was not quite up to par with non-Indian children.

Indian children are very much involved in decision making at home and are usually given choices. Perhaps they do not always decide wisely, but, nonetheless, they have a part in the decision. Counselors working with Indian children should always present a choice: "Either this or that," "Do you or don't you want to?" For example, in counseling toward more school participation, a counselor could say, "I see that you are a good basketball player; you shoot well and you are fast. We would like to have you join us. Will you play on our team?" It calls for a definite yes or no answer. If the student says no, he will supply the reason.

Indian children are very much aware of nonverbal communication. One of the greatest factors in counseling is the counselor's own individual personality and his perception of people and children around him. If the counselor gives the impression of being busy, communication is broken. The Indian child would not dream of being in the way or taking up anyone's time. The Indian's concept of time is not the number of conferences, the number of minutes, or racing the clock. Rather, it is a relaxed few minutes of listening and talking. This is especially true of Indians who have not spent much time living and working within the urban structure.

As most counselors know, what works for one child may not work for another. This is even more so for Indian children. The key word is patience. Patience and more patience!

The sincerity of a person is a trait that most Indian children are very much aware of. A child brought up in the Indian culture is going to observe how closely the counselor lives with what he says. One of the reasons an Indian is slow to open up is because he is going to watch and observe whether the counselor says one thing and does another. A counselor who shows sincere friendliness, perhaps by visiting the home and developing interest in the entire family, will be more likely to find Indian children confiding in him more often.

Friendly inquisitiveness is considered nosiness by Indians. It can slam doors of communication shut. In counseling a child on being late, one counselor said, "I'm happy you made it to school even though you are late.

Do you have to help clean house or wash dishes before you come to school?'' (Yes) ''Let's find ways to help you get your work done on time.'' Some choices were given, such as ''You could do more at night; you could talk to your mother to see if you could do more work when you get home from school.'' The problem was handled without embarrassment to the child or family.

There are no set rules for working with Indian children because of different tribal backgrounds. If there are a large number of Indian children in school, the counselor might find out the tribal background and do some research before approaching the child. Use a slow approach: The first session may be all one sided with the counselor doing the talking or it might just be a comfortable silent session. Counselors should have open minds and understand the need for patience and time. Keep in mind that the child's response is apt to be slow. The Indian people have a lot to contribute, but they have learned to be careful in dispensing any knowledge.

Working with Indian children who have different beliefs and values may cause a counselor to question his own beliefs and values. For the young Indians who are caught in the middle, with the dominant society urging them to forge ahead and achieve according to certain standards and the Indian culture saying it is not important to be the ''top cheese,'' there can be paths to tragic ends, which must be carefully avoided. Remember—before coming to any conclusion regarding any Indian child try to put yourself in his mocassins.

Selected Readings

American Indian Historical Society. *Indian Voices*. San Francisco: The Indian Historian Press, 1970.

Deloria, V. *Custer Died for Your Sins: An Indian Manifesto*. New York: Macmillan Pub. Co., 1969.

Dinges, N.G., Yazzie, M.L., & Tolletson, G.D. Developmental intervention for Navajo family mental health. *Personnel and Guidance Journal,* 1974, *52* (6), 390-395.

Forbes, J.D. *The Indian in America's Past*. Englewood Cliffs, N.J.: Prentice Hall, Inc. 1964.

Forbes, J.D. *Native Americans of California and Nevada*. Healdsburg, Ca.: Naturegraph Pub., 1969.

Fuchs, E., & Havighurst, R.J. *To Live on this Earth*. Garden City, N.Y.: Doubleday & Co., 1972.

Henry, J. *The American Indian Reader*. San Francisco: American Indian Educational Publishers, 1972.

Tracks, J.G.G. Native American non-interference. *Social Work,* 1973, *18,* 30-34.

The American Indian Client
Cases and Questions

1. Assume you are an elementary school counselor for several rural elementary schools that enroll about twelve American Indian students each year (approximately five percent of the total enrollment). Although the American Indian children perform as well as the Anglo children in kindergarten, by fourth grade it is clear they are less advanced in reading, writing, and computational skills. The district in which these schools are located is quite poor, and you are one of the few specialists available to supplement the resources of the classroom teacher.

   a. Upon entering a teacher's lounge in one school, you hear the English teacher, in conversation with several other teachers, relate the American Indian students' poor performance to their family/cultural background in rather uncomplimentary terms. How would you react?
   b. What responsibility, if any, would you accept for attempting to offset the deficiencies in academic skills these Native American students have?
   c. What response would you expect to receive from American Indian students and their parents to your attempts to improve the students' academic performance (assuming you accept responsibility for doing this)?

2. Assume you are a community social worker employed by the BIA to work with reservation Indian families in which one or both of the parents have a history of chronic alcoholism.

   a. What are some of the factors you believe may contribute to alcoholism among American Indians, and how would this affect your role as a social worker?
   b. What personal and professional qualities which you possess would be helpful in your work with American Indians? What qualities might be detrimental?
   c. Would you attempt to work with several families at once through group counseling? If so, how would you structure the group experience?

3. Assume you are a counselor in an urban high school that enrolls a small number of Native American students whose parents have left reservation

life for the employment opportunities of a big city. Johnny Lonetree, an artistically gifted junior who regularly makes the honor roll, has just informed you that he is contemplating returning to the reservation to live with his grandparents. Johnny knows that for all practical purposes this will mean an end to his scholastic education, but he is intensely interested in being immersed in the tribal culture, specifically tribal art work.

a. How can you best assist Johnny in his decision-making process?
b. How might some of your own values affect how you proceed with Johnny?
c. What are some of the social pressures (exerted by administrators, colleagues, Johnny's parents) that are likely to be exerted upon both you and Johnny if he decides to return to the reservation?

Part 3 The Asian American Client

In contrast to many Third World groups, the contemporary image of Asian Americans is that of a highly successful minority that has "made it" in society. For example, the popular press has often portrayed Asian Americans as a "model" minority, using such headlines as "Success Story: Outwhiting the Whites" and "Success Story of One Minority Group in the U.S." (*U.S. News and World Report,* 1966; *Newsweek,* 1971). A superficial analysis of the 1970 Census seems to support this contention: Chinese, Japanese, and even Philippinos now exceed the median income; Asian Americans complete a higher medium number of grades than all other groups; studies consistently reveal that Asian Americans have low official rates of juvenile delinquency, psychiatric contact, and divorce. The conclusion one can draw from all of these statistics is that Asian Americans have never been victims of prejudice and discrimination.

Yet, a review of the Asian experience in America indicates the massive discrimination directed at them. Assaulted, murdered, denied ownership of land, denied rights of citizenship, and placed in concentration camps during World War II, Asian Americans have been subjected to some of the most flagrant forms of discrimination ever perpetrated against an immigrant group.

A closer analysis of the status of Asian Americans does not support their success story. Reference to the higher median income does not take into account (a) the higher percentage of more than one wage earner in the family, (b) an equal incidence of poverty despite the higher median income, (c) lower poverty assistance and welfare than the general population, and (d) the fact that salaries are not commensurate with the education levels of Asian American workers (lower salaries despite higher educational level). Statistics on educational levels are also misleading. Asian Americans present a picture of extraordinarily high educational attainment for some, while a large number remain undereducated.

There is also recognition that, apart from being tourist attractions, Chinatowns, Manilatowns, and Japantowns in major metropolitan cities represent ghetto areas. Unemployment, poverty, health problems, and juvenile delinquency are major facts of life. For example, San Francisco's Chinatown has the second greatest population density next to Harlem. It not only has a high tuberculosis rate, but a suicide rate three times the national average. Juvenile gangland warfare has also caught the public eye. Under-utilization of mental health facilities by Chinese Americans in San Francisco is now recognized to be due to cultural factors inhibiting self-referral (shame and disgrace associated with admitting to emotional problems, reliance on the family to prevent it from becoming public, etc.), and/or to inappropriate institutional policies and practices.

S. Sue and Kitano, in their leadoff article, "Stereotypes as a Measure of Success," deal with the myths and stereotypes of Asian Americans. They trace the historical evolution of Chinese and Japanese stereotypes and conclude that the social, economic, and political climate in America often determined how these two groups were portrayed. While most stereotypes were negative, Sue & Kitano point to the detrimental consequences of contemporary positive stereotypes (success story). They suggest that the belief that Asian Americans are a model minority is a notion which has (a) been used to reassert the erroneous belief that any group can succeed in a democratic society if they work hard enough, (b) acted as a devisive concept to pit one minority group against another, and (c) prevented Asian Americans from being eligible for certain programs and services. In the second article, "Ethnic Identity: The Impact of Two Cultures on the Psychological Development of Asians in America," D. Sue goes further in describing the psychological development of Asians in America, not only with respect to stereotypes, but also because of unique cultural values and the experience of racism. Personality characteristics, academic abilities, and vocational interests of both Chinese and Japanese Americans are described. These descriptions provide important information for counselors who work with Asian Americans and need to look behind the "success myth," and to understand the Asian experience in America.

It is increasingly recognized that traditional counseling approaches must be modified to fit the life experiences of minority clients. In the case of Chinese-Americans, D. Sue and S. Sue in their article "Counseling Chinese-Americans" suggest how such modifications in counseling can be made by taking into account such factors as cultural values and the experience of racism. Specific concrete strategies are presented and discussed. While this article deals only with Chinese American clients, it presents an example of how different approaches might be used for other Asian Americans (Japanese, Philippinos, Koreans, and Hawaiians) as well.

Newsweek. Success Story: Outwhiting the whites. June, 1971.
U.S. News and World Report. Success story of one minority group in the U.S. December, 1966.

6 Stereotypes as a Measure of Success

Sue, Stanley
Kitano, Harry H. L.

Chinese and Japanese stereotypes have undergone dramatic changes. Early stereotypes were uniformly negative, reflecting the social, economic, and political climate in America. Labor union members and gold miners were particularly vehement in their denunciation of Asian Americans because of the perceived threat of job competition. With the passage of numerous discriminatory laws and the entrance of other ethnic minorities, the Chinese and Japanese were considered less dangerous and the favorability of stereotypes increased. World War II revived negative stereotypes against the Japanese. Currently, these Asian American groups are viewed as highly successful, model minorities. To what extent are these positive stereotypes and views accurate? Methodological and conceptual problems in the study of stereotypes have hindered a clear analysis of this question. It is suggested that some stereotypes have kernels of truth. The potential negative consequences of favorable stereotypes are also discussed.

Stereotypes have been an important area of concern in the study of interracial relationships. They presumably reflect prevalent attitudes and feelings and/or, in some way, influence behaviors toward members of racial minorities. While most studies have focused on black Americans, stereotypes of Asian Americans seem particularly interesting. Asian Americans are, for the most part, identifiable by their appearance, have a different subculture, and represent an anthropologically-defined racial group distinct from Caucasians and blacks. In addition, attitudes toward two major Asian groups, the Japanese and Chinese, have drastically changed.[1] Ogawa (1971) characterizes the change as a positive one from "Jap to Japanese"; similarly, a "Chink to Chinese" image has evolved.

The dramatic changes in the views of Japanese and Chinese Americans raise important questions. What are the social, economic, and political correlates of these stereotypes? Do stereotypes accurately characterize groups of individuals? Why are stereotypes undesirable?

Public stereotypes and sentiments toward Chinese and Japanese were not systematically sampled until 1933, when Katz and Braly published their

This article originally appeared in the *Journal of Social Issues*, 1973, Vol. 29, and is reprinted with permission.

---

[1] Although the term "Asian American" covers a diversity of groups, the central focus of this paper is on Chinese and Japanese, whose public stereotypes have shown relatively similar changes over time.

empirical study of ethnic stereotypes. Therefore the nature and extent of the stereotypes in the 1800s and the early 1900s can only be inferred from early newspapers, books, and public policies toward Asian Americans. Investigators who have analyzed historical documents show a high degree of consensus regarding the early attitudes toward Chinese and Japanese.

The Chinese

The significant immigration of Chinese occurred in the 1850s. Coming during the rapid rise of industrialization and urbanization in America, they were initially well received as "exotic curiosities [Lyman, 1970]." The severe shortage of women on the Pacific Coast enabled Chinese to fill much needed services as cooks, laundry workers, and houseboys. America at this time also needed a supply of docile and cheap labor in textile, shoe, and cigar factories and in railroad construction. The Chinese not only quickly assumed these labor positions but also began to enter the mines with great visions of finding gold. Exaggerated fears that these foreigners would carry away American gold (Paul, 1970) and that Chinese would drive whites into starvation by working for lower wages (tenBroek, Barnhart, & Matson, 1954) made them the object of much hostility. Anti-Chinese feelings were most violent during the 1870s when America was experiencing a depression (Wollenberg, 1971).

The early stereotypes of Chinese exhibited an interesting parallel to these historical events. Initially they were used descriptively to denote racial and cultural differences. The Chinese people were "yellow," "slant eyed," and "pigtailed." As they came into direct job competition with Caucasians, the stereotypes evolved from descriptions to negative characterizations. Whereas the customs and behaviors of Chinese were previously labeled as strange and exotic, they now indicated "filthy habits" and "moral evils [tenBroek et al., 1954]." McLeod (1947) cites the following resolution passed by a group of miners in 1852:

> Be it resolved: That it is the duty of the miners to take the matter into their own hands...to erect such barriers as shall be sufficient to check this Asiatic inundation....That the Capitalists, ship owners and merchants and others who are encouraging or engaged in the importation of these burlesques on humanity would crowd their ships with the long-tailed, horned and cloven-hoofed inhabitants of the infernal regions [p. 36].

Other traits which were attributed to Chinese included the coolies' unassimilable nature, treacherous and shrewd facade, low intellect, foul smell, natural cowardice, and willingness to eat rats (Lyman, 1970; Paul, 1970). These stereotypes were assumed to be an inherent part of the Chinese character, and they served to justify continuing discrimination and legislation against Chinese. By attributing these "immutable" traits to the Chinese nature and inferring that those with such characteristics must be subhuman, many Americans could maintain the philosophy that "all *men* are created equal" and continue to treat the Chinese as less than equal.

In retrospect, it is quite apparent that the actions of the majority group were responsible for many of the Chinese behaviors. For example, the "unassimilable nature" of Chinese who frequently banded in Chinatowns was due not only to desires to find fellowship and a common tongue but also to the constant harassment from white Americans. Beliefs that the Chinese were engaging in immoral acts such as the kidnaping of Chinese girls for prostitution were both exaggerated and had some basis in fact since Chinese males outnumbered females in a ratio of over 10 to 1 in the 1870s. The Chinese Exclusion Act of 1882 served to restrict the further immigration of Chinese and to perpetuate the shortage of Chinese females which in turn exacerbated the sexual problem. With the closing of Chinese immigration, the Chinese "Yellow Peril" ceased to be a problem for the majority group.

The Japanese

The exclusion of the Chinese resulted in an acute labor shortage for menial and unskilled jobs. The first significant influx of Japanese after the 1880s was thus received with joy by business and farm employers. Many of the Japanese immigrants seemed more respectable than Chinese since they brought their wives and children and invested their money into businesses or farms. Labor unions, however, felt threatened by the new "Yellow Peril." Revived fears of competition for employment and the physical similarity to Chinese made the Japanese likely targets for hostility. Stereotypes of the Chinese were now applied to the Japanese with increased vigor: Japanese were worse than the Chinese; they exhibited no morality; and they took unfair advantage of Americans because of their tricky nature (tenBroek et al., 1954). Daniels and Kitano (1970) list the following headlines appearing in the *San Francisco Chronicle,* a major newspaper in that city, during 1905: "Crime and Poverty Go Hand In Hand With Asiatic Labor; Japanese a Menace to American Women; The Yellow Peril—How Japanese Crowd out the White Race [p. 47]." Arguing from a Darwinian view of races in 1900, Edward Ross, a sociologist from Stanford University, advanced the idea that " . . .owing to its high, Malthusian birth rate, the Orient is the land of 'cheap men,' and that the coolie, though he cannot outdo the American, can underlive him [Mathew, 1970, pp. 270-271]." Stereotypes during this period included the Japanese as highly un-American, inferior citizens, sexually aggressive, and part of an international menace (Ogawa, 1971).

Anti-Japanese sentiment forced the passage of several state and federal laws. The Gentlemen's Agreement of 1907 limited immigration; the Alien Land Law of 1913 prevented additional ownership of California farm property. Hostility subsided somewhat during the late 1920s and the early 1930s. America had succeeded in controlling the alleged threat created by the Japanese. To be sure, negative stereotypes persisted but not with the same vigor and force. A California field study during 1927 even suggested that Nisei Japanese had actively assimilated into American life (Mathew, 1970).

However, the threat of Japan's power as a nation and the bombing of Pearl Harbor in 1941 reawakened hostile feelings. People felt helpless, frightened, and angry. Again old stereotypes were applied; Japanese were inscrutable, treacherous, and dangerous. At the same time new beliefs and rumors spread. Japanese were perceived as likely spies and saboteurs (Ogawa, 1971), and the slogan "a Jap is a Jap" regardless of birthplace came into being. Specific rumors included the notion that some Japanese had hidden transmitters and that others had knowledge of Japan's mission. The press, politicians, farm organizations, and patriotic groups demanded that all Japanese on the Pacific Coast show their patriotism by submitting themselves to concentration camps, and soon over 110,000 Japanese were ordered to evacuate. The evacuation, often termed as America's greatest wartime mistake, became an ugly reality (Daniels, 1971).

The Post World War II Stereotypes

The decline of negative stereotypes toward Chinese and Japanese Americans has been phenomenal. For the most part, Chinese and Japanese are now considered as being model minorities. They are described as patient, clean, courteous, and Americanized. Daniels and Kitano (1970) suggest that the Oriental image is "whiter than white," reflecting high achievement status according to white middle-class standards. These new stereotypes point to the success of Asian Americans by virtue of their hard work, thrift, family cohesion, and obedience.

> At a time when Americans are awash in worry over the plight of racial minorities—One such minority, the nation's 300,000 Chinese-Americans, is winning wealth and respect by dint of its own hard work. . . . At a time when it is being proposed that hundreds of billions be spent to uplift negroes and other minorities, the nation's 300,000 Chinese-Americans are moving ahead on their own—with no help from anyone else [*U.S. News and World Report, 1966*].
>
> The Japanese Americans, in short, ought to be a central focus of social studies. Their experience converts our best sociological generalizations into partial truths at best; this is a laboratory case of an exception to test a rule. Conceivably in such a more intensive analysis, we might find a means of isolating some of the element of this remarkable culture and grafting it onto plants that manifestly need the pride, the persistence, and the success of our model minority [Kitano, 1969a, p. 257].

What factors accounted for the dramatic changes in the stereotypes of these Asian groups? In the late 1800s, Chinese and Japanese competed for jobs in America. Obviously, fears that whites were being economically dislocated caused much anti-Oriental feeling. To be sure, Asians often worked for lower wages. It is interesting to note, however, that many positions assumed by Asians were those avoided by white males. Even when the Chinese entered the gold mines, these mines had usually been abandoned by white diggers (Wollenberg, 1971).

In order to understand the hostile reaction on the part of Americans beyond the economic factor, it is necessary to view the Asian immigration as occurring during a period in which America was developing its modern form of institutional racism (Lyman, 1970). The misuse of Darwinian concepts, notions of white supremacy, and the appearance of visually and culturally identifiable foreigners set the stage for the outrageous treatment of Asians. Further, they were small enough in number so that they could not effectively retaliate, and the scattered West needed the convenient scapegoat as one technique of achieving a degree of unity.

With the defeat of Japan, Japanese Americans were no longer a threat. The drastic action of imprisoning Japanese Americans was found to be unnecessary; massive acts of sabotage did not happen. In addition both the Japanese and the Chinese demonstrated their willingness to become ''good'' Americans by working hard, despite the historical abuses. Asians exhibited low rates of juvenile delinquency, divorce, and mental illness and a high educational level. Allport (1954) reported that negative stereotyping was beginning to fade, and was weakening in the mass media. Figure 1 shows the hypothesized relationship between the positive and negative Asian stereotypes from the past to the present.

Figure 1 Hypothesized stereotyping patterns for Chinese and Japanese over time.

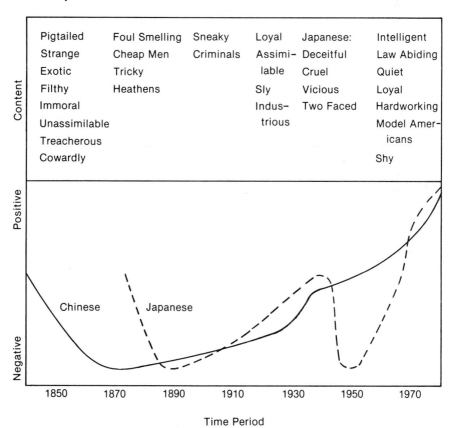

Research on Asian Stereotypes

Although it is not possible to assess precisely the nature and extent of early stereotypes, there can be little doubt that American views of the Chinese and Japanese prior to the 1920s were strongly negative. The publication of Lippman's book (1922) and of the classic study by Katz and Braly (1933) brought the subject of stereotypes within the domain of social scientists. Katz and Braly asked college students to select from a list of 84 adjectives those words which seemed typical characteristics of various groups. Japanese were described as intelligent, industrious, progressive, shrewd, shy, and quiet; stereotypes of Chinese included superstitious, sly, conservative, tradition loving, and loyal to family ties. At this stage, both positive and negative stereotypes were given to these Asian groups although most views in the mass media were primarily negative.

World War II strongly influenced the positivity and negativity of Japanese stereotypes. Seago (1947) found that while the Japanese had mildly favorable stereotypes prior to Pearl Harbor, the attack resulted in strongly negative stereotypes so that words such as deceitful, treacherous, sly, shrewd, cruel, and nationalistic became dominant. During the five-year period (1941-1945) of Seago's study which compared Japanese, blacks, and Germans, Japanese were often regarded more unfavorably than blacks. Interestingly, although positive German stereotypes also declined in this period, they never dropped far below the neutral level. There are several hypotheses as to why the Japanese were viewed more unfavorably than the equally "dangerous" Germans. Many Americans were more angered by the surprise attack on the part of the Japanese. Seago also suggests that Americans could perhaps discriminate between German Americans and Nazi Germans, and that German atrocities in Europe left America relatively untouched. The former hypothesis is weak since one can question why there was no distinction between Japanese Americans and their counterparts in Japan. Although the "untouched America" explanation proposed by Seago remains a possibility, the discrepancy can also be attributed to the fact that Germans, unlike the physically identifiable Japanese, were still members of a white race. As Daniels (1971) indicates, acts of German atrocities were attributed to evil *individuals* while the Japanese actions were attributed to an evil *race*.

Negative stereotypes of Japanese persisted into the early 1950s. Gilbert (1951) found that Japanese were still characterized as being immature, sly, treacherous, and nationalistic; Chinese, on the other hand, started gaining positive stereotypes and losing more negative ones such as sly and superstitious. More recent studies have indicated a uniformly "positive" view of Chinese and Japanese (Karlins, Coffman, & Walters, 1969; Maykovich, 1971, 1972). Chinese and Japanese are considered intelligent, industrious, loyal to the family, quiet, and shy. Ayabe (1971) was so impressed by the quietness exhibited by Asian students that he conducted a study to determine if Japanese students had the physical ability to speak as loudly as Caucasian students; no differences in voice strength were noted.

Validity of Stereotypes

Some Asian stereotypes have persisted for years. Asians were and still are considered intelligent, industrious, quiet, and loyal to the family. These persistent stereotypes have led some researchers to ask whether there are kernels of truth to stereotypes and whether stereotyping is necessarily bad (Brigham, 1971).

The Determination of Stereotypes

In order to answer the question regarding the validity of stereotypes, one must be able accurately to assess the stereotypes and the characteristics of the group. The assessment procedures typically used in determining stereotypes have been criticized by Brigham (1971). Stereotypes attributed to the same ethnic groups may vary according to (a) whether studies employ open-ended or checklist questionnaires (Ehrlich & Rinehart, 1965), (b) whether subjects are asked to endorse or show knowledge of group stereotypes, (c) whether personal or social stereotypes are considered (Karlins et al., 1969), (d) personal familiarity and contact with the groups being rated (Cobb, 1949), (e) assumed social class of the ethnic members (Bayton, McAlister, & Hamer, 1956), (f) order of presentation for the ethnic groups being rated (Diab, 1963), (g) the sophistication of subjects regarding the fallacies of making overgeneralizations (Gilbert, 1951), and (h) the social desirability of giving positive rather than negative stereotypes (Sigall & Page, 1971). Brigham concludes his analysis by offering suggestions for improving the research strategies involved in the assessment of stereotypes and of their validity.

Although the extent to which these methodological problems have influenced Asian American stereotypes is largely unknown, it appears to be minimal. As noted previously, there is a high degree of consensus regarding the traits attributed by the public to Chinese and Japanese. Members of these two ethnic groups are considered industrious, quiet, loyal to family ties, and courteous. In short they are viewed as model minorities. Moreover, these stereotypes obtained by asking respondents to endorse traits characteristic of Chinese and of Japanese have also been confirmed by content analysis of newspapers, magazine articles, or films. Ogawa (1971) concludes that the following stereotypes of Japanese have emerged in the mass media: highly Americanized and assimilated, well educated, and superior in citizenship. A similar finding was obtained by Weiss (1970) in the case of Chinese Americans.

Interestingly, in the studies by Ogawa and by Weiss, sex differences emerged in the favorability of stereotypes. Ogawa found that Japanese males were considered quiet, shy, timid, and interested in gardening; females were purported to be graceful, lovely, delicate, and servile. Although the male stereotypes are not intrinsically negative, the characterizations do not convey a charismatic, adventuresome, hero image. Japanese females, on the other hand, possess stereotypes that have been traditionally considered as desirable female qualities. The Chinese male image of being honest, studious, and obedient does not foster a masculine figure but the "Suzy Wong" stereotype of females (i.e., slim, sexy, feminine, and charming) can be viewed as a more positive one. The Chinese male image in films is best summed up by Weiss (1970):

> Chinese character profiles include the evil and cunning Dr. Fu Manchu, the inscrutable Charlie Chan, and the agreeable but puzzled and simple proprietor of a hand-laundry shop. . . .Although the Chinese male has also been popularly characterized as "clever, honest, industrious and studious," "a paragon of family virtue," "respectfully obedient to his elders" (traits acceptable in business and family success), he is still identified as "shy," "introverted," "withdrawing" and "tongue-tied" (traits unacceptable to current ideas of romanticism). . . .Furthermore, the Occidental stage, screen and television image of the "hero". . .includes too few physical or cultural features of Oriental men [p. 274].

In summary, various studies do seem to agree upon the attitudes and beliefs held by the public toward Chinese and Japanese. Although the stereotypes are generally favorable, the image of the Asian female appears more positive than that of the Asian male.

The Relationship Between Stereotypes and Group Characteristics

Comparing these stereotypes with studies of Chinese and Japanese characteristics, it is apparent that there is some validity to the stereotypes. First, the "success" of Chinese and Japanese is a matter of record. They generally show low rates of juvenile delinquency and of hospital admissions for psychiatric problems (Abbott & Abbott, 1968; Kitano, 1969a). The divorce rate for Japanese is quite low (Kitano, 1969b), and the educational level particularly in the proportion of Chinese and Japanese college graduates exceeds that of whites (Daniels & Kitano, 1970; Schmid, Nobbe, & Mitchell, 1968). The recent study by Levine and Montero (1973) indicates that almost 90% of the Sansei have or are attending college. These statistics give credence to the "model" status of these Asian Americans. Second, research on Chinese and Japanese students reveals some consensus between stereotypes and personality traits. On the Edwards Personal Preference Schedule, Fenz and Arkoff (1962) found that Chinese and Japanese males were significantly lower than Caucasians in dominance, autonomy, aggression, exhibitionism, and heterosexuality. Chinese and Japanese females showed more deference than their Caucasian counterparts. Other studies tend to support current stereotypes in the following characteristics: introversion of Japanese males (Meredith & Meredith, 1966); passivity of Japanese (Kitano, 1969b); Chinese introversion and conformity (Sue & Kirk, 1972); and Japanese quietness

(Ayabe, 1971). Several investigators (Meredith & Meredith, 1966; Weiss, 1970) share the view that Asian females are assimilating quicker than males and that stereotypes of Asian females may be more favorable, which facilitates interracial dating and marriage (Tinker, 1973; Weiss, 1970).

Although it can be argued that there seems to be a relationship between current stereotypes and the status of these two Asian groups, the relationship is far from being unequivocal. First, comparisons between stereotypes and ethnic group characteristics depend on the ability to accurately assess the latter. Official statistics on the status of Asians may not be valid. For example, Chinese and Japanese may be reluctant to seek mental health services which would lower official rates of mental illness (Kitano, 1970; Sue, 1973). Traditional values of Chinese and Japanese make it difficult for the individual to admit emotional problems and to undergo treatment. In regard to the low Japanese divorce rates, cultural factors may dictate against formal divorce; the number of "emotional divorces" is unknown (Kitano, 1969a). Only recently have the problems of Chinatowns, such as poverty, unemployment, gang wars among youths, and poverty conditions, been publicized (see Jacobs, Landau, & Pell, 1971; Lyman, 1970). If we accept Brigham's notion (1971) that whether stereotypes are accurate depends upon the observer, then who the observer is and what criteria of accuracy are used become exceedingly important.

Second, most studies of personality have compared mean differences between traits of different ethnic groups. To say that Chinese are more conforming than Caucasians actually tells us very little about Chinese as individuals or as a group. Allport (1954) mentioned that some traits ascribed to a group are rare within the group but never exist within other groups. Thus Chinese may be significantly more conforming than Caucasians; however, in both groups the vast majority of individuals may not be conforming. In one sense, the stereotype is accurate (Chinese are more conforming than Caucasians); and yet it is inaccurate (Chinese are conforming) when overgeneralized.

Third, the nature of stereotypes often seems to depend upon the moods or conditions of society rather than upon any real characteristics of the stereotyped group. During the late 1800's when America experienced economic problems and unemployment, attitudes toward Asians were extremely unfavorable. The war with Japan in the 1940s also resulted in negative attitudes and beliefs toward the Japanese. Beliefs that Asians were unassimilable, sexually aggressive, and treacherous were grossly false. In his classic book on prejudice, Allport (1954) has discussed the effects of societal events on the attitudes and behaviors toward minority group members. Factors such as the nation's employment situation, changes in social mobility, and the relative density of minority groups often influence attitudes toward minorities.

The current mood of the country has been more concerned than ever before with civil rights and racial equality. Stereotypes toward minorities are less negative. More realistic, or at least more favorable, images of Asians can be seen in television programs or films. Asian Americans are no longer merely portrayed as cooks, busboys, laundry men, sinister villains, and geishas. Although Paik (1971) feels that stereotypes are still perpetuated, he notes that there have been attempts to break stereotypes in movies.

> *Flower Drum Song* (1961) used Asian stereotypes as the punch lines of jokes and the themes for songs creating a happy contented image of the Asian living in Chinatown San Francisco. . . .The father and aunt are not wise ancestors, but practical stubborn activists. The younger son is interested, not in karate, but baseball. The older son is not the quiet studious hardworking number one son, but a young man in love. The leading Asian girl is a loud, hip, shapely swinging night club dancer. The friend of the family is a hustler and nightclub entrepreneur [Paik, 1971, pp. 33-34].

The relationship between the United States and the country associated with a particular minority group may also influence stereotypes. The favorability of Japanese American stereotypes over the past 30 years has gone from extremely negative to extremely positive. The major events that transpired during this time period were the war and, more recently, the trade relationship between the United States and Japan. Indeed Japan has emerged as an industrious, progressive, and economically important country. In a similar sense, the increased friendliness between the People's Republic of China and the United States may give Chinese Americans more favorable stereotypes. However, the correlation between stereotypes and international events is less clear in the case of Chinese since Chinese Americans cannot be easily identified with a particular country or form of government. The People's Republic of China, Nationalist Free China, and Hong Kong represent quite different life styles.

The Consequences of Stereotypes

Brigham (1971) feels that there is a paucity of evidence regarding the validity of stereotypes, there is little agreement on what aspects of stereotypes are undesirable (i.e., rigidity, faulty thinking, ethnocentrism, inaccuracy), and the relationship between stereotypes and behaviors is unclear. Although most investigators believe that stereotypes are bad, he notes that it has been difficult to specify the reasons why.

Much research has focused on the stereotypist's thought processes, personality, and behaviors toward minorities. The effects of being victimized by stereotypes have been studied to a lesser degree. A few studies suggest that negative stereotypes can have detrimental effects on self-image. Evaluations of colors are related to the evaluation of races (Williams, 1965). White is considered most favorable, followed by yellow, red, brown, and black; Caucasians and blacks are respectively most and least favorably evaluated, with Asians in an intermediate position. Although cause and effect cannot be determined, Williams and Roberson (1967) did find that color evaluation and racial awareness appear to develop concurrently with the former possibly reinforcing the latter. In the past, black children have preferred white dolls or white playmates (Morland, 1966; Clark & Clark, 1947), although there is now evidence that the trend may be changing (Hraba & Grant, 1970). Furthermore, negative stereotypes often result in self-fulfilling prophecies. Blacks may learn to fulfill the role of being intellectually dull (Katz, 1969), since to act bright is a sign of being "uppity" (Pettigrew, 1964). Rosenthal and Jacobson (1968) suggest that disadvantaged students fall behind in school because of teachers' expectations; when teachers were led to believe some students could be expected to improve, at the end of the year these students made dramatic changes in IQ scores.

As mentioned previously, the Asian male projects a demasculinized stereotype. Weiss (1970) believes that many Chinese American females are contemptuous of Chinese males, who are perceived to be lacking in confidence, assertiveness, and sexual attractiveness. Many Asian females have the same view of males as portrayed by the mass media, and they also share the same negative evaluations of these "unmasculine" characteristics. As a consequence, some Chinese have developed racial self-hatred (Sue & Sue, 1971). Thus stereotypes and expectancy often influence self-images.

In another sense, however, the beliefs that Asians are quiet, unobtrusive, hard working, and intelligent can be viewed as positive. For one, they are more favorable than past images of Asians. The problem is that such stereotypes, although positive, may also have negative side effects. An Asian student may remain passive, unquestioning, and obedient in order to conform to his teachers' expectations. A rebellious or low achieving student is likely to face the wrath of his teachers for violating their stereotypes of Asians (Sue & Sue, 1971). Indeed, with the rise in militancy among Asian youths, one can wonder how well received Asian Americans will be in the future. Uniformly "positive" stereotypes also make it difficult to realize that Asians may have problems. Many of the current Chinese and Japanese youths reject the "model minority" status of Asians (Tachiki, Wong, Odo, & Wong, 1971) as another technique of white racism.

Stereotypes of groups can be abused. The apparent success of Asian Americans, as reflected by stereotypes, is often held as a model for other minorities. It is argued that blacks should copy the Asians and that America is not really racist since some nonwhite minorities are able to achieve the "American dream." This ignores the tremendous variations among ethnic groups and is a gross oversimplification of complex phenomena. The sudden change in the stereotypes of Japanese and Chinese also provides a note of warning. Stereotypes often reflect rather than determine national policies (Brigham, 1971), so that any change in relations with Japan and China could easily revive old stereotypes. A quick conversion to the use of stereotypes may also indicate a tendency to change to negative stereotypes when conditions warrant. Finally, stereotypes whether of a positive or negative nature ignore the humanity of the object. No person is all good or all bad, as is inferred by most stereotypes.

Conclusion

There can be no doubt that Chinese and Japanese stereotypes are exceedingly favorable. To some extent, the stereotypes indicate a greater willingness of white Americans to view Asians in a more positive fashion. They also reflect the achievement of Chinese and Japanese. If stereotypes are an inescapable product of man's thinking, then strong efforts must be made to control their side effects and potential misuse—even in the case of positive stereotypes.

References

Abbott, K.A., & Abbott, E.L. Juvenile delinquency in San Francisco's Chinese-American community: 1961-1966. *Journal of Sociology,* 1968, 4, 45-56.

Allport, G.W. *The nature of prejudice.* Reading, Mass.: Addison-Wesley, 1954.

Ayabe, H.L. Deference and ethnic differences in voice levels. *Journal of Social Psychology,* 1971, 85, 181-185.

Bayton, J.A., McAlister, L.B., & Hamer, J. Race-class stereotypes. *Journal of Negro Education,* 1956, 25, 75-78.

Brigham, J.C. Ethnic stereotypes. *Psychological Bulletin,* 1971, 76, 15-38.

Clark, K.B., & Clark, M.K. Racial identification and preference in Negro children. In T.M. Newcomb & E.L. Hartley (Eds.), *Readings in social psychology.* New York: Holt, Rinehart, & Winston, 1947.

Cobb, J.W. Personal familiarity and variations in stereotypes regarding Japanese. *Sociology and Social Research,* 1949, 33, 441-448.

Daniels, R. *Concentration camps, U.S.A.* New York: Harper & Row, 1971.

Daniels, R., & Kitano, H.H. *American racism.* Englewood Cliffs, N.J.: Prentice Hall, 1970.

Diab, L.N. Factors affecting studies of national stereotypes. *Journal of Social Psychology,* 1963, 59, 29-40.

Ehrlich, H.J., & Rinehart, J.W. A brief report on the methodology of stereotype research. *Social Forces,* 1965, 43, 564-575.

Fenz, W.D., & Arkoff, A. Comparative need patterns of five ancestry groups in Hawaii. *Journal of Social Psychology,* 1962, 58, 67-89.

Gilbert, G.M. Stereotype persistence and change among college students. *Journal of Abnormal and Social Psychology,* 1951, 46, 245-254.

Hraba, J., & Grant, G. Black is beautiful: A reexamination of racial preference and identification. *Journal of Personality and Social Psychology,* 1970, 16, 398-402.

Jacobs, P., Landau, S., & Pell, E. *To serve the devil. Vol. 2. Colonials and sojourners.* New York: Vintage, 1971.

Karlins, M., Coffman, T.L., & Walters, G. On the fading of social stereotypes: Studies in three generations of college students. *Journal of Personality and Social Psychology,* 1969, 13, 1-16.

Katz, D., & Braly, K. Racial stereotypes in one hundred college students. *Journal of Abnormal and Social Psychology,* 1933, 28, 280-290.

Katz, I. A critique of personality approaches to Negro performance, with research suggestions. *Journal of Social Issues,* 1969, 25 (3), 13-27.

Kitano, H.H. Japanese-American mental illness. In S.C. Plog & R.B. Edgerton (Eds.), *Changing perspectives in mental illness.* New York: Holt, Rinehart, & Winston, 1969. (a)

Kitano, H.H. *Japanese Americans: The evolution of a subculture*. Englewood Cliffs, N.J.: Prentice Hall, 1969. (b)

Kitano, H.H. Mental illness in four cultures. *Journal of Social Psychology*, 1970, 80, 121-134.

Levine, G.N., & Montero, D.M. Socioeconomic mobility among three generations of Japanese Americans. *Journal of Social Issues*, 1973, 29 (2).

Lippman, W. *Public opinion*. New York: Harcourt, Brace, 1922.

Lyman, S.M. *The Asian in the west*. Reno: Desert Research Institute, 1970.

Mathew, F.H. White community and "Yellow Peril." In L. Dinnerstein & F.C. Jaher (Eds.), *The aliens*. New York: Appleton-Century-Crofts, 1970.

Maykovich, M. White-yellow stereotypes: An empirical study. *Pacific Sociological Review*, 1971, 14, 447-467.

Maykovich, M. Reciprocity in racial stereotypes: White, black, and yellow. *American Journal of Sociology*, 1972, 77, 876-897.

McLeod, A. *Pigtails and golddust*. Caldwell, Idaho: Caxton Printers, 1947.

Meredith, G.M., & Meredith, C.G. Acculturation and personality among Japanese-American college students in Hawaii. *Journal of Social Psychology*, 1966, 68, 175-182.

Morland, J.K. A comparison of race awareness in northern and southern children. *American Journal of Orthopsychiatry*, 1966, 36, 22-31.

Ogawa, D. *From Japs to Japanese: The evolution of Japanese-American stereotypes*. Berkeley: McCutchan, 1971.

Paik, I. That oriental feeling. In A. Tachiki, E. Wong, F. Odo, & B. Wong (Eds.), *Roots: An Asian American reader*. Los Angeles: Continental Graphics, 1971.

Paul, R.W. The origin of the Chinese issue in California. In L. Dinnerstein & F.C. Jaher (Eds.), *The aliens*, New York: Appleton-Century-Crofts, 1970.

Pettigrew, T.F. *A profile of the Negro American*. Princeton: Van Nostrand, 1964.

Rosenthal, R., & Jacobson, L.F. Teacher expectations for the disadvantaged. *Scientific American*, 1968, 218, 19-23.

Schmid, C.F., Nobbe, C.E., & Mitchell, A.E. *Nonwhite races: State of Washington*. Olympia, Washington: Washington State Planning and Community Affairs Agency, 1968.

Seago, D.W. Stereotypes: Before Pearl Harbor and after. *The Journal of Psychology*, 1947, 23, 55-63.

Sigall, H., & Page, R. Current stereotypes: A little fading, a little faking. *Journal of Personality and Social Psychology*, 1971, 18, 247-255.

Sue, D.W., & Kirk, B.A. Psychological characteristics of Chinese-American students. *Journal of Counseling Psychology*, 1972, 19, 471-478.

Sue, S. Third world student counselors. *Journal of Counseling Psychology*, 1973, 1, 73-78.

Sue, S., & Sue, D.W. Chinese American personality and mental health. *Amerasia Journal*, 1971, 1, 36-49.

Tachiki, A., Wong, E., Odo, F., & Wong, B. (Eds.) *Roots: An Asian American reader*. Los Angeles: Continental Graphics, 1971.

tenBroek, J., Barnhart, E.N., & Matson, F.W. *Prejudice, war and the constitution*. Berkeley: University of California Press, 1954.

Tinker, J.N. Intermarriage and ethnic boundaries: The Japanese American case. *Journal of Social Issues*, 1973, 29 (2).

U.S. News and World Report. December 26, 1966.

Weiss, M.S. Selective acculturation and the dating process: The Patterning of Chinese-Caucasian interracial dating. *Journal of Marriage and the Family,* 1970, 32, 273-278.

Williams, J.E. Connotations of racial concepts and color names. *Journal of Personality and Social Psychology,* 1965, 3, 531-540.

Williams, J.E., & Roberson, K.A. A method for assessing racial attitudes in preschool children. *Educational and Psychological Measurement,* 1967, 27, 671-689.

Wollenberg, C. Ethnic experiences in California history: An impressionistic survey. In R. Olsted & C. Wollenberg (Eds.), *Neither separate nor equal.* San Francisco: California Historical Society, 1971.

7 Ethnic Identity
The Impact of Two Cultures on the Psychological Development of Asians in America
Sue, Derald Wing

Among the many determinants of Asian-American identity, the cultural influences (values, norms, attitudes, and traditions) are of considerable importance. While social scientists agree that psychological development is not an isolated phenomenon apart from socio-cultural forces, most theories of personality are culturally exclusive. Furthermore, empirical studies tend not to deal adequately with the impact of cultural racism on the behavior of ethnic minorities. To understand the psychological development of Chinese- and Japanese-Americans, the cultural and historical forces of racism which serve to shape and define the Asian-American's identity must be examined.

Most studies which focus on the effects of culture on Asian-Americans tend to be highly compartmentalized. For example, one can find research investigating the relationship of culture to (a) personality characteristics (Abbott, 1970; Fong & Peskin, 1969; Meredith, 1966; Arkoff, Meredith & Iswahara, 1964; 1962; Fenz & Arkoff, 1962), (b) child-rearing practices (DeVos & Abbott, 1966; Kitano, 1964), (c) the manifestation of behavior disorders (Marsella, Kinzie, Gordon, 1971; Kitano, 1970; 1969a; Arkoff & Weaver, 1966; Sommers, 1960; Kimmich, 1960), (d) the ineffectiveness of traditional therapy (Sue & Sue, 1972a; 1971; Yamamoto, James & Palley, 1968), (e) acculturation (Matsumoto, Meredith & Masuda, 1970; Meade, 1970; Weiss, 1969; Fong, 1965; Kitano, 1962; Arkoff, 1959), and (f) use of English (Meredith, 1964; Smith & Kasdon, 1961; Smith, 1957). Few attempts integrate these findings into a global description of how cultures influence the socio-psychological functioning of the "whole" person.

Cultural impact is clearly demonstrated in the study of Chinese- and Japanese-Americans, where remnants of Asian cultural values collide with European-American values. The historical meeting of these two cultures and their consequent interaction in a racist society have fundamental importance in understanding the personality characteristics, academic abilities, and vocational interests of Asians in America.

Reprinted by permission of the editors and the publisher from D.W. Sue "Ethnic Identity: The Impact of Two Cultures on the Psychological Development of Asians in America." In S. Sue and N.N. Wagner (Eds.), *Asian-Americans: Psychological Perspectives.* Palo Alto, CA: Science and Behavior Books, 1973.

Asian Cultural Values

Although it is acknowledged that the Asian-American family structure and its subcultural values are in transition, they still retain their many values from the past. Because the primary family is generally the socializing agent for its offspring and because parents interpret appropriate and inappropriate behavior, a description of traditional Asian families will lead to greater understanding of their cultural values.

Chinese and Japanese family interaction patterns have been described as being similar by many social scientists (Sue & Sue, 1971; Abbott, 1970; Kitano, 1969a; 1969b; DeVos & Abbott, 1966; Kimmich, 1960). The Asian family is an ancient, complex institution, the fundamental unit of the culture. In China and Japan, it has long been more or less independent of political alliances; its form has survived political upheavals and invasions of foreigners.

The roles of family members are highly interdependent. Deviations from traditional norms governing behavior are suppressed to keep the family intact. Independent behavior which might upset the orderly functioning of the family is discouraged. The family structure is so arranged that conflicts within the family are minimized; each member has his own role to play which does not interfere with that of another. If a person has feelings which might disrupt family peace and harmony, he is expected to hide them. Restraint of potentially disruptive emotions is strongly emphasized in the development of the Asian character; the lack of outward signs of emotions has given rise to the prevalent opinion among Westerners that Asians are "inscrutable."

The Chinese and Japanese families are traditionally patriarchal with communication and authority flowing vertically from top to bottom. The father's behavior in relationship to other family members is generally dignified, authoritative, remote, and aloof. Sons are generally highly valued over daughters. The primary allegiance of the son is to the family, and obligations as a good father or husband are secondary. Asian women are expected to carry on the domestic duties, to marry, to become obedient helpers of their mothers-in-law, and to bear children, especially males.

The inculcation of guilt and shame are the principal techniques used to control the behavior of family members. Parents emphasize their children's obligation to the family. If a child acts independently (contrary to the wishes of his parents), he is told that he is selfish and inconsiderate and that he is not showing gratitude for all his parents have done for him. The behavior of individual members of an Asian family is expected to reflect credit on the whole family. Problems that arise among Asian-Americans such as failure in school, disobedience, juvenile delinquency, mental illness, etc., are sources of great shame. Such problems are generally kept hidden from public view and handled within the family. This fact may explain why there are low *official* rates of juvenile delinquency (Abbott & Abbott, 1969; Kitano, 1967) and low utilization of mental health facilities among Asians (Sue & Sue, 1972a;

Kitano, 1969a; Yamamoto, James & Palley, 1968; Kimmich, 1960). On the other hand, outstanding achievement in some aspect of life (especially educational and occupational success) is a source of great pride for the entire family. Thus, each family member has much at stake in the behavior of others.

In summary, traditional Asian values emphasize reserve and formality in interpersonal relations, restraint and inhibition of strong feelings, obedience to authority, obligations to the family, high academic and occupational achievement, and use of shame and guilt to control behavior. These cultural values have a significant impact on the psychological characteristics of Asians in America.

Historical Experience: Cultural Racism

Kovel (1970) believes that White racism in America is no aberration but an ingredient of our culture which serves as a stabilizing influence and a source of gratification to Whites. In defining cultural racism, Jones (1972) states that it is "...the individual and institutional expression of the superiority of one race's cultural heritage over that of another race. Racism is appropriate to the extent that racial and cultural factors are highly correlated and are a systematic basis for inferior treatment." (p. 6) Any discussion concerning the effects of racism on the psychological characteristics of minorities is necessarily fraught with hazards. It is difficult to distinguish the relevant variables which affect the individual and to impute cause-effect relations. However, a historical analysis of Asians in America suggests that cultural racism has done great harm to this ethnic group.

Unknown to the general public, Asian-Americans have been the object of much prejudice and discrimination. Ironically, the American public is unaware that no higher walls of prejudice have been raised, historically, around any other ethnic minority than those around the Chinese and Japanese. Asians have generally attempted to function in the existing society without loud, strong, or public protest (Sue & Sue, 1972a).

The first Chinese immigrants came to the United States during the 1840s. Their immigration from China was encouraged by the social and economic unrest in China at that time and by overpopulation in certain provinces (DeVos & Abbott, 1966). During this period, there was a demand for Chinese to help build the transcontinental railroad. Because of the need for cheap labor, they were welcomed into the labor force (Daniels, 1971). However, a diminishing labor market and fear of the "yellow peril" made the Chinese immigrants no longer welcome. Their pronounced racial and cultural differences from the White majority made them conspicuous, and they served as scapegoats for the resentment of White workers. Although Daniels (1971) mainly discusses the economic aspect for the hostility expressed against the Chinese, he points out that the anti-Chinese movement soon developed into an ideology of White supremacy which was compatible with the mainstream of American racism. Chinese were seen as "subhuman" or "heathens," and their mode of living was seen as undesirable and detrimental to the well-being of America. Laws which were passed to harass the Chinese denied them the rights of citizenship, ownership of land, the right of marriage, etc. At the height of the anti-Chinese movement, when prejudice and discrimination against the Chinese flourished, many Chinese were assaulted and killed by mobs of Whites. This anti-Chinese sentiment culminated in the passing of the Federal Chinese Exclusion Act of 1882 which was the first exclusion act against any ethnic group. This racist immigration law, justified by the alleged need to exclude masses of "cheap Chinese labor" from the United States, was not repealed until 1943 as a gesture of friendship toward China, an ally of the United States during World War II.

Likewise, the Japanese in America faced severe hostility and discrimination from White citizens. Japanese began immigrating to the United States during the 1890s when anti-Chinese sentiment was great. As a result, they shared in the pervasive anti-Oriental feeling. Originally brought in to fill the demand for cheap agricultural labor and coming from an agrarian background, many Japanese became engaged in these fields (Kitano, 1969b). Their fantastic success in the agricultural occupations, coupled with a racist climate, enraged many White citizens. Legislation similar to the anti-Chinese acts was passed against the Japanese, and individual-mob violence repeated itself. Such cries as "The Japs must go" were frequently echoed by the mass media and labor and political leaders. In response to hostility toward members of their race, both Chinese and Japanese formed their own communities to isolate and protect themselves from a threatening racist society.

Within this background of White racism, it became relatively easy for White society to accept the relocation of 110,000 Japanese-Americans into camps during World War II. Their pronounced racial and cultural characteristics were enough justification for the atrocious actions taken against the Japanese. The dangerous precedent created by American reaction to the Japanese is an ever-present threat that racial strains can again result in a repeat of history.

There can be no doubt that cultural racism has been practiced against the Chinese and Japanese. Many people would argue that, today, Asian-Americans face no such obstacles as their ancestors. The myth that Asians represent a "model minority" and are successful and functioning well in society is a popular belief often played up by the press (Newsweek, 1971; U.S. News & World Report, 1966). The 1960 Census reveals that Chinese and Japanese, indeed, have higher incomes and lower unemployment rates than their *non-White* counterparts. A further analysis, however, reveals that Chinese and Japanese are lower in income and higher in unemployment rates than the *White* population. This disparity is even greater when one considers that, generally, Chinese and Japanese achieve higher educational levels than Whites. It can only be concluded that social and economic discrimination are still flagrantly practiced against Asian-Americans.

Thus far, the fact that cultural racism has and is being practiced against Asian minorities has been documented. Attention now will be focused on the psychological costs of culture conflict.

Culture Conflict

Jones (1972) believes that many forms of culture conflict are really manifestations of cultural racism. Although there is nothing inherently wrong in acculturation and assimilation, he believes that "...when it is forced by a powerful group on a less powerful one, it constitutes a restriction of choice; hence, it is no longer subject to the values of natural order." (p. 166)

When an ethnic minority becomes increasingly exposed to the values and standards of the dominant host culture, there is progressive inculcation of those norms. This has been found for both the Chinese (Abbott, 1970; Meade, 1970; Fong & Peskin, 1969; Fong, 1965) and Japanese (Matsumoto, Meredith & Masuda, 1970; Kitano, 1962; Arkoff, 1959). However, assimilation and acculturation are not always smooth transitions without their pitfalls. As they become Westernized, many Asian-Americans come to view Western personality characteristics as more admirable qualities than Asian characteristics. Constantly bombarded with what constitutes desirable traits by a society that has low tolerance for differing life styles, many Asian males and females begin to find members of their own race undesirable social partners. For example, Weiss (1969) found many Chinese-American girls coming to expect the boys they date to behave boldly and aggressively in the traditional Western manner. They could be quite vehement in their denunciation of Asian-male traits. Unfortunately, hostility to a person's minority cultural background may cause Asians to turn their hostility inward. Such is the case when Japanese-American females express greater dissatisfaction with their body image than Caucasian females (Arkoff & Weaver, 1966). The individual may develop a kind of racial self-hatred that leads to lowered self-esteem and intense conflicts (Sue & Sue, 1971; Sommers, 1960). Among individuals of minority cultural background, we find many instances of culture conflict; the individual finds that he is heir to two different cultural traditions, and he may have difficulty in reconciling their effects on his own personality; he may find it difficult to decide to which culture he owes primary loyalty. Such a person has been called a Marginal Man. Because of his marginal status, he often experiences an identity crisis and feels isolated and alienated from both cultures.

In previous articles (Sue & Sue, 1972a; 1971), three different reactions to this stress were described. A person may remain allied to the values of his own culture; he may attempt to become over-Westernized and reject Asian ways; or he may attempt to integrate aspects of both cultures which he believes are functional to his own self-esteem and identity. The latter mode of adjustment is being advocated by the ethnically conscious Asians on many college campuses. In an attempt to raise group esteem and pride, Asian-Americans are actively exploring and challenging the forces in White society which have served to unfairly shape and define their identity (Sue & Sue, 1972b). No longer are they content to be a "banana," a derogatory term used to designate a person of Asian descent who is "Yellow on the outside but White on the inside."

Psychological Characteristics of Chinese- and Japanese-American Students

The cultural background of both the Japanese and Chinese, the historical and continuing forces of White racism, and the cultural conflicts experienced in the United States have left their mark on the current life styles of Asian-Americans. Although it is difficult to impute a direct cause-effect relationship between these forces and the psychological characteristics of Asian-Americans, the following description, certainly, seems consistent with their past background. The remaining sections will focus upon the personality traits, academic abilities, and vocational interests of Chinese- and Japanese-American college students. Findings presented in these sections will rely heavily on research conducted at the University of California, Berkeley (Sue & Kirk, in press; forthcoming). Three tests consisting of the Omnibus Personality Inventory, the School and College Ability Tests, and the Strong Vocational Interest Blank were administered to an entire entering Freshman class. Chinese-American, Japanese-American, and all other students were compared to one another on these three instruments.

Personality Characteristics

The studies conducted at Berkeley reveal that Chinese- and Japanese-American college students tend to exhibit similar characteristics. This is not surprising in view of their similar cultural and historical backgrounds. Asian-Americans of both sexes tend to evaluate ideas on the basis of their immediate practical application and to avoid an abstract, reflective, theoretical orientation. Because of their practical and applied approach to life problems, they tend to be more intolerant of ambiguities and to feel much more comfortable in well-structured situations. Asian-Americans also appear less autonomous and less independent from parental controls and authority figures. They are more obedient, conservative, conforming, and inhibited. In interpersonal relationships, they tend to be cautious in directly expressing their impulses and feelings. In comparison to Caucasian norms, both Chinese- and Japanese-American students appear more socially introverted and will more often withdraw from social contacts and responsibilities. Other investigators have found similar results for the Chinese (Abbott, 1970; Fong & Peskin, 1969; DeVos & Abbott, 1966) and Japanese (Meredith, 1966; Fenz & Arkoff, 1962; Arkoff, 1959).

Asian cultural values, emphasizing restraint of strong feelings, obedience, dependence upon the family, and formality in interpersonal relations, are being exhibited by these students. These values are in sharp contrast to Western emphasis on spontaneity, assertiveness, and informality. Because of socialization in well-defined roles, there is a tendency for Asian students to feel more comfortable in structured situations and to feel uncomfortable in ambiguous ones. As a result, they may tend to withdraw from social contacts with those outside their ethnic group or family. As discussed later, their minority status and sensitivity to actual and potential discrimination from White society may make them suspicious of people. It is possible, also, that their concrete and pragmatic approach was reinforced because it possessed social and economic survival value.

The socio-emotional adjustment characteristics of Asian-Americans also seem to reflect their cultural background and experiences as minorities in America. Meredith (1966), in testing Sansei students at the University of Hawaii, found them to be more tense, apprehensive, and suspicious than their Caucasian counterparts. A study by Fenz & Arkoff (1962) revealed that senior high school students of Chinese and Japanese ancestry possessed significantly higher needs for abasement. This trait indicates a need to feel guilty when things go wrong and to accept personal blame for failure. The Berkeley studies also support the fact that Asian-Americans seem to be experiencing more stress than their Caucasian controls. Both Chinese- and Japanese-American students exhibited attitudes and behaviors that characterize alienated persons. They were more likely to possess feelings of isolation, loneliness, and rejection. They also appeared more anxious, worried, and nervous.

Three factors seem to be operating in these findings. First, cultural elements are obviously affecting these tests. For example, Asian values emphasizing modesty and the tendency to accept blame (guilt and shame) would naturally elevate their abasement score. However, clinical observations and the consistency of personality measures revealing higher experienced stress point to real problems. Second, past and present discrimination and the isolation imposed by a racist society would affect feelings of loneliness, alienation, and anxiety. Last, the earlier discussion of culture conflict leading to a negative self-image could be a strong component of these findings.

Academic Abilities

Using the School and College Ability Tests, the Berkeley studies revealed that Chinese- and Japanese-Americans of both sexes scored significantly lower on the verbal section of the test than their control counterparts. In addition, Chinese-Americans of both sexes scored significantly higher on the quantitative section of the test. Although Japanese-American students tended to obtain higher quantitative scores, the differences were not significant.

Although the possibility of inherited racial characteristics cannot be eliminated, greater explanatory power seems to lie in a sociocultural analysis. The Asian-American's lowered verbal performance probably reflects his bilingual background (Smith & Kasdon, 1961; Smith, 1957). The nature of Asian society also stresses filial piety and unquestioning respect for authority. Limited communication patterns in the home (parent to child) and the isolation imposed by a dominant society (one that rewarded silence and inconspicuousness and punished outspoken behavior from minorities) greatly restricted verbal interaction (Watanabe, 1971). The higher quantitative scores may represent compensatory modes of expression. Quantitative activities also tend to be more concrete, impersonal, and structured. These attributes are highly attractive to Asian-Americans.

Vocational Interests

Most educators, pupil personnel workers, and counselors throughout the West and East Coasts have frequently remarked on the abundance of Asian students entering the physical sciences. Surveys undertaken at the University of California, Berkeley, (Chu, 1971; Takayama, 1971) reveal that approximately 75 percent of Chinese and 68 percent of Japanese males enter the physical sciences. Using the Strong Vocational Interest Blank, the Berkeley studies compared the interests of Chinese-Americans, Japanese-Americans, and all other students. Chinese-American men expressed more interest in the physical sciences (Mathematician, Physicist, Engineer, Chemist, etc.) than all other students. Although not statistically significant, Japanese-American men also tended to express more interest in these occupations. Males from both ethnic groups appeared more interested in occupations comprising the skilled-technical trades (Farmer, Aviator, Carpenter, Printer, Vocational-Agricultural Teacher, Forest Service Man, etc.) and less interested in sales (Sales Manager, Real Estate Salesman, Life Insurance Salesman) and the verbal-linguistic occupations (Advertising Man, Lawyer, Author-Journalist). Although Chinese-American males exhibited less interest in the social sciences, this was not true for the Japanese-American males. Generally, both groups expressed more interest in the business fields, especially the detail (Senior Certified Public Accountant, Accounting and Office Man) as opposed to the business contact vocations. They tended to be less interested in the aesthetic-cultural fields (Musician and Artist). Although they did not differ significantly in the biological sciences as a group, they did express more interest in the clinically applied ones (Dentist and Veterinarian).

The Asian-American females had a profile similar to their male counterparts. Both ethnic groups exhibited more interest in business occupations, applied-technical fields, biological and physical sciences and less interest in verbal-linguistic fields, social service, and aesthetic-cultural occupations. Although Chinese- and Japanese-American females tended to express more interest in the domestically oriented occupations (Housewife, Elementary Teacher, Office Worker, and Stenographer-Secretary), only the Chinese-American females scored significantly higher.

An analysis of the relationship between personality traits, academic abilities, and vocational interests for Asian-Americans reveals a logical consistency among all three variables. Greater interest in the physical sciences and lower interest in sales, social sciences, and verbal-linguistic fields are consistent with the Asian-American's higher quantitative and lower verbal skills. Furthermore, the people-contact professions call for some degree of forceful self-expression. These traits are antagonistic to the Asian-American's greater inhibition, reserve in interpersonal relations, and lower social extroversion. Physical sciences and skilled-technical trades, also, are characterized by more of a structured, impersonal, and concrete approach.

The Asian-American's restricted choice of vocations can be explained by two factors. First, early immigrants came from a strongly agricultural and peasant background. This is especially true of the Japanese who, according to the 1960 Census, were over-represented in agricultural fields. Second, early immigrants may have encouraged their sons and daughters into occupations with potentially greater social and economic survival value. Thus, their concern with evaluating choice of vocations on the basis of pragmatism was reinforced by a racist society. Agricultural fields, skilled-technical trades, and physical sciences can be perceived as possessing specific concrete skills that were functional in American society. Discrimination and prejudice were minimized in these occupations while people-contact professions were wrought with hazards of discrimination. Even though the Chinese and Japanese expressed more interest in the businesses, most of the fields were accounting and bookkeeping activities. Furthermore, business occupations which they have historically chosen tended to be within their ethnic community (import-export, family-owned businesses, restaurants, etc.) rather than within the larger society.

Differences Between Chinese- and Japanese-Americans

The discussion thus far has revealed many similarities between Chinese- and Japanese-American students. In light of their many common cultural values and experiences in America, this is not surprising. However, differences certainly exist. On all three measures (personality, abilities, and interests) administered at the University of California, Berkeley, Japanese-American students consistently fell into an intermediate position between the Chinese-American and the control students. In other words, Japanese-Americans are more similar to the controls than are the Chinese-Americans. This finding suggests two possibilities. It might be assumed that Japanese values are much more similar to European-American values than are those of the Chinese. An analysis of Japanese and Chinese cultural values would dictate against this as the sole interpretation. Additionally, the high rate of industrialization in Japan is a relatively recent phenomenon that may have minimal impact at this time. A more plausible explanation lies in the differential acculturation of both groups.

Arkoff, Meredith, & Iswahara (1962) conclude that Japanese-American females appear to be acculturating faster than their male counterparts. Weiss (1969) feels that Chinese females are much better accepted by American society than males. This leads to greater social contact with members of the host society and acculturation is fostered. If differential acculturation occurs between sexes of the same ethnic group, it might be possible that a similar phenomenon has and/or is affecting both the Chinese and Japanese. An answer to this question may lie in the historical past of both the Chinese and Japanese in America.

Prior to the outbreak of World War II, relations between Japan and the United States became noticeably strained. Many Japanese in America feared that their loyalty would be questioned. Fearing that war would break out between the two nations and bring retaliation against Japanese-Americans, many Japanese-American organizations such as the Japanese-American Citizens League emphasized the need to appear as American as possible. Pro-American proclamations were common, and offspring were encouraged to acculturate and identify themselves with the American people.

With the bombing of Pearl Harbor, war was declared on Japan and the relocation experience of 110,000 Japanese-Americans did much to foster acculturation (Umemoto, 1970; Kitano, 1969b). First, it broke up Japanese-American communities by uprooting their residents. Homes and properties of the Japanese were confiscated and lost. Even today, the Japanese communities (Japantowns) are not comparable to the cohesive Chinatowns in San Francisco and New York, which serve as visible symbols of ethnic identity for the Chinese. Second, the camp experience disrupted the traditional family structure and lines of authority. Elderly males no longer had a functional value as household heads. Control and discipline of children and women became noticeably weakened under these circumstances. Third, many Japanese-Americans chose to migrate to the East Coast and Midwest rather than suffer the humiliation of internment. Even after the termination of the relocation centers, some Japanese-Americans chose not to return to the West Coast because of the strong anti-Japanese feeling there. Their greater physical dispersal increased contact with members of the host society and probably aided acculturation.

Conclusions

The psychological characteristics exhibited by Asian-Americans are related to their culture and the Asian-American's interaction with Western society. Any study of ethnic minorities in America must necessarily deal with the forces of racism inherent in American culture. Since there are no Asian-Americans untouched by racism in the United States to use as a control group, the relationship of racism to psychological development becomes a complex issue that cannot easily be resolved. If an attempt is made to use control groups in Taiwan, Hong Kong, or China, the problem becomes clouded by a whole complex of other social and cultural differences. For these reasons, the analyses presented in this article must be seen as somewhat tentative and speculative. Hopefully, further research will help clarify this issue.

References

Abbott, K.A. *Harmony and Individualism,* Taipei: Orient Cultural Press, 1970.
Abbott, K., and Abbott, E. "Juvenile Delinquency in San Francisco's Chinese-American Community." *Journal of Sociology* 4, 1968, 45-56.

Arkoff, A. "Need Patterns of Two Generations of Japanese-Americans in Hawaii." *Journal of Social Psychology* 50, 1959, 75-79.

———; Meredith, G.; and Iswahara, S. "Dominance-Deference Patterning in Motherland-Japanese, Japanese-American, and Caucasian-American Students." *Journal of Social Psychology* 58, 1962, 61-63.

———; Meredith, G.; and Iswahara, S. "Male-Dominant and Equalitarian Attitudes in Japanese, Japanese-American, and Caucasian-American Students." *Journal of Social Psychology* 64, 1964, 225-229.

———, and H. Weaver. "Body Image and Body Dissatisfaction in Japanese-Americans." *Journal of Social Psychology* 68, 1966, 323-330.

Chu, Robert. "Majors of Chinese and Japanese Students at the University of California, Berkeley, for the Past 20 Years." Project report, AS 150, Asian Studies Division, University of California, Berkeley, Winter, 1971.

Daniels, R. *Concentration Camps USA: Japanese-Americans and World War II*. New York: Holt, Rinehart, and Winston, Inc., 1971.

DeVos, G., and Abbott, K. "The Chinese Family in San Francisco." MSW dissertation, University of California, Berkeley, 1966.

Fenz, W., and Arkoff, A. "Comparative Need Patterns of Five Ancestry Groups in Hawaii." *Journal of Social Psychology* 58, 1962, 67-89.

Fong, S.L.M. "Assimilation of Chinese in America: Changes in Orientation and Social Perception." *American Journal of Sociology* 71, 1965, 265-273.

———, and Peskin, H. "Sex-Role Strain and Personality Adjustment of China-born Students in America: A Pilot Study." *Journal of Abnormal Psychology* 74, 1969, 563-567.

Jones, J.M. *Prejudice and Racism*. Massachusetts: Addison-Wesley Publishing Company, 1972.

Kimmich, R.A. "Ethnic Aspects of Schizophrenia in Hawaii." *Psychiatry* 23, 1960, 97-102.

Kitano, H.H.L. "Changing Achievement Patterns of the Japanese in the United States." *Journal of Social Psychology* 58, 1962, 257-264.

———. "Inter and Intra-Generational Differences in Maternal Attitudes Toward Child Rearing." *Journal of Social Psychology* 63, 1964, 215-220.

———. "Japanese-American Crime and Delinquency." *Journal of Psychology* 66, 1967, 253-263.

———. "Japanese-American Mental Illness." In S.C. Plog and R.B. Edgerton (eds.), *Changing Perspectives in Mental Illness*. New York: Holt, Rinehart, and Winston, 1969a.

———. *Japanese-Americans: The Evolution of a Subculture*. New Jersey: Prentice-Hall, 1969b.

———. "Mental Illness in Four Cultures." *Journal of Social Psychology* 80, 1970, 121-134.

Kovel, J. *White Racism: A Psychohistory*. New York: Vintage Books, 1971.

Marsella, A.J.; Kinzie, D.; and Gordon, P. "Depression Patterns among American College Students of Caucasian, Chinese, and Japanese Ancestry." Paper presented at the Conference on Culture and Mental Health in Asia and the Pacific. March, 1971.

Matsumoto, G.M.; Meredith, G.; and Masuda, M. "Ethnic Identification: Honolulu and Seattle Japanese-Americans." *Journal of Cross-Cultural Psychology* 1, 1970, 63-76.

Meade, R.D. "Leadership Studies of Chinese and Chinese-Americans." *Journal of Cross-Cultural Psychology* 1, 1970, 325-332.

Meredith, G.M. "Personality Correlates of Pidgin English Usage among Japanese-American College Students in Hawaii." *Japanese Psychological Research* 6, 1964.

———. "Amae and Acculturation among Japanese-American College Students in Hawaii. *Journal of Social Psychology* 70, 1966, 171-180.

Smith, M.E. "Progress in the Use of English after Twenty-Two Years by Children of Chinese Ancestry in Honolulu." *Journal of Genetic Psychology* 90, 1957, 255-258.

———, and Kasdon, L.M. "Progress in the Use of English after Twenty Years by Children of Filipino and Japanese Ancestry in Hawaii." *Journal of Genetic Psychology* 99, 1961, 129-138.

Sommers, V.S. "Identity Conflict and Acculturation Problems in Oriental-Americans." *American Journal of Orthopsychiatry* 30, 1960, 637-644.

Success Story: "Out-Whiting the Whites." *Newsweek,* June, 1971.

Success Story of One Minority Group in the U.S. *US News and World Report,* December, 1966.

Sue, D.W., and Sue, S. "Counseling Chinese-Americans." *Personnel and Guidance Journal* 50, 1972a, 637-644.

———, and Sue, S. "Ethnic Minorities: Resistance to Being Researched." *Professional Psychology* 2, 1972b, 11-17.

———, and Kirk, B.A. "Psychological Characteristics of Chinese-American College Students." *Journal of Counseling Psychology* in press [1972].

———, and Kirk, B.A. "Differential Characteristics of Japanese- and Chinese-American College Students." Research in progress at the University of California, Berkeley.

Sue, S., and Sue, D.W. "Chinese-American Personality and Mental Health." *Amerasia Journal* 1, 1971, 36-49.

Takayama, G. "Analysis of Data on Asian Students at UC Berkeley, 1971." Project report, AS 150, Asian Studies Division, University of California, Berkeley, Winter, 1971.

Unemoto, A. "Crisis in the Japanese-American Family." In *Asian Women.* Berkeley: 1971.

Watanabe, C. "A College Level Reading and Composition Program for Students of Asian Descent: Diagnosis and Design." Asian Studies Division, University of California, Berkeley, 1971.

Weiss, M.S. "Selective Acculturation and the Dating Process: The Patterning of Chinese-Caucasian Interracial Dating." *Journal of Marriage and the Family* 32, 1970.

Yamamoto, J.; James, Q.C.; and Palley, N. "Cultural Problems in Psychiatric Therapy." *General Archives of Psychiatry* 19, 1968, 45-49.

8 Counseling Chinese-Americans

Sue, Derald Wing
Sue, Stanley

The Chinese-American student's cultural background plays an important part in his expression of personality traits and the manifestation of his problems. This article presents an analysis of Chinese values and suggests that the counseling situation may arouse intense conflicts for many Chinese-American students. It also suggests a modified counseling approach that can be used in working with these students.

Many people believe that the Chinese in America represent a model minority group. Unlike the blacks and Chicanos, the Chinese have tried to function in the existing social structure with a minimum of visible conflict with members of the host society. Historically, they have accepted much prejudice and discrimination without voicing strong public protest (DeVos & Abbott, 1966). Their traditional nonthreatening stance and the public's lack of knowledge about Chinese people have masked their problems of poverty, unemployment, and juvenile delinquency. The notion that Chinese people experience few problems in American society is also shared by many educators, counselors, and mental health workers. The Chinese-Americans' strong emphasis on educational achievement (DeVos & Abbott, 1966), their custom of handling problems within the family, and their limited use of mental health facilities (Kimmich, 1960; Kitano, 1969) have reinforced this misconception.

Since many Chinese-American college students find it difficult to label themselves as having emotional problems, they tend to under-use psychiatric facilities on campuses when they encounter personal problems (Sue & Sue, 1971). Rather, they often seek the less threatening services of campus counseling centers with an educational-vocational orientation, because they feel that less social stigma is involved. It is especially important for guidance workers to understand the Chinese-American students' cultural background and the conflicts they experience. These cultural influences may, in fact, hinder the development of a therapeutic relationship between counselor and client. However, very few counselors know enough about the Chinese-Americans' background to understand their reaction to the counseling-therapy situation. An examination of Chinese culture and family interaction patterns suggests that the counseling situation may cause a great deal of conflict for many Chinese-American students.

Chinese Culture and Personality

Although the Chinese family in America is changing, it still retains many of the cultural values from its past (DeVos & Abbott, 1966). The Chinese family is an ancient and complex institution, and the roles of family members have long been rigidly defined. Chinese are taught to obey parents, to respect elders, and to create a good family name by outstanding achievement in some aspect of life, for example, by academic or occupational success. Since misbehaviors (juvenile delinquency, academic failure, and mental disorders) reflect upon the entire family, an individual learns that his behavior has great significance. If he has feelings whose expression might disrupt family harmony, he is expected to restrain himself. Indeed, the Chinese culture highly values self-control and inhibition of strong feelings (Abbott, 1970).

Sue and Kirk (1972, in press) found that the personality traits of Chinese-American students reflect this family and cultural background. The investigators studied the entire entering freshman class in the fall of 1966, at the University of California in Berkeley. Chinese-American students seemed to be more conforming to authority, inhibited, and introverted than the general student body. They also tended to be more practical in their approach to tasks and to be less tolerant of ambiguity, preferring to deal with concrete facts and events. Although their quantitative skills appeared high, their verbal scores were lower than that of the general student body, perhaps reflecting a bilingual background and limited communication patterns in the home.

The Acculturation Process

The Chinese individual in America is in a position of conflict between the pulls of both his cultural background and the Western values he is exposed to in school and by the mass media. American values emphasizing spontaneity, assertiveness, and independence are often at odds with many Chinese values. As Chinese people progressively adopt more of the values and standards of the larger community as their own, the transition is not always smooth. Indeed, culture conflict seems to be an intimate part of the Asian-American experience.

It is our impression that Chinese students do not react in any stereotyped manner to culture conflict (Sue & Sue, 1971), but we have most frequently observed three main types of reaction. Some tend to resist assimilation by maintaining traditional values and by associating predominantly with other Chinese. Others try to become assimilated into the dominant culture by rejecting their Chinese culture. The Asian-American movement on college campuses has attracted yet another group of students by stressing pride in racial identity.

Obviously, each Chinese student does not fall neatly into one of the three groups, and there are quantitative differences in the types of conflicts exhibited in counseling situations, depending upon the cultural orientation of individuals. To illustrate the many conflicts experienced by Chinese-American students in their personal life and in their reactions to counseling, in this article we will use case descriptions of clients we have seen for counseling. We have taken care to insure the anonymity of all case materials.

Maintaining Traditional Values

John C. is a 21-year-old student majoring in electrical engineering. He first sought counseling because he was having increasing study problems and was receiving failing grades. These academic difficulties became apparent during the first quarter of his senior year and were accompanied by headaches, indigestion, and insomnia. Since he had been an excellent student in the past, John felt that his lowered academic performance was caused by illness. However, a medical examination failed to reveal any organic disorder.

During the initial interview, John seemed depressed and anxious. He was difficult to counsel because he would respond to inquiries with short but polite statements and would seldom volunteer information about himself. He avoided any statements that involved feelings and presented his problem as a strictly educational one. Although he never expressed it directly, John seemed to doubt the value of counseling and needed much reassurance and feedback about his performance in the interview. In view of John's reluctance to open up, it seemed unwise to probe immediately into areas that aroused much anxiety in him.

As the sessions progressed, John became less anxious and more trusting of the counselor. Much of his earlier difficulties in opening up were caused by his feelings of shame and guilt at having come to a counselor. He was concerned that his family might discover his seeking of help and that it would be a disgrace to them. This anxiety was compounded by his strong feelings of failure in school. However, when the counselor informed him that many Chinese students experienced similar problems and that these sessions were completely confidential, John seemed quite relieved. As he became increasingly able to open up, he revealed problems such as we have found are typical of Chinese students who have strongly internalized traditional cultural values and whose self-worth and identity are defined within the family nexus.

John's parents had always had high expectations of him and constantly pressured him to do well in school. They seemed to equate his personal worth with his ability to obtain good grades. This pressure caused him to spend endless hours studying, and generally he remained isolated from social activities. This isolation did not help him to learn the social skills required in peer relationships. In addition, John's more formalized training was in sharp contrast to the informality and spontaneity demanded in Caucasian interpersonal relationships. Therefore, his circle of friends was small, and he was never really able to enjoy himself with others.

John experienced a lot of conflict, because he was beginning to resent the pressure his parents put on him, and also their demands. For example, they stated that it would be nice if he would help his brothers through school after graduation. This statement aroused a great amount of unexpressed anger in John toward them. He felt unable to lead his own life. Furthermore, his lack of interest in engineering was intensified as graduation approached. He had always harbored secret wishes about becoming an artist but was pressured into engineering by his parents. His deep-seated feelings of anger toward his parents resulted in his passive-aggressive responses of failure in school and in his physical symptoms.

The case of John C. illustrates some of the following conflicts encountered by many Chinese students attempting to maintain traditional Chinese values: (a) there is often a conflict between loyalty to the family and personal desires for independence; (b) the learned patterns of self-restraint and formality in interpersonal relationships often result in a lack of social experience and subsequent feelings of loneliness, and furthermore, they can act as impediments to counseling; (c) the family pressure to achieve academically accentuates feelings of shame and depression when the student fails.

Rejecting Chinese Customs

Many Chinese-Americans attempt to become Westernized and reject traditional Chinese customs. Vontress (1970) points out that many blacks develop a hatred of their own group and culture, and many Chinese counselees experience a similar type of conflict, especially in their social life. It is typified in the following counseling interchange.

Counselor: You seem to prefer dating Caucasians...

Client: Well...It's so stupid for my parents to think that they can keep all their customs and values. I really resent being Chinese and having to date all those Chinese guys. They're so passive, and I can make them do almost anything I want. Others [Chinese] are on a big ego trip and expect me to be passive and do whatever they say. Yes...I do prefer Caucasians.

Counselor: Is that an alternative open to you?

Client: Yes...but my parents would feel hurt...they'd probably disown me. They keep on telling me to go out with Chinese guys. A few months ago they got me to go out with this guy—I must have been the first girl he ever dated—I wasn't even polite to him.

Counselor: I guess things were doubly bad. You didn't like the guy and you didn't like your parents pushing him on you.

Client: Well...actually I felt a little sorry for him. I don't like to hurt my parents or those [Chinese] guys, but things always work out that way.

The client's last statement reflected some feelings of guilt over her rudeness toward her date. Although she was open and honest, her desire to be independent was confused with a constant rejection of her parents' attempts to influence her life. During a later session, she was able to express her conflict:

Client: I used to think that I was being independent if I went out with guys that my parents disapproved of. But that isn't really being independent. I just did that to spite them. I guess I should feel guilty if I purposely hurt them, but not if I *really* want to do something for myself.

Although the rejection of Chinese culture is often a developmental phase adequately resolved by most Chinese-Americans, many come to look upon Western personality characteristics as more admirable. For example, some Chinese-American girls come to expect the boys they date to behave boldly and aggressively in the Western manner. Weiss (1969) found that many Chinese-American college females were quite vehement in their denunciation of their male counterparts as dating partners. They frequently described the Chinese male as immature, inept, and sexually unattractive. Although the males denied the more derogatory accusations about themselves, they tended to agree that they were more inhibited and unassertive than Caucasians.

The Asian-American Movement

Recently, a growing number of Chinese students on college campuses throughout the nation are, like the blacks and Chicanos, emphasizing their own heritage, pride, and self-identity. They feel that the role of a conforming "banana" (a derogatory term used to describe a person of Asian ancestry who is "yellow on the outside but white on the inside") is too degrading. In an attempt to gain the self-respect they feel has been denied them by white society, they have banded together in an attempt to reverse the negative trend of bananaism among their own group. This group of individuals seem much more aware of political, economic, and social forces that have shaped their identity. They feel that society is to blame for their present dilemma and are actively challenging the establishment. They are openly suspicious of institutions, such as counseling services, because they view them as agents of the establishment. Very few of the more ethnically conscious and militant Asians will use counseling—because of its identification with the status quo. When they do, they are usually suspicious and hostile toward the counselor. Before counseling can proceed effectively, the counselor will have to deal with certain challenges from these students, such as the following:

Client: First of all . . . I don't believe in psychology . . . I think it's a lot of bullshit. People in psychology are always trying to adjust people to a *sick* society, and what is needed is to overthrow this goddamned establishment. . . . I feel the same way about those stupid tests. Cultural bias . . . they aren't applicable to minorities. The only reason I came in here was . . . well, I heard your lecture in Psychology 160 [a lecture on Asian-Americans], and I think I can work with you.

The counselee in this case happened to be hostile and depressed over the recent death of his father. Although he realized he had some need for help, he still did not trust the counseling process.

Client: Psychologists see the problem inside of people when the problem is in society. Don't you think white society has made all minorities feel inferior and degraded?

Counselor: I know that. White society has done great harm to minorities.

The client was posing a direct challenge to the counselor. Any defense of white society or explanations of the value of counseling might have aroused greater hostility and mistrust. It would have been extremely difficult to establish rapport without some honest agreement on the racist nature of American society. Later, the counselee revealed that his father had just died. He was beginning to realize that there was no contradiction in viewing society as being racist and in having personal problems.

Often, growing pride in self-identity makes it difficult for students who are having emotional problems to accept their personal difficulties. This is not to say that militance and group pride are signs of maladjustment. On the contrary, the Asian-American movement is a healthy attempt to resolve feelings of inferiority and degradation fostered by discrimination and prejudice.

The Counseling Process as a Source of Conflict

Chinese students are often caught between the demands of two cultures, but individuals react differently to this conflict. The counseling situation reflects the cultural conflicts encountered by Chinese students in their everyday life.

First, counselors and other mental health professionals are often at a loss to explain why Chinese counselees do not actively participate in the counseling process. Our colleagues have remarked that Chinese students are difficult to counsel because they repress emotional conflicts. These remarks indicate that counselors expect their counselees to exhibit some degree of openness, psychological-mindedness, or sophistication. Such characteristics are often beneficial in counseling. However, openness is quite difficult for many Chinese students who have learned to inhibit emotional expression, and direct or subtle demands by the counselor for openness may be quite threatening to them.

Second, Chinese students frequently find it difficult to admit they have emotional difficulties, because such problems arouse a great deal of shame and a sense of having failed one's family. Often, Chinese students may indirectly ask for help with personal difficulties by presenting educational problems or somantic complaints. Some investigators (Abbott, 1970; Marsella, Kinzie, & Gordon, 1971) feel that Chinese frequently express psychological distress through indirect routes, such as bodily complaints and passive-aggressive responses. Since emotional problems are felt to reflect shamefully on family upbringing, somatization could represent a more acceptable means of expressing psychological disturbance. Such was the case of John C.

Third, the counseling or therapy situation is often an ambiguous one. The counselee is encouraged to discuss any problems; the counselor listens and responds. Many Chinese students prefer concrete and well-structured situations, and the well-defined role expectations in the Chinese family are in sharp contrast to the ambiguity of the counseling process.

Implications for the Counseling Process

Just as it is unwise to suggest definite guidelines in dealing with all Chinese-Americans in counseling, it seems equally unwise to ignore cultural factors that might affect the counseling process. The counselor's inability to recognize these factors may make the Chinese counselee terminate prematurely. The difficulty in admitting social and emotional problems despite a need for help places the Chinese-American in an intense conflict. A too-confrontive and emotionally intense approach at the onset of counseling can frequently increase the level of shame. The counselor may facilitate counseling by responding to what may be viewed as superficial problems, such as the educational difficulties and somatic complaints that may mask more serious emotional conflicts. The counselee is then in a position to move at his own rate in exploring more threatening material.

In addition, the counselor can often facilitate self-disclosure by referring to psychological material relevant to vocational choice or job demands. For example, test interpretation can be threatening to the Chinese student, especially when psychological problems are involved. Many students are able to talk more freely about their difficulties if test interpretations are related concretely to their vocational future. Therefore, counselors involved in vocational decision-making may be in an advantageous position not shared by other mental health professionals, as the following case illustrates.

Pat. H. was a 19-year-old pre-pharmacy major who came for vocational counseling. Since he was the eldest of three boys, his parents had high expectations of him. He was expected to set a good example for his younger brothers and enhance the good name of the family. Because his grades were mediocre, he was beginning to doubt his ability to handle pharmacy. However, results of his interest and ability tests and his counselor's impressions supported his choice of the pharmacy major. The counselor felt that his difficulty in courses reflected passive resistance to his parents' high expectations of him for being the oldest son.

On his Edwards Personal Preference Schedule, Pat showed high achievement, change, and abasement scores. Earlier attempts to explore his feelings dealing with parental expectations proved fruitless. However, the following transcript demonstrates how testing was used to open up exploration in a nonthreatening manner.

Counselor: Let's explore the meaning of your scores in greater detail as they relate to future vocations. All right?
Client: Okay.

Counselor: Your high score on achievement indicates that whatever you undertake you would like to excel and do well in. For example, if you enter pharmacy, you'd like to do well in that field [*client nods head*]. However, your high change score indicates that you like variety and change....You may tend to get restless at times...maybe feel trapped in activities that bore you.

Client: Yeah.

Counselor: Do you see this score [abasement score]?

Client: Yeah, I blew the scale on that one.... What is it? [*some anxiety observable*]

Counselor: Well, it indicates you tend to be hard on yourself..For example, if you were to do poorly in pharmacy school...you would blame yourself for the failure...

Client: Yea, yeah...I'm always doing that..I feel that...it's probably exaggerated.

Counselor: Exaggerated?

Client: I mean...being the oldest son.

Counselor: What's it like to be the oldest son?

Client: Well...there's a lot of pressure and you can feel immobilized. Maybe this score [*points to change scale*] is why I feel so restless.

This progression marked a major breakthrough in Pat's case and led to an increasingly personalized discussion.

The difficulty in self-disclosure for Chinese-American students indicates that assurances of confidentiality between counselor and counselee are of utmost importance. A frequent concern of many Chinese-American students is that their friends, and especially their parents, will find out that they are seeing a counselor. For this reason, group counseling or therapy is very threatening. It is difficult enough to share their thoughts with one individual, let alone an entire group. Chinese students frequently refuse to participate in groups, and when in a group, they are often quiet and withdrawn. It may be wise to discuss the issue of confidentiality, the feelings of trust and mistrust in one another, and the cultural barriers in talking about feelings. We have found that many Chinese-American counselees are able to open up and express feelings quite directly once they develop trust of the counselor.

Since many Chinese-American students tend to feel more comfortable in well-structured and unambiguous situations, counseling by providing guidelines in the form of explanations and suggestions may be helpful. Such guidelines might include an explanation of the counseling process. In addition, the Chinese-American's emotional inhibition and lower verbal participation may also indicate the need for a more active approach on the part of the counselor. The following case description is an example of an active structuring of interviews.

Anne W. was quite uncomfortable and anxious during the first interview dealing with vocational counseling. This anxiety seemed more related to the ambiguity of the situation than anything else. She appeared confused about the direction of the counselor's comments and questions. At this point the counselor felt that an explanation of vocational counseling would facilitate the process.

Counselor: Let me take some time to explain to you how we usually proceed in vocational counseling. Vocational counseling is an attempt to understand the whole person. Therefore, we are interested in your interests, likes and dislikes, and specific abilities or skills as they relate to different possible vocations. The first interview is usually an attempt to get to know you . . . especially your past experiences and reactions to different courses you've taken, jobs you've worked at, and so forth. Especially important are the hopes and aspirations that you have. If testing seems indicated, as in your case, you'll be asked to complete a battery of tests. After testing we'll sit down and interpret them together. When we arrive at possible vocations, we'll use the vocational library and find out what these jobs entail in terms of background, training, etc.

Client: Oh! I see . . .

Counselor: That's why we've been exploring your high school experiences. . . . Sometimes the hopes and dreams in your younger years can tell us much about your interests.

After this explanation, Anne participated much more in the interviews.

Culture and Counseling

Since guidance workers may lack understanding of cultural influences, they frequently encounter difficulty in working with minority groups. Because there are cultural determinants of behavior, and counseling is essentially a white middle class activity, it may be necessary to modify counseling approaches. This is especially true in working with many Chinese-American counselees. The suggestions we have offered are primarily directed to the establishment of a working relationship of rapport and trust. Once a strong relationship has been established, the counselor has greater freedom in varying his therapeutic approach. To avoid oversimplification and the creation of an artificial situation, we have purposely kept our discussion of techniques somewhat general. The use of counseling techniques should be evaluated on the basis of the client's needs and their compatibility with the counselor's style and personality. Perhaps the most important tool a counselor could possess is knowledge of the Asian-American experience and its relationship to counseling. The counselor must address himself to problems of guilt and shame and lack of openness in the case of the traditionalist, to problems of independence and self-hate in the marginal man, and to racism in society with the Asian-American.

Finally, a word of caution must be noted. Most Chinese-Americans are able to handle cultural conflicts and adequately resolve them. This article has been mainly concerned with that relatively small number who seek counseling help when they feel that they cannot resolve their conflicts.

References

Abbott, K.A. *Harmony and individualism.* Taipei: Orient Cultural Service, 1970.

DeVos, G., & Abbott, K. The Chinese family in San Francisco. Unpublished master's thesis, University of California, Berkeley, 1966.

Kimmich, R.A. Ethnic aspects of schizophrenia in Hawaii. *Psychiatry,* 1960, *23,* 97-102.

Kitano, H.H.L. Japanese-American mental illness. In S.C. Plog and R.B. Edgerton (Eds.), *Changing perspectives in mental illness.* New York: Holt, Rinehart & Winston, 1969.

Marsella, A.J., Kinzie, D., & Gordon, P. Depression patterns among American college students of Caucasian, Chinese, and Japanese ancestry. Paper presented at the Conference on Culture and Mental Health in Asia and the Pacific, March 1971.

Sue, D.W., & Kirk, B.A. Psychological characteristics of Chinese-American students. *Journal of Counseling Psychology,* 1972 in press.

Sue, S., & Sue, D.W. Chinese-American personality and mental health. *Amerasia Journal,* 1971, *1*(2), 36-49.

Vontress, C.E. Counseling blacks. *Personnel and Guidance Journal,* 1970, *48,* 713-719.

Weiss, M.S. Inter-racial romance: The Chinese-Caucasian dating game. Paper presented at the Southwestern Anthropological Association. Las Vegas, Nevada, April 1969.

Selected Readings

Atkinson, D.R., Maruyama, M. & Matsui, S. Effects of Counselor race and counseling approach on Asian Americans' perceptions of counselor credibility and utility. *Journal of Counseling Psychology,* 1978, *25* (1), 76-83.

Fong, S.L.M. Assimilation and changing social roles of Chinese-Americans. *Journal of Social Issues,* 1973, *29* (2), 115-127.

Hayasaka, P. The Asian experience in White America. *Journal of Intergroup Relations,* 1973, *2,* 67-73.

Kim, B.C. Asian-Americans: no model minority. *Social Work,* 1973, *18* (1), 44-53.

Kitano, H.H.L., & Sue, S. The model minorities. *Journal of Social Issues,* 1973, *29* (2), 1-9.

Levine, G.N., & Montero, D.M. Socioeconomic mobility among three generations of Japanese Americans. *Journal of Social Issues,* 1973, *29* (2), 33-48.

Maykovich, M.F. Political activation of Japanese-American youth. *Journal of Social Issues,* 1973, *29* (2), 167-185.

Sue, D.W., & Kirk, B.A. Differential characteristics of Japanese-American and Chinese-American college students. *Journal of Counseling Psychology,* 1973, *20* (2), 142-148.

Sue, D.W., & Sue, D. Understanding Asian-Americans: The neglected minority. *Personnel and Guidance Journal,* 1973, *51,* 386-389.

Sue, S., & McKinney, H. Asian Americans in the community mental health care system. *American Journal of Orthopsychiatry,* 1975, *45* (1), 111-118.

Sue, S., & Wagner, N.N. *Asian Americans: Psychological Perspectives.* Ben Lomand, California: Science and Behavior Books, Inc., 1973.

Watanabe, C. Self-expression and the Asian-American experience. *Personnel and Guidance Journal,* 1973, *51,* 390-396.

The Asian American Client
Cases and Questions

1. Assume you are a high school counselor in a large suburban high school. A Japanese American student whom you have seen for academic advising on several occasions has just shared with you his involvement as a marijuana dealer. Although attempting to hide his emotions, the student is clearly distraught. He is particularly concerned that a recent arrest of a marijuana supplier will eventually lead authorities to him.

    a. How *might* the student's cultural background affect his feelings as he shares this problem?
    b. What kind of input from you as a counselor do you think this student wants/needs most?
    c. Can you anticipate any prejudicial reaction on the part of the school administration (if the student's behavior is uncovered) as a result of the student's racial/ethnic background?

2. Assume you are a community psychologist employed by a community agency which provides psychological services to a population of middle class Japanese American families, among others. A Young Buddhist Association (YBA) has asked you to speak on, "resolving inter-generational conflict" at their next meeting. (Your agency is aware that generational conflict has become a major problem in this community in recent years.)

    a. What do you think are some of the causes of the inter-generational conflict being experienced by these young people and their parents?
    b. Other than your talk, what services do you feel qualified to render these young Japanese Americans and their families?
    c. How do you think these services will be received by the YBA members and their families?

3. Assume you are a high school counselor who has been asked by the Dean of Guidance to organize and moderate a number of value clarification groups. You plan to set up six groups of eight students each from a list of volunteers, although seven students were referred by

teachers because they are non-participators in class. Six of the seven students referred by teachers are Asian Americans.

a. Will the composition of your six groups be determined by the fact six of seven teacher referrals are Asian American?
b. What goals do you have for your six groups and for the individual members of these groups?
c. How will your own cultural/educational background affect the way in which you relate to the six Asian American students?

Part 4 **The Black Client**

More than any other ethnic group in modern history, Black Americans have been caught up in the throes of social change (Anderson, 1971, p. 260). This process was set in motion nearly four hundred years ago as a Dutch vessel set sail for the port of Jamestown, Virginia. It carried on board a very special and economically promising commodity—twenty African slaves. "Darkies for sale" the signs at port-side read, "strong as oxen and guaranteed to fulfill your needs." This infamous event of 1619 marked the beginning of what came to be recognized as the most destructive and inhumane institution ever to be applied by one group of human beings to another. Bennet (1969), describing life under American slavery, writes:

> A curtain of cotton rang down on some four million human beings; it became a crime to teach these men and women to read and write. . . .Behind the cotton curtain four million human beings were systematically deprived of every right of personality. Vice, immorality and brutality were institutionalized. The sanction of the family was violated; children were sold from mothers, and fatherhood, in effect, was outlawed (p. 271).

This cruel and brutal system was to legitimately continue for two hundred years until, on January 1, 1863, President Lincoln proclaimed it "illegal."

But the jubilation and rejoicing of the newly freed Negro quickly disappeared. Biesanz and Biesanz (1969) point out that from 1890 to 1930 the conditions of the Negro were, in general, worse than those experienced under slavery. In the North, Blacks were unemployed or, if fortunate enough to be employed, poorly paid; in the South, they typically worked farms, often as sharecroppers, and were vulnerable to White exploitation and oppression (p. 275).

Nor was the oppression of Blacks limited to economic discrimination. According to John Hope Franklin (1967), there were more than 2,500 lynchings of Negroes in the last sixteen years of the nineteenth century; in the first fourteen years of the new century, approximately 1,100 lynchings took place. In Philadelphia and New York as well as other cities North and South, there were race riots, not of Negro protest, but riots in which Whites pillaged, burned and killed in the Negro section (p. 439-444).

A number of laws were passed which specifically addressed the issue of "ex-slave" entitlement to equality and justice under the United States Constitution. More often than not, laws which granted the Negro equal rights were so badly phrased that they were, for all practical purposes, nullified. The Thirteenth, Fourteenth and Fifteenth Amendments to the Constitution, for instance, asserted that the freed Negro had all the rights granted every American citizen. Yet in 1896 the U.S. Supreme Court ruled in Plessy vs Ferguson that the provision of "separate but equal" facilities in public transportation did not violate the "equal rights" amendment of the constitution. This decision, in effect, cleared the way for the Negro community to be isolated and neglected.

Outraged by the court's decision, a number of outspoken Negroes and White sympathizers united in opposition to what they considered as the "legal reenslavement" of the Negro. Organizations such as the National Association for the Advancement of Colored People (NAACP) were formed. Their first decisive victory came on May 17, 1954. On that date, the U.S. Supreme Court decided in Brown vs. Board of Education Topeka (1954) that "separate school facilities were unequal" and to "separate children from others of similar age and qualification solely because of their race generated a feeling of inferiority as to their status in the community that may affect their hearts and minds in ways unlikely ever to be undone." While this decision reinstated Negro rights under the equal rights amendment, it did not end racial discrimination and prejudice and, in some ways, only marked the beginning of a battle to end unequal treatment in public supported education.

According to the Current Population Report of 1976 (U.S. Bureau of Census, 1977), over eight million Black Americans enrolled in public education programs in the United States for that year. This figure is expected to increase considerably as more and more Black Americans are now turning to higher education as a means of gaining greater social mobility. The increasing number of middle income Blacks in the United States suggests this faith in education as the key to upward social and economic mobility may not be entirely unfounded. Yet Blacks are likely to find the present educational system ill-prepared to deal with the distinct problems which they bring with them as product of a racist and discriminatory society. Swick (1974) in a review of the research in this area, suggests that public education, like many other institutions found in our society, often reflects the general attitudes, values and traditions of the dominant group. Prejudices and unequal treatment procedures are frequently perpetuated by administrators, teachers and counselors who operate under the consoling illusion that, by attending a prestigious college and receiving the required credentials and licenses, they have somehow freed themselves of the negative and inhumane attitudes and practices that are so much a part of American life and culture.

The impact of the struggle for political, economic, and educational freedom and equality by Black Americans is reflected in the articles to follow. In the first, "What Counselors Must Know About the Social Science of Black Americans," Harper stresses the need for counselors to expand their awareness of the Black American experience. According to Harper, counselors need to be versed in the history, sociology, economics, and psychology of Black Americans. In addition to presenting an excellent overview of these four social sciences, the author cites numerous readings in each area to aid the reader who wishes to further explore the Black experience.

In the second contribution to this section, "Race and the Counseling Process: An Overview," Bryson and Bardo draw upon the historical, sociological, economical, and psychological experiences of Blacks to help the reader comprehend how Black/White relations have developed over the years. As one of the first attempts to analyze issues of cross-racial counseling dissonance, this article has heavily influenced subsequent writings in the area, not excluding the present text. Bryson and Bardo group earlier research and writing on the Black client into three categories: client analysis, counselor analysis, and analysis of the counseling process. Their discussion suggests that research and writing which examines the counseling process is most likely to provide valid and useful insight into cross-cultural counseling.

In the final article in this section, "Counseling Black Students: A Model in Response to the Need for Relevant Counselor Training Programs," Mitchell succinctly summarizes the plight of Black students in a White dominated institution. Much to his credit, Mitchell then presents an alternative model for training counselors to the unique needs experienced by the Black student population.

Anderson, C.H. *Toward a new sociology: A critical view.* Homewood, Ill. The Dorsey Press, 1971.

Bennet, L. *Before the Mayflower: A history of the Negro American 1619-1964.* Baltimore: Penguin Books, 1969.

Biesanz, J. & Biesanz, M. *Introduction to sociology.* Englewood Cliffs, New Jersey: Prentice Hall, 1969.

Brown vs. Board of Education of Topeka. 347 U.S. 483 (1954).

Franklin, J.H. *From slavery to freedom: A history of Negro Americans.* New York: Alfred A. Knopf, 1967.

Swick, K.J. Challenging Preservice and inservice teachers' perceptions of minority group children: A review of research. *Journal of Negro Education,* 1974, *43,* 194-201.

U.S. Bureau of Census, Current population report, Series P20, No. 309. School enrollment-socio economic characteristics of students, October, 1976 (Advance report) U.S. Government Printing Office, 1977.

9 What Counselors Must Know about the Social Sciences of Black Americans

Harper, Frederick D.

Wrenn emphasizes the need for the counselor to gain a strong background in the social sciences in order to better understand the world of the counselee.[1] Recognizing that such an experience can be a boon to broadening the counselor's perceptual field, the bugaboo remains that the general social sciences tend to limit or omit examining the black American experience. In addition, a number of social scientists tend to examine black experiences from a negative perspective as related to white middle-class Protestant norms.[2] In the counseling profession, several counselor educators have written counseling textbooks including at least one chapter on social sciences and the counselor since the recommendation of Gilbert Wrenn. Among these, Blocher, in his *Developmental Counseling,* presents a chapter on "The Counselor as a Behavioral Scientist,"[3] while Shertzer and Stone, in their *Fundamentals of Counseling,* present a chapter on "Counseling and the Social Sciences."[4] Unfortunately, both chapters have little, if anything, to say about black Americans as related to the social sciences. Shertzer and Stone fail to mention the status of black Americans in the social sciences, while Blocher briefly examines the limited topic of "Negro families."

In a time of school desegregation, racial conflict, political and socioeconomic rhetoric of black protesters, and a fast changing society, there is dire need for counselors to be aware of the historical, sociological, economic, and psychological dynamics of black American life. If the school counselor is to broaden his perceptual field, understand the world of the black counselee, and, even more, be able to interpersonalize across racial lines, then he must gain strength in the history, the sociology, the economics, and the psychology of black Americans.

History: Because of ethnocentrism, racial discrimination, and plain unawareness, researchers and authors have tended to omit, if not discredit, the contributions and participations of blacks in American history. Various historians have attempted to fill the vacuum. Among the most comprehensive and well-documented books of blacks in American history are Franklin's *From Slavery to Freedom*[5] and Woodson and Wesley's *The Negro in Our History.*[6] Other historians have written scholarly works on the black American in selected eras of American history. The more prominent of these authors are Benjamin Quarles, Rayford Logan, and Lerone Bennett.

© 1975 National Association of Social Workers, Inc. Reprinted from *Social Work,* Vol. 20, No. 5 (September, 1975), pp 379-382.

Regarding the history of Negro education, Bond,[7] Bullock,[8] and McGrath[9] have written excellent documents.

Within various periods of history, counselors must be aware of influential black leaders and heroes such as Frederick Douglass,[10] Martin Luther King, Jr.,[11] W.E.B. Du Bois,[12] Marcus Garvey[13] and Malcolm X.[14] Counselors must be familiar with black heroes that black students have recently begun to discover and to claim. The awareness and acknowledgement of black leaders can aid in counseling the black student toward a positive racial identity and toward a positive self-concept.

Counselors cannot afford to be prejudiced by the superficial accounts and classic stereotypes of blacks in the traditional American history. Instead, they must fully develop awareness and understanding of the rich African heritage of blacks; the social, political, and economic dynamics of slavery; the social and political progress of blacks during the post Civil War (or Reconstruction) period; and the disenfranchising effects of "Jim Crowism" on blacks during the late 1800s and the early 1900s. Counselors must also be abreast of the civil rights and the militant movements of the post World War II period along with the many contributions of black Americans in fields such as literature and poetry, music, sports, the natural and social sciences, the military, education, drama and theatre, and politics.

Sociology: Counselors need to grasp the social forces that affect their black clientele. There are numerous social forces and social systems that shape the behavior of black counselees who come for help and assistance. A classic document in the sociology of race relations is Myrdal's *An American Dilemma.*[15] A recent parallel to Myrdal's report is the *Report of the National Advisory Commission on Civil Disorders.*[16] In the study of the black family, Frazier's *The Negro Family in the United States*[17] is best noted among the earlier studies, while the more recent works of the black family include reports by Moynihan,[18] Bernard,[19] Liebow,[20] and Billingsley.[21] Clark[22] describes the nature and dynamics of the ghetto; and Bailey[23] edits a comprehensive work on black politics in America. In *Black Power,* Carmichael and Hamilton write of black politics and the damaging effects of institutional racism.[24] Furthermore, in a recent publication, Knowles and Prewitt examine institutional racism as the cause of many problems among blacks and whites.[25] The sociology of education includes the names of Havighurst and Levine,[26] and Clark.[27] Analyses of the civil rights movement and racial conflict can be found in the works of Lomax,[28] Killian,[29] and Grant.[30]

In perusing such sociological literature, there is need for the counselor to seek to understand the effects of history on the present status of race relations. In examining black families, one must understand the various black families that stratify on socioeconomic lines and the fact that all black families are not centered around one stereotype model. The urban black family is very much different from the rural black family, and the middle-class black family differs from the lower-class black family. In a similar way, the politics of the black community vary between the North and the South and between the rural town and the urban ghetto. However, one generality in politics has been that blacks are more likely to vote for the person or candidate as opposed to voting for the political party. It is also generally acknowledged that all areas of the country have attempted to disenfranchise the black voter through various chicanerous approaches.

Institutional racism and individual racism are concepts that the counselor must understand and deal with in terms of external forces that inhibit the growth of black people. Such forces have been historically ingrained in American society and hitherto permeate every strand of it. The corollary here is realizing that racism has basically been the reason for inequality in education between blacks and whites along with the cause for the perennial acting out of black protesters for human rights and citizen's rights.

Economics: Economically, the majority of blacks are poor and they have always been poor. This phenomenon has been primarily due to racial discrimination in employment, in training, and in business opportunities. Drake takes the view that the socio-economic stratification of black Americans takes the shape of a triangle with very few upper-income families at the smaller and upper end of the triangle and a great majority of lower-income black families at the wider base of the triangular structure.[31] Job and training discrimination resulting in unemployment and underemployment are not the only impasses to higher incomes for blacks. In addition, blacks employed in the same job or position as whites have often earned less money due to pay discrimination. Miller mentions that blacks earn less than whites with comparable family background, educational attainment, and occupational level.[32] *The Social and Economic Status of Negroes in the United States, 1969* reveals that the median income of black families in 1968 was only 60 percent of the median income of white families, that is, a median income of $5,400 for blacks compared with $8,900 for whites.[33] Economic discrimination in employment is a phenomenon that counselors must know about in understanding the dilemma of many black families and the consequences of stress, shame, and hunger that their children must face in attempting to meet their needs in school and out of school.

The popularizing of "black capitalism" and the emphasis by black protesters on black economic control of black communities by black people have stimulated new literature on the topics of economics and the ghetto and black economic development. Counselors must peruse such literature in understanding the economic powerlessness of black Americans and its sociological and psychological consequences. Such recent contributions include a descriptive account of joint business-government efforts in the ghetto,[34] a synthesis of writings on black economic development edited by Haddad and Pugh,[35] and an analysis of the political economy of the ghetto explaining the economic etiology of the black ghetto and the various mechanisms of exploitation and deprivation.[36] The counselor can also find a reasonable discussion of the black consumer in *The Poor Pay More* by Caplovitz[37] along with a discussion of the income of black Americans in Miller's *Rich Man Poor Man*.[38]

A number of current issues have been emphasized by students of black economics. Such issues include (1) the question of how white economic expertise can be employed in black economic development without subverting black leadership and control; (2) whether a joint partnership between blacks and whites is more feasible or whether ghetto businesses should be entirely owned and controlled by blacks; (3) the question of whether black capitalism should take priority over the job training of the masses of unemployed and underemployed blacks; and (4) the dilemma of what means are best for securing capital for black businesses and securing training for black managers.

Psychology: The behavior of black people has been long and widely studied, which is indicative of an orientation to study the effect instead of the priority of focusing on the many causes that mediate different behaviors of black people. The counselor must be careful not to stereotype blacks as possessing the same general cluster of behavioral traits. It is clear that the behavior of blacks differs across socio-economic and geographic lines, and that black females differ in behavior from black males.[39] Frazier[40] and Hare[41] write of the black middle class as being as middle class in overt behavior and values as typical white middle-class Americans. In *Black Rage,* Grier and Cobbs examine the behavioral effects of blacks in "achieving womanhood" and in "achieving manhood" under the elusive shadow of American slavery and the damaging cloak-and-dagger of institutional racism.[42] On the topic of behaviors among black lower-income groups, a number of descriptions are delineated in works by Liebow,[43] Clark,[44] and Pettigrew.[45] Regarding the black college student, Edwards[46] and Clark and Plotkin[47] write about the nature and dynamics of the various behaviors of black students. In general, one of the most comprehensive reviews of psychological studies of black Americans is a 58 page article by Dreger and Miller which synthesizes psychological studies published between the years 1959 and 1965.[48]

In looking at black behavior, the counselor should be careful not to compare such behavior to a white, middle-class, Anglo-Saxon, Protestant norm in terms of being deviant or normal—healthy or unhealthy. Along this line, Jahoda,[49] Shoben,[50] and Maslow[51] emphasize that positive psychological health is not based on whether a person acts like the typical behavior of society; but, rather, whether a person is satisfactorily meeting his needs and developing his potential. The implication here for the counselor is that he should not attempt to make a white carbon copy out of the black counselee. Instead he should help the black counselee to fulfill his basic needs for physiological maintainance, physical and psychological security, love and belongingness, esteem, and self-actualization or self-development of his common and unique potential.

In the main, the theoretical propositions of psychological models have been primarily based on the experiences of white populations. Counselors must be careful in applying various concepts and propositions of psychological theory to the behavior of black counselees, especially poor blacks. Of the general categories of psychological models, it appears that various humanistic models and behavioristic models might be more meaningful in counseling blacks than psychoanalytic models, especially classical psychoanalysis. The original theory of Freud's psychoanalysis was based on middle- and upper-class white Europeans of the 1800s which has little, if anything, to do with a black ghetto child of America in 1973. Another weakness of psychoanalysis is that it is a post-dictive therapeutic approach, explaining the why's of behavior. Although this approach can be cathartic to a neurotic middle-class person, it means nothing to a poor black ghetto dweller who is trying to get food to quell his hunger.

Regarding techniques of behaviorism or behavior modification, Gordon, indicates that the behavior of black children of the ghetto has already been conditioned and even predestined by the dehumanizing conditions in which they are born and incarcerated.[52] Therefore, it is the moral duty of the counselor to recondition the behavior of the black child in helping him to learn new ways of meeting his needs and new ways of relating to the world. Maslow's humanistic psychology of self-actualization posits that all human beings, regardless of race and culture, have the same basic human needs; and that the medium toward mental health and maturity is by way of one satisfying his basic needs for physiological maintainance, safety, love, esteem, and self-actualization. A recent compromise view has been the use of a combination of a humanistic model and a behavioristic model[53] or a combination of a passive therapeutic model with an active model.[54]

Crystallization

To empathize with the black counselee and to understand him, the counselor must be able to crystallize the external and internal worlds of the counselee's life; in other words to crystallize or interrelate the social sciences that surround the behavior of the black counselee. In order to crystallize such worlds, the counselor must have knowledge in the form of new perceptions that make up a frame of reference in helping him to see through the eyes of the black counselee. Such perceptions must be based on a knowledge of the social sciences of black Americans. In testing his framework, the counselor should ask himself: "Do I know the past of the black counselee's world?" "Do I know the sociological parameters that currently impinge upon him?" "Do I understand or even know of his economic status?" And, "Do I understand how all of these factors tune in to mediate his present intrapsychic and external behavior?" It is relatively clear that America's economic system compounded with institutional racism has created a history that affects the present status of society and thus the behavior of all black Americans who are destined to grow up in it. Thus the social sciences of blacks compose a concurrent chain of interrelated links or disciplines.

The counselor must see the interrelationships of the dynamics of the social sciences that determine the behavior of black Americans. That rare admixture of a history couched in the cruel institution of slavery and "Jim Crowism"; a sociology confounded in the miseries of poverty and the suppression of racism; an economy of powerlessness and inequality, and a psyche of hope, self-despair, and rage. Although some blacks have transcended this admixture of victimization, the number of such quasi-freedmen is yet to be significant. The masses of blacks are still incarcerated in the ghettoes and in the rural backwoods of America. If black Americans are to be liberated from poverty, racial discrimination, and their correlates, then counselors must be about their work with tools of the social sciences.

Implementation

The question follows then, "How do counselors get such knowledge and experience of the social sciences of blacks?" and, "How do they use this new knowledge?" In gaining such an experience, a good start would be the medium of the counselor education program where counselors-in-training are prepared for their professional responsibilities in the real world. Many of these future counselors will more likely be working in a situation where in part a black clientele is served, situations such as a desegregated public school, a junior college, or a university—an all-black (or almost black) ghetto school, a private college, or a community program. Counselor education programs can no longer assume that their students will go on to work in all-white situations; therefore, such programs must begin to include the integration of black experiences into the curriculum. Several well-chosen paperback books can provide a beginning for the counselor in learning something about the history, sociology, economics, and psychology of black people in the United States. There are even inexpensive paperbacks that cover a number of different social science disciplines all in one volume. Such information can be explored in integrated or open-ended seminars and should provide a background for the student's first encounter in cross-racial and cross-cultural counseling. Such theoretical and scholarly readings can be supplemented with field trips to social settings in the black community that can provide live perceptions of the various worlds of the black counselee and the various factors that affect him.

A pitfall in the counselor education program is that many counselor educators, themselves, know little of the social sciences of blacks and little of counseling blacks which leaves a vacuum of expertise on the subject of black populations. An answer to this inequity is that counselor educators must free themselves from their mythical perceptions of black people and begin to gain new and broad awareness of black Americans through media such as personal readings, workshops and professional meetings, interdisciplinary and interprofessional collaboration, and greater cross-racial encounters. Counselor educators must begin to recruit more black students to their programs, students who may be able to contribute a different and valuable perspective to the classroom experience for the education of their students and for the education of counselor educators themselves.

Another question relates to the counselor who has finished his graduate program and who is already in the professional field of work. That counselor must develop his own internal motivation to read such literature about blacks instead of confining his reading to novels with only white characters or nonfiction materials that discuss white populations and white personalities only. Counselor staff meetings can also allow time on the agenda for recommendations or presentations along this line. Even film and other media can be employed in a type of inservice experience. Moreover, counselors can read various journals oriented to the black social sciences such as *Afro-American Studies: An Interdisciplinary Journal* or *The Journal of Black Studies*. Since the literature in professional journals might lag time wise and be somewhat specialized at times regarding topics, the counselor may want to subscribe to popular black magazines such as *Ebony, Essence, Encore* and *Jet* to receive a current presentation of black experiences and events.

It cannot be assumed that all black counselors and black counselor educators are aware of the dynamics of the social sciences of blacks; neither can it be assumed that black counselors are effective in interpersonalizing with black counselees just because they are black. Although black counselors are closer to understanding the black American experience, it still remains that many blacks, just as a great number of whites, have been handicapped in the helping relationship due to ethnocentrism in society and in educational programs, along with a lack of exposure to the social sciences of black Americans. Although a few black counselors and white counselors have been strong enough to transcend the Anglocentric and ethnocentric socialization of American culture, a greater number have dire need to seek new knowledge and experiences in broadening their perceptual framework.

All the counselors must be able to perceive the interrelationships of the social sciences of blacks in order to grasp the dynamics that affect black behavior. This approach will help counselors to crystallize a frame of reference in more effectively interpersonalizing with black counselees. Counselors must use this information in helping the black counselee to develop a positive outlook of himself and his ethnic group, to learn new ways of relating to the world, and in helping him to meet his basic needs.

Notes

1. C. Gilbert Wrenn, *The Counselor in a Changing World* (Washington, D.C.: American Personnel and Guidance Association, 1962).
2. Lee Rainwater, "Crucible of Identity: The Negro Lower-Class Family," in Talcott Parsons and Kenneth B. Clark (eds.), *The Negro American* (Boston: Beacon Press, 1965).
3. Donald H. Blocher, *Developmental Counseling* (New York: The Ronald Press, 1966).
4. Bruce Shertzer and Shelley Stone, *Fundamentals of Counseling* (Boston: Houghton Mifflin, 1968).
5. John Hope Franklin, *From Slavery to Freedom: A History of Negro Americans* (3rd Ed.; New York: Vintage Books, 1967).
6. Carter G. Woodson and Charles H. Wesley, *The Negro in Our History* (11th ed.; Washington, D.C.: The Associated Publishers, 1966).

7. Horace Bond, *The Education of the Negro in the American Social Order* (New York: Octagon Books, 1966).
8. Henry A. Bullock, *A History of Negro Education in the South: From 1619 to the Present* (Cambridge: Harvard University Press, 1967).
9. Earl J. McGrath, *The Predominantly Negro Colleges and Universities in Transition* (New York: Bureau of Publications of Teachers College at Columbia University, 1965).
10. Philip S. Foner, *Frederick Douglass* (New York: The Citadel Press, 1950).
11. William R. Miller, *Martin Luther King, Jr.* (New York: Avon Books, 1968).
12. Francis L. Broderick, *W.E.B. Du Bois, Negro Leader in a Time of Crisis* (Stanford: Stanford University Press, 1959).
13. Edmund D. Cronon, *Black Moses* (Madison: University of Wisconsin Press, 1968).
14. Malcolm X (with the assistance of Alex Haley), *The Autobiography of Malcolm X* (New York: Grove Press, 1964).
15. Gunnar Myrdal, *An American Dilemma* (New York: Harper and Brothers, 1944).
16. *Report of the National Advisory Commission on Civil Disorders* (Washington: U.S. Government Printing Office, 1968).
17. E. Franklin Frazier, *The Negro Family in the United States* (revised; Chicago: University of Chicago Press, 1966).
18. Daniel P. Moynihan, *The Negro Family: The Case for National Action* (Washington: U.S. Government Printing Office, 1965).
19. Jessie S. Bernard, *Marriage and Family Among Negroes* (Englewood Cliffs: Prentice-Hall, 1968).
20. Elliot Liebow, *Tally's Corner* (Boston: Little, Brown and Co., 1967).
21. Andrew Billingsley, *Black Families in White America* (Englewood Cliffs: Prentice-Hall, 1968).
22. Kenneth B. Clark, *Dark Ghetto* (New York: Harper and Row, 1965).
23. Harry A. Bailey (ed.), *Negro Politics in America* (Columbus, Ohio: Charles E. Merrill Books, 1967).
24. Stokely Carmichael and Charles Hamilton, *Black Power: The Politics of Liberation in America* (New York: Vintage Books, 1967).
25. Louis L. Knowles and Kenneth Prewitt, *Institutional Racism in America* (Englewood Cliffs: Prentice-Hall, 1969).
26. Robert J. Havighurst and Daniel U. Levine, *Education in Metropolitan Areas,* (2nd ed.; Boston: Allyn and Bacon, Inc., 1971).
27. Kenneth B. Clark, "Alternative Public School Systems," *Harvard Educational Review,* 38 (1968), 100-118.
28. Louis Lomax, *The Negro Revolt* (New York: Harper and Row, 1962).
29. Lewis M. Killian, *The Impossible Revolution? Black Power and the American Dream* (New York: Random House, 1968).
30. Joanne Grant, *Black Protest: History, Documents, and Analyses, 1619 to the Present* (Greenwich, Connecticut: Fawcett Publications, Inc., 1968).
31. St. Clair Drake, "The Social and Economic Status of the Negro in the United States," in Talcott Parsons and Kenneth B. Clark (eds.), *The Negro American* (Boston: Beacon Press, 1965).
32. Herman P. Miller, *Rich Man Poor Man* (New York: Thomas Y. Cromwell, Co., 1971).
33. *The Social and Economic Status of Negroes in the United States, 1969* (Washington, D.C.: U.S. Government Printing Office, 1970).

34. Sar A. Levitan, *et al.*, *Economic Opportunity in the Ghetto: The Partnership of Government and Business* (Baltimore: The Johns Hopkins Press, 1970).

35. William F. Haddad and G. Douglas Pugh (eds.), *Black Economic Development* (Englewood Cliffs: Prentice-Hall, 1967).

36. William K. Tabb, *The Political Economy of the Black Ghetto* (New York: W.W. Norton and Co., Inc., 1970).

37. David Caplovitz, *The Poor Pay More* (New York: Free Press, 1967).

38. Miller, *op. cit.* 1971.

39. Clemmont E. Vontress, *Counseling Negroes,* in Bruce Shertzer and Shelly Stone (eds.), *Guidance Monograph Series,* Vol. 6 (Boston: Houghton Mifflin, Co., 1971).

40. E. Franklin Frazier, *Black Bourgeoisie* (New York: Collier, 1962).

41. Nathan Hare, *The Black Anglo-Saxons* (New York: Collier, 1970).

42. William H. Grier and Price M. Cobbs, *Black Rage* (New York: Basic Books, 1968).

43. Liebow, *op, cit.,* 1967.

44. Clark, *op. cit.,* 1965.

45. Thomas F. Pettigrew, *A Profile of the Negro American* (Princeton: D. Van Nostrand, 1964).

46. Harry Edwards, *Black Students* (New York: The Free Press, 1970).

47. Kenneth B. Clark and Lawrence Plotkin, *The Negro Student at Integrated Colleges* (New York: National Scholarship Service and Fund for Negro Students, 1963).

48. Ralph M. Dreger and Kent S. Miller, "Comparative Psychological Studies of Negroes and Whites in the United States: 1959-1965," *Psychological Bulletin,* 70 (1968), 1-58.

49. Marie Jahoda, *Current Concepts of Positive Mental Health* (New York: Basic Books, 1958).

50. Edward J. Shoben, "Toward a Concept of the Normal Personality," *The American Psychologist,* 12 (1957), 183-189.

51. Abraham H. Maslow, *Motivation and Personality,* (2nd ed.; New York: Harper and Row, 1970).

52. Edmund Gordon, "Counseling the Disadvantaged: Avenues to Effectiveness," *Capsule* (Winter, 1969), 3-9.

53. Lawrence M. Brammer and Everett L. Shostrom, *Therapeutic Psychology* (Englewood Cliffs: Prentice-Hall, 1960).

54. Robert R. Carkhuff and Bernard G. Berenson, *Beyond Counseling and Therapy* (New York: Holt, Rinehart and Winston, Inc., 1967).

10 Race and the Counseling Process
An Overview
Bryson, Seymour
Bardo, Harold

Professional literature has lately paid increased attention to the problems facing counselors of Blacks and other minority group members. Although the source of these problems is not strictly racial, it is becoming increasingly clear that there is dissonance in client-counselor interactions when the client is Black and the counselor is white. There is considerable disagreement among professionals over the cause and the nature of the dissonance, but they are beginning to recognize and accept that there is a problem. This review of the writings and research efforts of theorists who have attempted to clarify and articulate some of these issues will provide a rationale for recommendations concerning counselor behavior in such situations.

Since World War II, American society has experienced a great change in its racial relationships and attitudes. One of the salient outcomes of the civil rights movement is that the white population has lost some of its power to dominate race relations. The constant reduction of the proportion of acquiescent Black Americans has resulted in a qualitatively different relationship between whites and Blacks (Thompson 1963). Concurrently, most interactions between whites and Blacks can be conceptualized as a complex interpersonal encounter. In this period scientists, educators, writers, and others have attempted to examine and explain this complex and perplexing Black/white phenomenon. Rohrer (1970) stated that "every great public issue currently engaging the nation is beclouded by Negro/White relations. Therefore, resolving relations between Negro and White is perhaps the predominate concern" (p. xvi). Johnson (1966) stated that Blacks should regard with a certain degree of caution efforts by white America to examine the Negro problem. He stated that attempts of white Europeans and their descendants to divide the Negro has taken the form of trying to explain away the Negro. He stated that Negroes were explained away for nearly 100 years by the contention that they were not yet ready for the white culture. The Negroes were "protected" by courts that said that legally Negroes should be kept separate though equal—second-class citizens. Then came World War II, the communist conspiracy, the Black nations' fight for freedom from colonialism and a reexamination of the Christian faith. These occurrences highlighted the idea that skin color was not a true measure of a person's humanity. After 1954, the U.S. Supreme Court ruled that the doctrine of separate but equal was untenable under the Constitution. Today, according to Johnson, the explaining away continues, but it is much more difficult to do. It takes the form of "Things are better today than they were yesterday and will be better tomorrow than they are today," and "Have patience, don't demonstrate, everything will come about in due time."

Such developments in the relations between races have effects peculiar to many special activities in our culture. Perhaps no area has been more intimately affected than counseling. The problems arising from interaction between Whites and Blacks—manifested by feelings of mistrust, suspicion, anger, pessimism, and negativism—characterize and affect many helping relationships, including counseling and psychotherapy. The counseling relationship is probably one of the most personal contacts established within a behavioral science framework. Communication is an emotional bridge between the counselor and the client. This phenomenon is referred to in the literature by varied terms; the medically oriented prefer *establishing rapport,* and behavioral scientists use the term *developing a relationship.*

Due to the intent of a therapeutic relationship, the importance of and the need to establish mature trust and understanding are critical. There must be warmth, acceptance, and understanding, and the client should be permitted maximum expression of feelings, attitudes, and problems. Anything that might interfere with the relationship may make counseling less effective. Doubts or concerns over differences in color seem unwarranted in counseling.

Many of the earlier articles written by white behavioral scientists focus on Black pathology. The concept of Black pathology is an approach favored and used by many white educators and behavioral and social scientists to explain, describe, and discuss Black reactions to oppressive practices. The Black pathology theme is used to describe Black behavior in terms of its deviation from the white norm. This theme came into prominence after the 1954 Supreme Court decision on segregation in the public schools. Prior to that time the traditional view was that Negroes were genetically inferior; this view was replaced with the belief that Negroes were not genetically inferior but, rather, that their behavior was pathological in the social sense due to the history of slavery in this country. Baratz (1968) stated that the replacement of the genetic inferiority theory with the social pathology theory encouraged a great deal of research in the social sciences, which were primarily interested in describing how Negro behavior deviated from the white norm. Consequently, the professional literature consisted of a body of knowledge (more appropriately called misinformation) that described Negroes as "not conforming" to the code of behavior that whites had established as normal and appropriate. This body of misinformation has been and unfortunately still is being used by many educators and trainers, both Black and white, to help their students understand Black people, thus creating a picture of the Negro as a pathologically ill white. By using white control groups and samples of behavior of white populations, researchers developed white norms and then emphasized the ways Negro behavior deviated from them. A mythical illness for the Black population was thus created and is readily identified in the professional literature of the 50s and 60s.

Many professionals attempted to explain their inability to provide quality services to Blacks by rationalizing that because of a client's particular personality imperfection he or she was unable to benefit from the professional helping services provided. In other words, the services were good but the clientele were beyond help.

In the past 25 years there has been a proliferation of literature in which the effects of race on the counseling process have been discussed. Obvious trends appear in the writing, and they may be classified into three distinct groups: analysis of the client, description of the counselor, and discussion of the counseling process.

Client Analysis

Articles that focus on the client apparently had greatest appeal during the early 50s, the period that Smith (1967) described as the time of the "acquiescent Negro." Many of these articles were written by white psychiatrists who were trying to explain why they were ineffective with their Negro clients. Some of the authors were: Adams (1950), Heine (1950), St. Clair (1951), Kennedy (1952), Brown (1950), English (1957), Shane (1960), and Rosen and Frank (1962). Several symptoms were identified by these authors: Black patients demonstrate far more submissiveness, suspiciousness, and initial fear than do white patients when interviewed by white psychiatrists (Frank 1947; St. Clair 1951); fully educated Blacks and those reared in highly prejudicial areas behave in a manner compatible with the traditional expectations of the majority group by being passive, polite, and essentially noncommunicative when in the presence of a white therapist (Heine 1950); Negroes are preoccupied with the Negro problem (Frank 1947; Heine 1950; St. Clair 1951; Shane 1960).

During this period, the majority of the written articles were classified as position papers or commentaries; research studies investigating the variables of race were meager. The investigations by St. Clair (1951) and Phillips (1960) were among the few studies presented. The purpose of St. Clair's study was to focus on details observed during individualized clinical contacts with psychotic Negro servicemen. Generalizations from his results must be made with caution, for he did not employ a rigorous method or design for discerning which variables should be observed. He categorized them into clinical features he had observed in treating Negro servicemen. Interviews were conducted over a three-year period, and most of the observations were with adult males, the majority of whom were from the lower socioeconomic levels. Included among the clinical characteristics he had observed and generalized to all Negroes were the following: (a) difficulty in establishing rapport and developing a therapeutic relationship, (b) race consciousness, (c) prestige factors, (d) the tendency to act out, and (e) problems of sexuality and hostility.

In a study that gained support from St. Clair's work, Phillips (1960) investigated whether white counselors could attain positive results in counseling Negro pupils. The Negro and Caucasian counselors in this investigation were candidates for doctoral degrees in counseling. Each counselor had had three years of counseling experience and two years of teaching experience. The participants in the study were twelve middle-class Negro students who had been referred repeatedly for counseling because of antisocial behavior: tardiness, uncooperative attitudes, and failure to use their assets or abilities.

Each counselor conducted weekly nondirective interviews with each of the six students assigned to him for one semester. The findings of the study suggested that there was very little observable change in the behavior or attitudes of the students who worked with the Caucasian counselor. It was theorized that the Caucasian counselors were easily manipulated and controlled by the students' deceptive and defensive techniques. Conversely, the results indicated that there were significant attitudinal and behavioral changes in those students assigned to Negro counselors.

Many of the conclusions of both St. Clair and Phillips appear plausible; however, there is not enough data to substantiate them. The investigators failed to define adequately what they were looking for, to control for experimenter bias, and to explain how they arrived at conclusions. Therefore, the results did not justify many of the findings that the investigators claimed.

One of the most pervasive and popular themes that emerged during the 60s and, to some degree, continues today was the Black self-hate construct suggested by Vontress (1966). He stated that "the most significant component of the Negro personality is his self-hatred for being a member of a downtrodden group" (p. 210). This thesis enjoyed wide circulation among many professionals who were interested in explaining away Blacks. In attempting to substantiate his position, Vontress stated that discrimination based on skin color existed among Negroes themselves. He contended that the Black bourgeoisie, a group with a greater number of the preferred, light-skinned Negroes, are most interested in pleasing and associating with whites. If this is true then it follows that Blacks feel some hate for their color and seek to identify with the "preferred," white population.

Counselor Analysis

Pervasive in professional counseling literature is the thesis that therapists' behavior and particularly their attitudes toward clients interact with other variables and significantly affect the counseling process and its outcome. Strupp (1960) suggested six therapist attitudinal components that interact to influence therapeutic interaction. Included in this group is the color of the client. He postulated that the client's station in life, socioeconomic status, intellect, sex, age, and color may evoke attitudes in the therapist that are conditioned by the culture of which client and therapist are a part. He also stated that cultural values may partly determine the meaning and the clinical significance the therapist will attach to attitudes and behaviors of the clients.

The importance of the therapist's attitude in the therapeutic process is also pointed out in Stieper and Wiener's (1965) review of the literature. It was noted that social class influences both the patient's behavior in psychotherapy and the therapist's diagnostic procedures. They concluded from their findings that, despite its impact on therapists, social class has been relatively ignored by psychotherapy research. Stieper and Wiener also suggested that counselors generally like people who are most similar to them, judge successful therapy mainly in terms of the degree to which their clients become more like them, and frequently project responsibilities for therapeutic failures on to their clients.

The literature concerning counseling and psychotherapy with Blacks suggests that white counselors as they are currently being trained cannot usually counsel Blacks effectively. Authors who examined the role and color of the counselor are: Smith (1967), Arbuckle (1969), Sattler (1970), Ayers (1970), Williams and Kirkland (1971), Gunnings (1971), Cimbolic (1972), and Harper (1973).

Ayers (1970) considered counselor attitude the greatest single factor influencing the counseling relationship. Other factors he identified as partly influencing the counseling relationship were counselor familiarity with the clients' life styles, values, and attitudes and the communication patterns within the interaction. Arbuckle (1969) stated that the counselor who is an "expert" in human communications should be able to relate to the Black client. He attributed the problem to one of separation. He believed that counselors frequently separate themselves from clients; consequently, the counselor is alienated, not the client. Arbuckle agreed with Ayers that counselors' attempts to impose middle-class values or standards on clients is one of the biggest factors in interracial counseling because it completely neglects the value system of the client.

Jerome Sattler (1970), a psychologist at San Diego State College, reviewed studies concerned with effects of the experimenter's race on experimentation, testing, interviewing, and psychotherapy and concluded that there was a scarcity of research regarding the racial variable in counseling. In his review, he identified only three studies that he considered relevant to the issues of therapist-client interaction: Banks, Berenson, and Carkhuff (1967), Carkhuff and Pierce (1967), and Yamamoto and others (1967). Sattler concluded that Negro clients preferred Negro counselors and that more positive relationships result when clients and therapists are of the same race. His results were based on a postcounseling survey of client preferences.

The findings from the two studies conducted by Banks, Berenson, and Carkhuff (1967) and Carkhuff and Pierce (1967) suggested that the race of the counselor does have an effect on therapeutic movement and outcome in counseling.

The results of the investigation conducted by Banks, Berenson, and Carkhuff (1967) suggested that counselor race and the type of counselor orientation (i.e., process versus trait and factor orientation) were more important than the level of counselor experience. The investigators employed a counterbalanced design to determine the effectiveness of an inexperienced Negro counselor and three Caucasian counselors of varying degrees of experience and types of training with eight Negro clients in an initial clinical interview. Counselor A was an inexperienced, 20-year-old, Negro senior undergraduate student who had taken an undergraduate course in counseling theory and practice, which was oriented toward counseling as a communication process between two parties in a relationship. Counselor B was an inexperienced, 25-year-old, Caucasian second-year graduate student who had previously worked with several clients in a counseling psychology program oriented in the same manner. Counselor C was an experienced, 25-year-old, Caucasian third-year graduate student in a counselor education program with a different orientation. He had had a year of experience in guidance activities. The fourth counselor was a 32-year-old Caucasian PhD with eight years of experience from a nationally recognized counselor education program with a traditional trait-factor counseling system. The 3 Caucasian counselors were selected by 2 experienced clinicians to match the personal attractiveness, intelligence, politeness, quietness, and apparent sincerity of the Negro counselor. The Negro clients in the study were 4 male and 4 female undergraduate students at the University of Massachusetts.

Each counselor saw each client for one interview, which was recorded: then the clients filled out an inventory on each counselor. Using random excerpts from the recorded interviews, trained observers rated the counselors on five dimensions considered to be positively related to constructive client change in counseling: empathy, respect, genuineness, concreteness, and client's depth of self-exploration.

The results showed no significant differences among Counselors A, B, and C in ability to provide facilitative therapeutic conditions, and these three relationship-oriented counselors provided a significantly higher level of facilitative conditions than did the trait-factor counselor. It was also found that race and level of experience did not have differential effects on the counselors' ability to provide high levels of constructive therapeutic conditions. The authors gave the following as one of their most important findings: All of the Negro clients indicated that they would return to the Negro counselor, but none indicated that they would return to see the traditional counselor. The traditional counselor was the Caucasian PhD who had had eight years of counseling experience.

The clients ranked the inexperienced Caucasian counselor higher than the inexperienced Negro counselor and ranked both of the inexperienced counselors higher than the two experienced counselors. The experienced and traditionally trained counselor functioned at the lowest level; in fact, he proved to be the least effective counselor. In this study constructive therapeutic conditions were identified and defined in terms of a relationship theory of counseling. The findings suggested that counselor experience may be independent of counselor effectiveness with Negro clients. The authors contended that race and type of orientation and training appear to be the more relevant variables. Perhaps the most important finding was that, when Negro clients were required to assess the counselor by filling out inventories, differences were less pronounced than those found in objective tape ratings. These results suggest that the clients, when asked to evaluate Caucasian counselors directly, tended to provide those ratings that were socially acceptable. One particular weakness of this experiment was that it did not permit the experimenter to determine the effectiveness of Negro counselors with Caucasian clients. Another weakness is the disproportionate number of Caucasian counselors.

In a similar study, Carkhuff and Pierce (1967) concluded from their findings that both race and class variables have an effect on clients' depth of self-exploration. The findings of this study suggested that in a first session clients will not explore their problems at a very deep level with a counselor from a different race. They concluded that, generally, the clients most similar to the race and social class of the counselor involved tended to explore their problems most; clients most dissimilar in terms of race and social class tended to explore them least. The study was designed to investigate the effect of the therapist's race and social class on the client in relation to the depth of self-exploration. The procedures for this investigation varied from those reported previously. In the interviews, which were recorded, the patients were encouraged to discuss whatever was important to them at that moment of time. Afterward, six four-minute excerpts were randomly selected from each of the 64 recorded clinical interviews and rated on the scale "depth of self-exploration in the interpersonal process" by two experienced raters. The ratings ranged from level 1 to level 5, the lowest and highest respectively. At level 1 the second person did not discuss personally relevant material either because there was no opportunity to do so or because he or she was actively evading discussion, even when it was introduced by the first person. At Level 5 the second person actively and spontaneously engaged in an inward probing merely to discover feelings or experiences about self and the world.

The authors concluded that race and social class of both the client and the counselor appeared to affect significantly the depth of clients' self-exploration in initial clinical interviews. Two of the main limitations of this study were that all of the clients were southerners and that all were females.

Counseling Process

Several theorists (Banks 1972; Calia 1966; Gunnings 1971) have postulated that the counseling process itself is the primary reason that counseling is basically ineffective with Black clients. These theorists believed that the counselor's tendency to presume personal disorganization rather than societal or institutional dysfunctions is particularly detrimental to the welfare of Black clients.

Calia questioned the appropriateness of traditional techniques for culturally different clients. He stated that "counselors who are inexperienced in the ways of the poor are likely to be perplexed and ineffectual in their initial encounters with these strange and formidable clients" (p. 100). He postulated that this distressing state of affairs is likely to be compounded when the counselor finds normative concepts and methods wanting. He questioned the currently held views regarding sedentary talk as a medium for client-counselor interaction, unconditional positive regard as an essential therapeutic element, the goal of counseling as the facilitation of self-exploration, and self-referral as a necessary prerequisite for effective counseling. He suggested a much more action-oriented and externally focused approach to the difficulties of culturally different clients and he recommended a new conceptualization of the role and functions of counselors.

Hecht (1970) described a guidance program for minority students. He proposed a more active role for the counselor and recommended that

> ...counselors should: (1) act as change agents in the regular school system, (2) hold conferences with the students and teachers, (3) provide feedback to teachers regarding student reactions to them, (4) talk to students and accept their side of issues, and (5) provide motivations and alternatives to residents having academic problems. (p. 731)

Weinrach (1973) suggested that counselors interested in helping Blacks must leave their offices and become involved in the community by spending some time in the student's community.

Williams and Kirkland (1971) noted that traditional counseling programs are typically geared to the white client. They included among their recommendations the idea that counselors employ the student advocate role when working with Black clients. They stated that the counselor must "represent the student and not the institution, the system that produced the problems" (p. 114).

Authors who examine the counseling process as it relates to Blacks have concluded that the traditional intrapyschic model is ineffective and that what is needed is a process that attempts to treat the system. Problems confronting most Blacks are perceived as being system induced, and, consequently, a different therapeutic approach is suggested.

Banks (1972), in a discussion of training strategies, indicated that "what is needed is a move beyond analysis of and intervention with the victim. As a matter of emphasis, counselors and therapists might begin to pay more attention and exert more energy at the level of social environmental change" (p. 70). He further stated that

...when many of the environmental restrictions that retard the development of black people are removed, it is likely that the adaptive responses that evolve from the restrictions will become obsolete. The many forms of behavior that serve to insure viability of the black psyche and person will no longer be necessary. (p. 71)

Theorists attempting to explain the efficacy of white counselors with Black clients have progressed through several distinct stages. Initial emphasis was focused on analyzing the client's behavior. Subsequent attention was devoted to investigating the counselor's behavior and, finally, the counseling process itself. Evidence regarding the effects of race on interracial relationships in counseling suggests that both the counselor and the client enter the relationship with attitudes and behavior that may negatively affect the process and outcome.

The general conclusion seems to be that although counselor race as a single variable is insufficient qualification for predicting effectiveness, it is a factor that must be considered. Consequently, it is imperative that those involved in training counselors or others in helping roles design and implement programs that will correct or modify the negative aspects of counselors' attitudes and behaviors.

Recommendation

The issues discussed in this article suggest that counselor training programs as they exist have not provided students adequate preparation for working with the Black population. The counseling profession needs to reexamine its present approach to training counselors; it can no longer be assumed that techniques and strategies that are successful with one group of clients will work effectively with another group. Educators must ensure that their students are provided opportunities to have direct contact and experiences with individuals from varied cultural, educational, and socioeconomic backgrounds.

Counselors need to be made aware that clients are individuals with rights, needs, attitudes, and values that may conflict with or be different from the counselor's but must nevertheless be understood, appreciated, and accepted. Counselors should be trained to adjust to client needs, attitudes, and preferences.

Training programs should embrace systematic activities that provide students with experiences and skills in working with individuals from different cultures who have different needs, values, and expectations. Specifically, counselors need to acquire an awareness and appreciation of the influence of race on the counseling process and outcome. They need to acknowledge that the results of social conditions in this century are the lack of confidence in and basic distrust that many Blacks have of counselors who are white. One of the primary barriers that must be overcome in interracial relationships is counselors' insensitivity to Black clients' reactions to negative interracial experiences.

References

Adams, W.A. The Negro patient in psychiatric treatment. *American Journal of Orthopsychiatry*, 1950, *20*, 305-310.

Arbuckle, D.S. The alienated counselor. *Personnel and Guidance Journal*, 1969, *48*, 18-23.

Ayers, G.E. The disadvantaged. An analysis of factors affecting the counseling relationship, *Rehabilitation Literature*, 1970, *31*, 194-199.

Banks, G.P.; Berenson, B.G.; & Carkhuff, R.R. The effects of counselor race and training upon counseling process with Negro clients in initial interviews. *Journal of Clinical Psychology*, 1967, *23*, 70-72.

Banks, W. The Black client and the helping professionals. In R.L. Jones (Ed.), *Black Psychology*. New York: Harper & Row, 1972. Pp. 205-212.

Baratz, J. Language and cognitive assessment of Negro children. Paper presented at the meeting of the American Psychological Association, San Francisco, 1968.

Brown, L.B. Race as a factor in establishing a casework relationship. *Social Casework*, 1950, *31*, 91-97.

Calia, V.F. The culturally deprived client: A reformulation of the counselor's role. *Journal of Counseling Psychology*, 1966, *13*, 100-105.

Carkhuff, R., & Pierce, R. Differential effects of therapist race and social class upon patient depth of self-exploration in the initial interview. *Journal of Consulting Psychology*, 1967, *31*, 632-634.

Cimbolic, P. Counselor race and experience effects on Black clients. *Journal of Consulting and Clinical Psychology*, 1972, *2*, 328-332.

English, W.H. Minority group attitudes of Negroes and implications for guidance. *Journal of Negro Education*, 1957, *26*, 99-107.

Frank, J. Adjustment problems of selected Negro soldiers. *Journal of Nervous and Mental Diseases*, 1947, *105*, 647-650.

Gunnings, T. Preparing the new counselor. *The Counseling Psychologist*, 1971, *2*, 100-101.

Harper, F. What counselors must know about the social sciences of Black Americans. *Journal of Negro Education*, 1973, *112*, 109-116.

Hecht, E. Guidance program for a ghetto school. *Personnel and Guidance Journal*, 1970, *48*, 731-738.

Heine, R.W. The Negro patient in psychotherapy. *Journal of Clinical Psychology*, 1950, *6*, 373-376.

Johnson, J. *The white problem in America*. Chicago: Johnson Publishing, 1966.

Kennedy, J.A. Problems posed in the analysis of Negro patients. *Psychiatry*, 1952, *15*, 313-327.

Phillips, W.B. Section D: Counseling Negro pupils: An educational dilemma. *Journal of Negro Education*, 1960, *28*, 504-507.

Rohrer, W.C. *Black profile of white Americans*. Philadelphia: F.A. Davis, 1970.

Rosen, H., & Frank, J. Negroes in psychotherapy. *American Journal of Psychiatry*, 1962, *119*, 456-460.

Sattler, J. Racial "experimented effects" in experimentation, testing, interviewing and psychotherapy. *Psychological Bulletin*, 1970, *73*, 137-160.

Shane, M. Some subcultural considerations in the psychotherapy of a Negro patient. *Psychiatric Quarterly*, 1960, *34*, 9-27.

Smith, D.H. The white counselor in the Negro slum school. *School Counselor,* 1967, *14,* 268-272.

St. Clair, H.R. Psychiatric interview experiences with Negroes. *American Journal of Psychiatry,* 1951, *108,* 113-119.

Stieper, D., & Wiener, D. *Dimensions of psychotherapy.* Chicago: Aldine, 1965.

Strupp, H.S. *Psychotherapist in action.* New York: Grune & Stratton, 1960.

Thompson, D.C. *The Negro leadership class.* Englewood Cliffs, N.J.: Prentice-Hall, 1963.

Vontress, C.E. The Negro personality reconsidered. *Journal of Negro Education,* 1966, *35,* 210-217.

Weinrach, S. Integration is more than just busing. *School Counselor,* 1973, *20,* 276-279.

Williams, R.L., & Kirkland, J. The white counselor and the Black client. *Counseling Psychologist,* 1971, *4,* 114-117.

Yamamoto, J.; Qunton, J.; Bloombaum, M.; & Hatten, J. Racial factors in patient selections. *American Journal of Psychiatry,* 1967, *124,* 630-636.

11 Counseling Black Students
A Model in Response to the Need for Relevant Counselor Training Programs
Mitchell, Horace

The Counselor's Role

Any examination of the counseling psychology curriculum in terms of its relevance for preparing counselors to work with black students must begin with an assessment of what efforts the counselor is to produce.

If the assumption is that he will help "deviant" black clients in conforming to the white middle-class value system, then the traditional curriculum is adequate because its purpose was to train middle class white counselors to work with middle class clients. Any black student who happened into the training program was also trained to work with middle class clients and was expected (as were white counselors) to transfer his knowledge as best he could if he wanted to work with black clients. White counselors and black counselors who had internalized white middle class values were almost certainly doomed to failure when they attempted to impose a white perspective on viewing the problems of black clients. It has been this orientation of wanting blacks to conform to an alien value system while tacitly rejecting their own that has caused blacks to become suspicious of the usefulness of counseling.

If the assumption about role underlying a training program is that the counselor will help black students deal with their problems within the context of the status quo, then it is but one step beyond the first assumption. It allows blacks to have cultural and racial differences in values, but the counselor is quick to point out where the black client's aspirations are in conflict with what is available to him within the society. Benevolent advice, such as telling a black student whose I.Q. was measured as 82 by a test based on white norms that he should look for a job after high school graduation rather than trying to go into college, and the unchanging social order which it reflects has all too often led to a sense of futility on the part of black students.

Let us examine for a moment the current status of counseling vis-a-vis the needs of black clients. Counseling and guidance services are not reaching black students in an effective manner. As Russell (1970) states, "...The student perceives guidance as an instrument of repression, controlled by counselors who constitute a roadblock he must somehow manage to get around if he has ambitions that do not coincide with those his counselors consider appropriate for him. He sees guidance as a wellspring of frustration

This article originally appeared in *The Counseling Psychologist,* 1971, 2(4) 117-122 and is reprinted with permission.

and despair, not a source of hope and encouragement. He has a background of guidance experiences that have been demeaning, debilitating, patronizing, and dehumanizing. He believes with all his heart that his counselors have racial biases that preclude their regarding or treating him as an individual who possesses the same emotions, aspirations, and potential as whites. In short, the city-dwelling black and his suburban brother regard guidance as an anathema.'' Russell also points out that the image the black student has of guidance was created by counselors and must be changed by counselors.

In discussing the sense of futility which many blacks feel with regard to the status quo, Proctor (1970) states, ''...Like a spiral, it begins with the awareness of rejection, moves on to an assessment of the powers of those in authority, then goes to the invention of tactics that too often result in only sluggish and insignificant changes, and finally ends with an acceptance of the futility of the whole endeavor.'' He also states that in order to reverse this spiral, counselors must become innovators rather than defenders of the status quo.

If counseling as a profession is to be relevant to the needs of black clients within the context of the American social milieu, then the counselor roles discussed above must be rejected in favor of one which sees the counselor as an agent of social change who understands and relates to blacks from a black frame of reference. This role definition requires that the counselor examine what's wrong with a society which has consistently denied humanity to blacks since its inception. For example, this is a society that has asserted that black males don't want to work while at the same time denying them equal opportunities in employment. It is a society that points out that black youngsters score lower than white youngsters on standardized achievement tests while at the same time denying black youngsters equal access to a good education. This new role requires, in brief, that the counselor accurately understand the environment to which blacks must respond and interpret black behavior within the context of that environment.

Grier and Cobbs (1968) has provided the most succinct description of Black America's environment and how blacks have responded to that environment. In discussing *The Black Norm* they state:

"We submit that it is necessary for a black man in America to develop a profound distrust of his white fellow citizens and of the nation. He must be on guard to protect himself against physical hurt. He must cushion himself against cheating, slander, humiliation, and outright mistreatment by the official representatives of society. . . .For his own survival, then, he must develop a *cultural paranoia* in which every white man is a potential enemy unless proved otherwise and every social system is set against him unless he personally finds out differently.

*****

He can never quite respect laws which have no respect for him, and laws designed to protect white men are viewed as white men's laws. To break another man's law may be inconvenient if one is caught and punished, but it can never have the moral consequences involved in breaking one's own law. The result may be described as a *cultural antisocialism*, but it is simply an accurate reading of one's environment—a gift black people have developed to a high degree, to keep alive. These and related traits are simply adaptive devices developed in response to a peculiar environment. They are no more pathological than the compulsive manner in which a diver checks his equipment before a dive or a pilot his parachute. They represent normal devices for ''making it'' in America, and clinicians who are interested in the psychological functioning of black people must get acquainted with this body of character traits which we call *The Black Norm.*''

''Black is when they say '. . .one nation indivisible with liberty and justice for all . . .' and you wonder what nation they're talking about.'' (Brown, 1969)

But in addition to role definition a prior problem exists. Counselors are products of their prior educational experiences. The root of the problem is in the curriculum of their training programs, and it is here that reform must begin.

Traditional counseling psychology programs must be restructured in order to provide the counselor-in-training with techniques, theories, and experiences that will be relevant in preparing him for his new role definition. But before we propose a restructured model, let's examine more closely the shortcomings of current training programs.

Inadequacy of Current Training Models

Other contributors to this volume have already pointed out how current training programs are inadequate for preparing counselors to work with black students.

Gunnings has discussed what he considers the three major deficiencies: (1) irrelevant admissions criteria which allow only a few ''super blacks'' to be admitted and which do not take into account the prospective students' chances of success with the black community; (2) a curriculum that is inadequate because it is centered around clinical models and theories which have no linkage to the actual life styles of blacks; and (3) the absence of meaningful experiences in the form of black teachers to whom black student counselors can relate, in meaningful research and in relevant practicum experiences.

Sikes places his focus on the characteristics of the clientele with which the counselor will work. He states that blacks are psychologically maimed as a result of the effects of white racism. He points out that the counseling psychology curriculum should give some attention not only to the symptom but to the cause of the problem. He concludes that training programs are deficient in meeting the needs of those who wish to work in the black community because they do not speak to the black experience nor do they attend to white racism.

Bell points out that in many, if not most, counseling psychology programs the failure to provide adequate educational experiences for persons wishing to work in the black community lies not so much in what is included in the curriculum as in what is omitted from it. He states that much attention is focused on the existential problems of middle-class white youths, but little is focused on the raw survival level problems of low income groups. He states, as does Gunnings, that courses concerned with counseling theory and methodology do not include in an integrated fashion black "deviations" from the white norm in such areas as values, attitudes toward self, work, and the world, future expectation and motivation. He also points out that while many black counselor trainees recognize that their training is irrelevant for preparing them to work in the black community, they make the assumption, usually erroneous, that they can transfer techniques devised for one culture to another culture. Bell concludes that it is imperative for blacks to be actively involved in the design and implementation of training programs in order that information about blacks and experiences with black clients will be systematically integrated into the training program rather than left to chance.

Franklin states that if black counselors are to serve the black community effectively, a new concept of counselor training must emerge, one which develops the training within the context of contemporary issues confronting the counselor and client as black men. He suggests that one possible way to refine the student's development of theory and professional methods is by a modified "seminar-encounter" group built on daily professional issues. These "seminar-encounter" groups would have components relating to: (1) the client and his environment (consumer orientation); (2) the discussion of theory, method and practice within the context of daily experiences of the student counselor (student orientation); and (3) a final phase of professional orientation in which the academic, consumer and any other information is blended into a professional position.

These criticisms and others found in the literature make it obvious that new training models are imperative for counselors, both black and white, who plan to work with black clients. The counselor who emerges from these new training programs must have a genuine concern and empathy for his black clients. He must be a student of blackness who understands the black life style. He must understand why blacks have developed a "cultural paranoia," a "cultural depression" and a "cultural antisocialism" (Grier and Cobbs, 1968). He must possess facts and skills which are applicable to a black population and be committed to changing the social status quo which is mainly responsible for the perpetuation of many of the problems of blacks. The counselor must have also come to grips with his feelings about race. I have previously discussed (Mitchell, 1970) the issues involved in counseling blacks for white counselors and for black counselors who may be out of touch with their blackness. Williams and Kirkland (in this volume) have also discussed the problems involved in counseling between a white counselor and a black client.

A New Model

Lewis and Lewis (1970) have proposed an innovative model for training inner-city counselors. The model which I will discuss is similar to theirs in some respects, but has the advantage of being more than a proposed model. It was recently instituted as part of the masters program in counseling at Washington University. The problem with the program previously, lay in what was omitted. Previously only one or two black students per year had been admitted to the program and they generally did their internships with white populations. The curriculum did not include any systematic in-put of a black perspective nor consideration of special problems of black counselors of clients.

For the class that began in June, 1971, twelve black students (one-fourth of the total class) were recruited and admitted. Each of these students was interviewed with the question in mind, "Does this student have the personal qualities which, when combined with relevant professional training, could lead to his being successful in counseling black students?" Usual admissions criteria, Miller Analogies Test scores and previous grade point averages, were not emphasized.

The curriculum was modified in order to provide a systematic in-put of a black perspective. Some reading lists were expanded to include books and articles by black writers. In theory courses where readings by blacks and meaningful research about blacks are not available, the large number of black students in the program will assure that these issues will be dealt with in class discussions. Significantly, the faculty will be pressed to become more knowledgeable about the counseling needs of black clients than they have been in the past when only one or two black students were in the program. A number of curriculum options have also been made available through the Black Studies Program. "Sociology of the Black Community," "Afro-American History," and "Black Psychology" are but a few examples. Students who will work with black clients may take "Black Psychology" instead of the usual required course in personality theory. The author will also offer a "Seminar in Counseling Minority Group Students" which will be added to the counseling curriculum for the spring semester.

Since the most significant portion of the old program was the clinical experiences which students received through their year-long internships, it was obvious that if the program was to train black counselors, then the most pressing need was to provide them with relevant practicum experiences. To this end, an arrangement was worked out with the St. Louis Public Schools under which they have provided several internships for our students in predominantly black high schools in St. Louis. Internships were also secured for the first time in the high school of an all-black school district in St. Louis County; in a predominantly black elementary school within a suburban school system; and in high schools, junior high and elementary schools within predominantly white suburban school systems which are enrolling larger numbers of black students. For students who wish to work in settings other than educational institutions, internships are being sought in social agencies.

These changes in the Washington University program deal with most of the criticisms leveled at traditional counseling psychology programs. This revised program has been set up within the framework of the existing program for the purpose of training black counselors, white counselors who plan to work with black populations and to give the class as a whole some exposure to a black perspective. The main inadequacy of the revised program is that there is no black instructor who devotes half-time or more to the program. The masters program requires thirty units of credit plus an internship. It begins with four courses in the summer, with the academic year being devoted to the internship and nine units of credit each semester. A typical sequence for students planning to work with black clients is outlined below.

Summer

1. *Introduction to Guidance.* Survey of the policies and practices of guidance services in elementary, high school, and college settings. Emphasis is placed on the psychological bases of student personnel services, and of their relationship to the field of education as a whole.

2. *Group Testing and Individual Inventory.* Methods of inferring measures of achievement, aptitude, personality, and interests by means of group testing techniques are studied. Consideration is given to the role of group tests in the assessment procedure, and to their relation to other techniques of individual appraisal such as questionnaires, projective techniques, and individual tests. The student is expected to develop an awareness of the use of non-test information in the school folder about a student as it relates to the test information and to the process of psychological assessment.

3. *Vocational Development Theory and Information.* Three major themes will be developed: an introduction to vocational development theory with special emphasis on the career as part of the total life history; a survey of national manpower trends, educational and vocational choice patterns; and a review of informational materials and services.

4. *Introduction to Counseling.* Theoretical approaches and related techniques involved in the counseling process are studied by means of reading, discussion of recorded counseling interviews, and role-play methods. The student is expected to develop his personal conception of the nature of man and relate this to the counseling process.

All four courses will demonstrate how they are relevant to a black population by dealing specifically with the problems of a hypothetical black student. This procedure has the added advantage of providing a consistent frame of reference from course to course. Toward the end of the summer as students approach the time when they will be working with clients at their placements, this hypothetical black student will also be presented as a coached-client with whom the student counselor will have to relate. The four summer courses must also attempt to answer questions like these: (1) "What is the role of the counselor in effecting changes in institutional policies which cause problems for black students by denying them outlets for expression of a black life style and black culture?" (2) "Which counseling theories and techniques are most appropriate in working with black clients?" (3) "How applicable are tests which use different racial and cultural norms in making inferences about black clients? Interpret test results in terms of "The Black Norm" proposed by Grier and Cobbs." (4) "Consider the effects of institutional racism and job discrimination on the vocational choices of blacks."

Fall Semester

5. *Counseling Internship*. As part of their internship training, students will meet for a seminar for two and one half hours per week. Each seminar group will consist of from six to eight students with primary attention focused on their experiences as counselors in their particular settings. Black students and white students who will counsel black clients will be grouped together. These seminars will be set up like the "seminar-encounter" groups discussed by Franklin. Role-playing, audio tapes, video tapes and personal encounters between group members will be the media by which students assess the effects that they have on their counselees and the extent to which they are viewing client problems from a black frame of reference.

In addition to this seminar each student will meet for one hour per week with a faculty member for individual supervision. Students will discuss problems with specific cases and receive constructive criticism. In some instances it might be necessary for the supervisor to counsel the intern regarding problems which he may have in establishing his legitimacy with black clients. This is an added opportunity for students to work through their feelings about race. Students will also receive supervision from a staff member at their placement.

6. *Black Psychology*. This course is offered through the Black Studies Program and will deal with an analysis of the formation of black identity; black psyche and life styles; a study of such concepts as prejudice, racism, oppression; and intelligence testing and ethical considerations in conducting research.

7. *Elective*. Students may take a course within the counseling program, the psychology department, or from the offerings of the Black Studies Program. Examples of electives are:

Psychology of Personality
Sociology of the Black Community
Afro-American History
Group Procedures in Counseling
Problems in Elementary School Counseling
Problems in Secondary School Counseling
College Student Personnel Work

Spring Semester:

8. *Counseling Internship*. Continuation of the "seminar-encounter" groups and individual supervision.

9. *Individual Assessment in Educational Settings: Wechsler.* Theory and intensive experience in administering and interpreting individual tests of intelligence, the Wechsler Intelligence Scale for Children and the Wechsler Adult Intelligence Scale. In light of current criticisms about the irrelevancy of standardized intelligence tests in measuring the abilities of blacks, students will take this course with the intention of examining consistent response patterns of blacks and discussing the validity of those responses within the context of a black perspective.

10. *Seminar in Counseling Minority Group Students.* This course will represent an extension of the third stage of Franklin's "seminar-encounter" groups. This will be a final phase of professional orientation in which the theories and techniques which students have learned will be combined with all information available about the black client from readings and internship experiences so that the counselor acquires a professional position on the issue of counseling minority group students.

In addition to required coursework and the internship, a series of black-white encounter groups will be available for students who wish to participate.

Evaluation

The program outlined above has much potential for promoting the personal and professional growth of counselors-in-training. The merits of this model will be examined at the end of the academic year when students assess the program in terms of how well it prepared them for their roles as counselors for black students.

References

Brown, Turner, Jr. *Black is.* New York: Grove Press Inc., 1969.

Grier, W.H. and Cobbs, P.M. *Black rage.* New York: Bantam Books, 1968.

Lewis, M.D. and Lewis, J.A. Relevant training for relevant roles: A model for educating inner-city counselors. *Counselor Education and Supervision,* Vol. 10, No. 1, 1970, 31-38.

Mitchell, H. The black experience in higher education. *The Counseling Psychologist,* Vol. 2, No. 1, 1970, 30-36.

Proctor, S.A. Reversing the spiral toward futility. *Personnel & Guidance Journal,* 1970, 48, 707-712.

Russell, R.D. Black perceptions of guidance. *Personnel & Guidance Journal,* 1970, 48, 721-728.

Selected Readings

Bryson, S., Bardo, H., & Johnson, C. Black Female counselor and the Black Male client. *Journal of Non-White Concerns in Personnel and Guidance,* 1975, *3*, 53-58.

Burrell, L., & Rayder, N.F. Black and white students' attitudes toward white counselors. *Journal of Negro Education,* 1971, *40,* 48-52.

Calnek, M. Racial factors in the countertransference: The black therapist and the black client. *Amer. J. Orthopsychiat.,* 1970, *40* (1), 39-46.

Cimbolic, P. Counselor race and experience effects on Black clients. *Journal of Consulting & Clinical Psychology,* 1972, *39* (2), 328-332.

Cross, W.E. The Negro-to-Black conversion experience. *Black World,* July, 1971, 13-27.

Ewing, T.N. Racial similarity of client and counselor and client satisfaction with counseling. *Journal of Counseling Psychology* 1974, *21* (5), 446-449.

Gardner, L.H. The therapeutic relationship under varying conditions of race. *Psychotherapy: Theory, Research and Practice,* 1971, *8* (1), 78-87.

Grantham, R.J. Effects of counselor sex, race, and language style on Black students in initial interviews. *Journal of Counseling Psychology,* 1973, *20* (6), 553-559.

Haettenschwiller, D.L. Counseling black college students in special programs. *Personnel and Guidance Journal,* 1971, *50* (1), 29-35.

Hall, W.S., Cross, W.E., & Freedle, R. Stages in the development of Black awareness: An exploratory investigation. In Reginald L. Jones' (Ed.) *Black Psychology,* New York: Harper & Row, 1972, 156-165.

Harper, F.D. What counselors must know about the social sciences of Black Americans. *The Journal of Negro Americans,* 1973, *42* (2), 109-116.

Hayes, E., Hill, J. & Young, H. Superfly, the mack, black youth, and counselors. *The School Counselor,* 1975, *22* (3), 174-179.

Hecht, E. Guidance program for a ghetto school. *Personnel and Guidance Journal,* 1970, *48,* 731-738.

Jackson, A.M. Psychotherapy: Factors Associated with the race of the therapist. *Psychotherapy: Theory Research and Practice,* 1973, *10* (3), 273-277.

Jackson, B. Black identity development. *MEFORM: Journal of Educational Diversity and Innovation,* 1975, *2,* 19-25.

Jackson, G.G., & Kirschner, S.A. Racial self-designation and preference for a counselor. *Journal of Counseling Psychology,* 1973, *20* (6), 560-564.

Jefferies, D. Counseling for the strengths of the Black woman. *The Counseling Psychologist,* 1976, *6,* 20-22.

Merluzzi, T.V., & Merluzzi, B.H. Counselor race and power base: Effects on attitudes and behavior. *Journal of Counseling Psychology,* 1977, *24* (5), 430-436.

Rousseve, R. Reason and reality in counseling the student-client who is Black. *School Counselor,* 1970, *17,* 337-344.

Russell, R.D. Black perceptions of guidance. *Personnel and Guidance Journal,* 1970, *48* (9), 721-728.

Smith, E.J. Counseling Black individuals: Some stereotypes. *Personnel and Guidance Journal,* 1977, *55,* 390-396.

Smith, P.M. Black Activists for liberation, not guidance. *Personnel and Guidance Journal,* 1971, *49,* 721-726.

Thomas, C.W. Boys no more: Some social psychological aspects of the new Black ethic. *The American Behavior Scientist,* 1969, *12,* 38-42.

Ward, E.J. A gift from the ghetto. *Personnel and Guidance Journal,* 1970, *48,* 753-756.

Williams, R.L., & Kirkland, J. The white counselor and the black client.''
    Counseling Psychologist, 1970, *2,* 114-116.
Wilson, W., & Calhoun, J.F. Behavior therapy and the minority client.
    Psychotherapy Theory, Research & Practice, 1974, *11* (4), 317-325.
Woods, E., & Zimmer, J.M. Racial effect in counseling-like interviews: An
    experimental analogue. *Journal of Counseling Psychology,* 1976, *23* (6), 527-531.

1. Assume you have just been hired by a social service agency that has contracted to provide home-liaison services between the local schools and the parents of students attending these schools. Although a large number of the students are Black (approximately 35%), your agency to date has hired only one Black home-liaison counselor (of a staff of 12 counselors). As a home-liaison counselor, your responsibilities include home visits to acquaint parents with community services available to them and to establish rapport between the parents and the schools.

   a. What expectations would you have for your first home visit with a Black family?
   b. What are some examples of "small talk" you might use to "break the ice" with the parents of a fourteen year old Black student who is consistently truant from school?
   c. Assuming none exists when you are hired, what courses and experiences related to Black culture would you recommend that the school district offer to students?

2. Assume you have just accepted a counseling position in a correctional facility where a large number of Black inmates are incarcerated, most of whom come from nearby urban centers.

   a. What expectations do you have for your own performance as a counselor in this setting?
   b. Do you anticipate Black inmates will avail themselves of your services as a counselor? Why?
   c. What psychological needs can you anticipate Black inmates may have which you as a counselor might attempt to fulfill? How will you attempt to fulfill them?

3. Assume you are a counselor in a small midwestern college that is predominately White but recruits Black athletes. One of the Black athletes (Bill) has been dating a White cheerleader (Mary) you have seen before for counseling. Mary, seeing you alone, has just informed you that Bill has moved in with her and she fears her parents will disown her

when they find out. She has also asked you if she may bring Bill for an appointment the next day.

a. How do you feel about Mary and Bill's cross-racial living arrangement?
b. What are some of the issues you will want to explore with Mary and Bill when they come to see you together?
c. What do you suppose Mary and Bill each want to get out of meeting with a counselor?

Part 5 The Latino Client

As with the labels Asian American, Black, and American Indian, there is a danger that by identifying a group of people as Latino we tend to overlook very real differences that exist within the group. Yet these labels are not applied spuriously or capriciously in the present text. Individuals within each group share a common cultural heritage, knowledge of which can enhance the counselor's effectiveness when working with clients from each group. Latinos, primarily consisting of immigrants from Cuba, Mexico, and Puerto Rico, share a similar heritage with regard to language, values, and tradition. Beyond these similarities, very important differences exist among the various Latino populations, and these differences are discussed in some detail in Chapter 14.

Presently the second largest ethnic minority in the United States, it is projected that by the year 2030 or sooner, Latinos will represent the largest minority group. Although the Bureau of Census lists 12 million persons of Spanish origin, it is estimated that there are already 20 million Latinos in this country (Here comes the Latino era, 1977). It has also been estimated that in California, one of our most populated states, Latinos will comprise a majority of the population by the year 2000.

Despite these impressive statistics, there is evidence that Latinos have had less than their share of the American dream. Fewer than 40% of the Latinos over 25 years of age have completed a high school education as compared to 66% of all other groups (U.S. Bureau of Census, 1977). There is little evidence the situation is improving, since more than 60% of the Latinos aged 20-24 have less than four years of high school education, a percentage that compares unfavorably with Blacks of the same age (57.5%) and even more unfavorably with Whites of the same age (35.5%) (U.S. Bureau of Census, 1975). The median family income for Latino families in 1976 was $10,300 (despite larger families and more members who work) as compared to a $15,200 median for all other families. Twenty-three percent of all Latino families exist on incomes below the poverty level as compared to nine percent for all other families (U.S. Bureau of Census, 1977).

This situation can be accounted for to a large degree by a cycle of poverty set in motion with the earliest migration of Latinos to this country. Ancestral immigrants of many present-day Latinos came to the United States from non-industrial, agrarian-based countries and, for the most part, were unskilled and spoke little or no English. (A major exception was the Cuban population, many of whom were middle class and skilled when they migrated.) Their lifestyle, customs, and language set them apart from the dominant society, making them the objects of stereotyping, prejudice, and discrimination. Thus handicapped, Latinos were forced to join the millions of other American ethnic minorities in competition for scarce jobs and low pay. Hence the pattern was set, and each new generation has been condemned to the perpetual cycle of poverty and group discrimination. Inevitably, the result of this process is loss of hope and motivation.

As Rohrer (1970) suggests, however, a few minority persons do, on occasion, manage to break free of their social caste, although it is seldom accomplished without considerable sacrifice. Richard Rodríguez, in the first article to this section, "Going Home Again: The New American Scholarship Boy," reflects upon his life as a Mexican American graduate student in English Renaissance literature and the price he paid to succeed. Rodríguez discovered that his indigenous cultural orientation directly conflicted with that of the academic world and that in order to succeed it became necessary for him to abandon much of what he had learned and practiced within his native culture. The Spanish language, which provided his deepest sense of relationship to his family, became an impediment instead of an asset. Allegiance that was demanded by his family and cultural group was demanded by his instructors and the academic community. Rodríguez, like other minority intellectuals, found that the net result was a paradoxical situation in which he felt an increased appreciation of his native culture, while at the same time serving as an instrument to change it.

In the second article to this section, "Counseling Puerto Ricans: Some Cultural Considerations," Christensen provides a brief introduction to the Puerto Rican in America. Important differences between native-born Puerto Ricans and Neo-Ricans are discussed as well as the values and traits linked to the Puerto Rican ethos. Most helpful to the counselor is a section in which Christensen offers a number of specific suggestions that apply directly to counseling Puerto Ricans.

In the final article to this section, "Counseling Latinos," Ruiz and Padilla present a demographic picture of the various sub-groups which constitute the larger Latino population, demonstrating how these sub-cultures differ from the general population. Their examination of Latino ethno-history and culture is highly instructive. Similarities found in each of the various sub-cultures, as well as the distinguishing features which make each unique, are examined in some detail. The need to view both intra-psychic and extra-psychic sources of stress, a theme presented throughout this text, is emphasized by Ruiz and Padilla when counseling Latinos. In the final portion of this article, the authors present several case histories of Latino clients, with the intention of providing guidelines for developing culturally relevant counseling programs for Latinos.

Here comes the Latino era. *Nuestro: The Magazine for Latinos,* 1977, *1* (1), 12, 15, 17-19.

Rohrer, W.C. *Black profile of white Americans.* Philadelphia: F.A. Davis, 1970.

Rodriguez, A. Bilingual education: Profile '70. In Rudolph Gomez (Ed.) *The changing Mexican-American.* Boulder, Co.: Pruett, 1972.

U.S. Bureau of Census. Persons of Spanish Origin in the United States. March, 1975. In *Current population reports,* (Series P-20, No. 292). Washington, D.C.: U.S. Government Printing Office, 1975.

U.S. Bureau of Census. Persons of Spanish Origin in the United States. March, 1977. In *Current population reports,* (Series P-20, No. 317). Washington, D.C.: U.S. Government Printing Office, 1977.

12 Going Home Again
The New American Scholarship Boy
Rodriguez, Richard

At each step, with every graduation from one level of education to the next, the refrain from bystanders was strangely the same: "Your parents must be so proud of you." I suppose that my parents were proud, although I suspect, too, that they felt more than pride alone as they watched me advance through my education. They seemed to know that my education was separating us from one another, making it difficult to resume familiar intimacies. Mixed with the instincts of parental pride, a certain hurt also communicated itself—too private ever to be adequately expressed in words, but real nonetheless.

The autobiographical facts pertinent to this essay are simply stated in two sentences, though they exist in somewhat awkward juxtaposition to each other. I am the son of Mexican-American parents, who speak a blend of Spanish and English, but who read neither language easily. I am about to receive a Ph.D. in English Renaissance literature. What sort of life—what tensions, feelings, conflicts—connects these two sentences? I look back and remember my life from the time I was seven or eight years old as one of constant movement away from a Spanish-speaking folk culture toward the world of the English-language classroom. As the years passed, I felt myself becoming less like my parents and less comfortable with the assumption of visiting relatives that I was still the Spanish-speaking child they remembered. By the time I began college, visits home became suffused with silent embarrassment: there seemed so little to share, however strong the ties of our affection. My parents would tell me what happened in their lives or in the lives of relatives; I would respond with news of my own. Polite questions would follow. Our conversations came to seem more like interviews.

A few months ago, my dissertation nearly complete, I came upon my father looking through my bookcase. He quietly fingered the volumes of Milton's tracts and Augustine's theology with that combination of reverence and distrust those who are not literate sometimes show for the written word. Silently, I watched him from the door of the room. However much he would have insisted that he was "proud" of his son for being able to master the texts, I knew, if pressed further, he would have admitted to complicated feelings about my success. When he looked across the room and suddenly saw me, his body tightened slightly with surprise, then we both smiled.

For many years I kept my uneasiness about becoming a success in education to myself. I did so in part because I wanted to avoid vague feelings that, if considered carefully, I would have no way of dealing with; and in part because I felt that no one else shared my reaction to the opportunity provided by education. When I began to rehearse my story of cultural dislocation publicly, however, I found many listeners willing to admit to similar feelings from their own pasts. Equally impressive was the fact that many among those I spoke with were *not* from nonwhite racial groups, which made me realize that one can grow up to enter the culture of the academy and find it a "foreign" culture for a variety of reasons, ranging from economic status to religious heritage. But why, I next wondered, was it that, though there were so many of us who came from childhood cultures alien to the academy's, we voiced our uneasiness to one another and to ourselves so infrequently? Why did it take *me* so long to acknowledge publicly the cultural costs I had paid to earn a Ph.D. in Renaissance English literature? Why, more precisely, am I writing these words only now when my connection to my past barely survives except as nostalgic memory?

Looking back, a person risks losing hold of the present while being confounded by the past. For the child who moves to an academic culture from a culture that dramatically lacks academic traditions, looking back can jeopardize the certainty he has about the desirability of this new academic culture. Richard Hoggart's description, in *The Uses of Literacy,* of the cultural pressures on such a student, whom Hoggart calls the "scholarship boy," helps make the point. The scholarship boy must give nearly unquestioning allegiance to academic culture, Hoggart argues, if he is to succeed at all, so different is the milieu of the classroom from the culture he leaves behind. For a time, the scholarship boy may try to balance his loyalty between his concretely experienced family life and the more abstract mental life of the classroom. In the end, though, he must choose between the two worlds: if he intends to succeed as a student, he must, literally and figuratively, separate himself from his family, with its gregarious life, and find a quiet place to be alone with his thoughts.

After a while, the kind of allegiance the young student might once have given his parents is transferred to the teacher, the new parent. Now without the support of the old ties and certainties of the family, he almost mechanically acquires the assumptions, practices, and style of the classroom milieu. For the loss he might otherwise feel, the scholarship boy substitutes an enormous enthusiasm for nearly everything having to do with school.

How readily I read my own past into the portrait of Hoggart's scholarship boy. Coming from a home in which mostly Spanish was spoken, for example, I had to decide to forget Spanish when I began my education. To succeed in the classroom, I needed psychologically to sever my ties with Spanish. Spanish represented an alternate culture as well as another language—and the basis of my deepest sense of relationship to my family. Although I recently taught myself to read Spanish, the language that I see on the printed page is not quite the language I heard in my youth. That other Spanish, the spoken Spanish of my family, I remember with nostalgia and guilt: guilt because I cannot explain to aunts and uncles why I do not answer their questions any longer in their own idiomatic language. Nor was I able to explain to teachers in graduate school, who regularly expected me to read and speak Spanish with ease, why my very ability to reach graduate school as a student of English literature in the first place required me to loosen my attachments to a language I spoke years earlier. Yet, having lost the ability to speak Spanish, I never forgot it so totally that I could not understand it. Hearing Spanish spoken on the street reminded me of the community I once felt a part of, and still cared deeply about. I never forgot Spanish so thoroughly, in other words, as to move outside the range of its nostalgic pull.

Such moments of guilt and nostalgia were, however, just that—momentary. They punctuated the history of my otherwise successful progress from *barrio* to classroom. Perhaps they even encouraged it. Whenever I felt my determination to succeed wavering, I tightened my hold on the conventions of academic life.

Spanish was one aspect of the problem, my parents another. They could raise deeper, more persistent doubts. They offered encouragement to my brothers and me in our work, but they also spoke, only half jokingly, about the way education was putting "big ideas" into our heads. When we would come home, for example, and challenge assumptions we earlier believed, they would be forced to defend their beliefs (which, given our new verbal skills, they did increasingly less well) or, more frequently, to submit to our logic with the disclaimer, "It's what we were taught in our time to believe. . . ." More important, after we began to leave home for college, they voiced regret about how "changed" we had become, how much further away from one another we had grown. They partly yearned for a return to the time before education assumed their children's primary loyalty. This yearning was renewed each time they saw their nieces and nephews (none of whom continued their education beyond high school, all of whom continued to speak fluent Spanish) living according to the conventions and assumptions of their parents' culture. If I was already troubled by the time I graduated from high school by that refrain of congratulations ("Your parents must be so proud. . . ."), I realize now how much more difficult and complicated was my progress into academic life for my parents, as they saw the cultural foundation of their family erode, than it was for me.

Yet my parents were willing to pay the price of alienation and continued to encourage me to become a scholarship boy because they perceived, as others of the lower classes had before them, the relation between education and social mobility. Lacking the former themselves made them acutely aware of its necessity as prerequisite for the latter. They sent their children off to school in the hopes of their acquiring something "better" beyond education.

Notice the assumption here that education is something of a tool or license—a means to an end, which has been the traditional way the lower or working classes have viewed the value of education in the past. That education might alter children in more basic ways than providing them with skills, certificates of proficiency, and even upward mobility, may come as a surprise for some, but the financial cost is usually tolerated.

Complicating my own status as a scholarship boy in the last ten years was the rise, in the mid-1960s, of what was then called "the Third World Student Movement." Racial minority groups, led chiefly by black intellectuals, began to press for greater access to higher education. The assumption behind their criticism, like the assumption of white working-class families, was that educational opportunity was useful for economic and social advancement. The racial minority leaders went one step further, however, and it was this step that was probably most revolutionary. Minority students came to the campus feeling that they were representative of larger groups of people—that, indeed, they were advancing the condition of entire societies by their matriculation. Actually, this assumption was not altogether new to me. Years before, educational success was something my parents urged me to strive for precisely because it would reflect favorably on *all* Mexican-Americans—specifically, my intellectual achievement would help deflate the stereotype of the "dumb Pancho." This early goal was only given greater currency by the rhetoric of the Third World spokesmen. But it was the fact that I felt myself suddenly much more a "public" Mexican-American, a representative of sorts, that was to prove so crucial for me during these years.

One college admissions officer assured me one day that he recognized my importance to his school precisely as deriving from the fact that, after graduation, I would surely be "going back to [my] community." More recently, teachers have urged me not to trouble over the fact that I am not "representative" of my culture, assuring me that I can serve as a "model" for those still in the *barrio* working toward academic careers. This is the line that I hear, too, when being interviewed for a faculty position. The interviewer almost invariably assumes that, because I am racially a Mexican-American, I can serve as a special counselor to minority students. The expectation is that I still retain the capacity for intimacy with "my people."

This new way of thinking about the possible uses of education is what has made the entrance of minority students into higher education so dramatic. When the minority group student was accepted into the academy, he came—in everyone's mind—as part of a "group." When I began college, I barely attracted attention except perhaps as a slightly exotic ("Are you from India?") brown-skinned student; by the time I graduated, my presence was annually noted by, among others, the college public relations office as "one of the fifty-two students with Spanish surnames enrolled this year." By having his presence announced to the campus in this way, the minority group student was unlike any other scholarship boy the campus had seen before.

The minority group student now dramatized more publicly, if also in new ways, the issues of cultural dislocation that education forces, issues that are not solely racial in origin. When Richard Rodriguez *became* a Chicano, the dilemmas he earlier had as a scholarship boy were complicated but not decisively altered by the fact that he had assumed a group identity.

The assurance I heard that, somehow, I was being useful to my community by being a student was gratefully believed, because it gave me a way of dealing with the guilt and cynicism that each year came my way along with the scholarships, grants, and, lately, job offers from schools which a few years earlier would have refused me admission as a student. Each year, in fact, it became harder to believe that my success had anything to do with my intellectual performance, and harder to resist the conclusion that it was due to my minority group status. When I drove to the airport, on my way to London as a Fulbright Fellow last year, leaving behind cousins of my age who were already hopelessly burdened by financial insecurity and dead-end jobs, momentary guilt could be relieved by the thought that somehow my trip was beneficial to persons other than myself. But, of course, if the thought was a way of dealing with the guilt, it was also the reason for the guilt. Sitting in a university library, I would notice a janitor of my own race and grow uneasy; I was, I knew, in a rough way a beneficiary of his condition. Guilt was accompanied by cynicism. The most dazzlingly talented minority students I know today refuse to believe that their success is wholly based on their own talent, or even that when they speak in a classroom anyone hears them as anything but *the* voice of their minority group. It is scarcely surprising, then, though initially it probably seemed puzzling, that so many of the angriest voices on the campus against the injustices of racism came from those not visibly its primary victims.

It became necessary to believe the rhetoric about the value of one's presence on campus simply as a way of living with one's "success." Among ourselves, however, minority group students often admitted to a shattering sense of loss—the feeling that, somehow, something was happening to us. Especially from students who had not yet become accustomed, as by that time I had, to the campus, I remember hearing confessions of extreme discomfort and isolation. Our close associations, the separate dining-room tables, and the special dormitories helped to relieve some of the pain, but only some of it.

Significant here was the development of the ethnic studies concept—black studies, Chicano studies, et cetera—and the related assumption held by minority group students in a number of departments that they could keep in touch with their old cultures by making these cultures the subject of their study. Here again one notices how different the minority student was from other comparable students: other scholarship boys—poor Jews and the sons of various immigrant cultures—came to the academy singly, much more inclined to accept the courses and material they found. The ethnic studies concept was an indication that, for a multitude of reasons, the new racial minority group students were not willing to give up so easily their ties with their old cultures.

The importance of these new ethnic studies was that they introduced the academy to subject matter that generally deserved to be studied, and at the same time offered a staggering critique of the academy's tendency toward parochialism. Most minority group intellectuals never noted this tendency toward academic parochialism. They more often saw the reason for, say, the absence of a course on black literature in an English department as a case of simple racism. That it might instead be an instance of the fact that academic culture can lose track of human societies and whole areas of human experience was rarely raised. Never asking such a question, the minority group students never seemed to wonder either if as teachers their own courses might suffer the same cultural limitations other seminars and classes suffered. Consequently, in a peculiar way the new minority group critics of higher education came to justify the academy's assumptions. The possibility that academic culture could encourage one to grow out of touch with cultures beyond its conceptual horizon was never seriously considered.

Too often in the last ten years one heard minority group students repeat the joke, never very funny in the first place, about the racial minority academic who ended up sounding more "white" than white academics. Behind the scorn for such a figure was the belief that the new generation of minority group students would be able to avoid having to make similar kinds of cultural concessions. The pressures that might have led to such conformity went unexamined.

For the last few years my annoyance at hearing such jokes was doubtless related to the fact that I was increasingly beginning to sense that I was the "bleached" academic the minority group students found so laughable. I suppose I had always sensed that my cultural allegiance was undergoing subtle alterations as I was being educated. Only when I finished my course work in graduate school and went off to England for my dissertation year did I grasp how far I had traveled from my cultural origins. My year in England was actually my first opportunity to write and reflect upon the kind of material that I would spend my life producing. It was my first chance, too, to be free simultaneously of the distractions of course-work and of the insecurities of trying to find my niche in academic life. Sitting in the reading room of the British Museum, I no longer doubted that I had joined academic society. Ironically, this feeling of having finally arrived allowed me to look back to the community whence I came. That I was geographically farther away from my home than I had ever been lent a metaphorical resonance to the cultural distance I suddenly felt.

But the feeling was not pleasing. The reward of feeling a part of the world of the British Museum was an odd one. Each morning I would arrive at the reading room and grow increasingly depressed by the silence and what the silence implied—that my life as a scholar would require self-absorption. Who, I wondered, would find my work helpful enough to want to read it? Was not my dissertation—whose title alone would puzzle my relatives—only my grandest exercise thus far in self-enclosure? The sight of the heads around me bent over their texts and papers, many so thoroughly engrossed that they wouldn't look up at the silent clock overhead for hours at a stretch, made me recall the remarkable noises of life in my family home. The tedious prose I was writing, a prose constantly qualified by footnotes, reminded me of the capacity for passionate statement those of the culture I was born into commanded—and which, could it be, I had now lost.

As I remembered it during those gray English afternoons, the past rushed forward to define more precisely my present condition. Remembering my youth, a time when I was not restricted to a chair but ran barefoot under a summer sun that tightened my skin with its white heat, made the fact that it was only my mind that "moved" each hour in the library painfully obvious.

I did need to figure out where I had lost touch with my past. I started to become alien to my family culture the day I became a scholarship boy. In the British Museum the realization seemed obvious. But later, returning to America, I returned to minority group students who were still speaking of their cultural ties to their past. How was I to tell them what I had learned about myself in England?

A short while ago, a group of enthusiastic Chicano undergraduates came to my office to ask me to teach a course to high school students in the *barrio* on the Chicano novel. This new literature, they assured me, has an important role to play in helping to shape the consciousness of a people currently without adequate representation in literature. Listening to them I was struck immediately with the cultural problems raised by their assumption. I told them that the novel is not capable of dealing with Chicano experience adequately, simply because most Chicanos are not literate, or are at least not yet comfortably so. This is not something Chicanos need to apologize for (though, I suppose, remembering my own childhood ambition to combat stereotypes of the Chicano as mental menial, it is not something easily admitted). Rather the genius and value of those Chicanos who do not read seem to me to be largely that their reliance on voice, the spoken word, has given them the capacity for intimate conversation that I, as someone who now relies heavily on the written word, can only envy. The second problem, I went on, is more in the nature of a technical one: the novel, in my opinion, is not a form capable of being true to the basic sense of communal life that typifies Chicano culture. What the novel as a literary form is best capable of representing is solitary existence set against a large social background. Chicano novelists, not coincidentally, nearly always fail to capture the breathtakingly rich family life of most Chicanos, and instead often describe only the individual Chicano in transit between Mexican and American cultures.

I said all of this to the Chicano students in my office, and could see that little of it made an impression. They seemed only frustrated by what they probably took to be a slick, academic justification for evading social responsibility. After a time, they left me, sitting alone. . . .

There is a danger of being misunderstood here. I am not suggesting that an academic cannot reestablish ties of any kind with his old culture. Indeed, he can have an impact on the culture of his childhood. But as an academic, one exists by definition in a culture separate from one's nonacademic roots and, therefore, any future ties one has with those who remain "behind" are complicated by one's new cultural perspective.

Paradoxically, the distance separating the academic from his nonacademic past can make his past seem, if not closer, then clearer. It is possible for the academic to understand the culture from which he came "better" than those who still live within it. In my own experience, it has only been as I have come to appraise my past through categories and notions derived from the social sciences that I have been able to think of Chicano life in cultural terms at all. Characteristics I took for granted or noticed only in passing—the spontaneity, the passionate speech, the trust in concrete experience, the willingness to think communally rather than individually—these are all significant phenomena to me now as aspects of a total culture. (My parents have neither the time nor the inclination to think about their culture as a culture.) Able to conceptualize a sense of Chicano culture, I am now also more attracted to that culture than I was before. The temptation now is to try to preserve those traits of my old culture that have not yet, in effect, atrophied.

The racial self-consciousness of minority group students during the last few years evident in the ethnic costumes, the stylized gestures, and the idiomatic though often evasive devices for insisting on one's continuing membership in the community of the past, are also indications that the minority group student has gained a new appreciation of the culture of his origin precisely because of his earlier alienation from it. As a result, Chicano students sometimes become more Chicano than most Chicanos. I remember, for example, my father's surprise when, walking across my college campus one afternoon, we came upon two Chicano academics wearing serapes. He and my mother were also surprised—indeed offended—when they earlier heard student activists use the word "Chicano." For them the term was a private one, primarily descriptive of persons they knew. It suggested intimacy. Hearing the word shouted into a microphone by a stranger left them bewildered. What they could not understand was that the student activist finds it easier than they to use "Chicano" in a more public way, for his distance from their culture and his membership in academic culture permits a wider and more abstract view.

The Mexican-Americans who begin to call themselves Chicanos in this new way are actually forming a new version of what it means to be a Chicano. The culture that didn't see itself as a culture is suddenly prized and identified for being one. The price one pays for this new self-consciousness is the knowledge of just that—it is *new*—and this knowledge is not available to those who remain at home. So it is knowledge that separates as well as unites people. Wanting more desperately than ever to assert his ties with the newly visible culture, the minority group student is tempted to exploit those characteristics of that culture that might yet survive in him. But the self-consciousness never allows one to feel completely at ease with the old culture. Worse, the knowledge of the culture of the past often leaves one feeling strangely solitary. At home, I hear relatives speak and find myself analyzing too much of what they say. It is embarrassing being a cultural anthropologist in one's own family's kitchen. I keep feeling myself little more than a cultural voyeur. I often come away from family gatherings suspecting, in fact, that what conceptions of my culture I carry with me are no more than illusions. Because they were never there before, because no one back home shares them, I grow less and less to trust their reliability: too often they seem no more than mental bubbles floating before an academic's eye.

Many who have taught minority group students in the last decade testify to sensing characteristics of a childhood culture still very much alive in these students. Should the teacher make these students aware of these characteristics? Initially, most of us would probably answer negatively. Better to trust the unconscious survival of the past than the always problematical, sometimes even clownish, re-creations of it. But the cultural past cannot be assured of survival; perhaps many of its characteristics are lost simply because the student is never encouraged to look for them. Even those that do survive do so tenuously. As a teacher, one can only hope that the best qualities in his minority group students' cultural legacy aren't altogether snuffed out by academic education.

More easy to live with and distinguishable from self-conscious awareness of the past are the ways the past unconsciously survives—perhaps even yet survives in me. As it turns out, the issue becomes less acute with time. With each year, the chance that the student is unaware of his cultural legacy is diminished as the habit of academic reflectiveness grows stronger. Although the culture of the academy makes innocence about one's cultural past less likely, this same culture, and the conceptual tools it provides, increases the desire to want to write and speak about the past. The paradox persists.

Awaiting the scholarship boy who finally acknowledges the fact that his perceptions of reality have changed is the dilemma of action. The sentimental reaction to this knowledge entails merely a refusal to renew contact with one's nonacademic culture lest one contaminate it. The problem, however, with this sentimental solution is that it overlooks the way academic culture renders one capable of dealing with the transactions of mass society. Academic culture, with its habits of conceptualization and abstraction, allows those of us from other cultures to deal with each other in a mass society. In this sense academic culture does have a profound political impact. Although people intent upon social mobility think of education as a means to an end, education does become an end: its culture allows one to exist more easily in a society increasingly anonymous and impersonal. The truth is, the academic's distance from his own experience brings the capacity for communicating with bureaucracies and understanding one's position in society—a prerequisite for political action.

If the sentimental reaction to nonacademic culture is to fear changing it, the political response, typical especially of working-class and lately minority group leaders, is to see higher education solely in terms of its political and social possibilities. Its cultural consequences, in this view, are disregarded. At this time when we are so keenly aware of social and economic inequality, it might seem beside the point to warn those who are working to bring about equality that education alters culture as well as economic status. And yet, if there is one main criticism that I, as a minority group student, must make of minority group leaders in their past attacks on the "racism" of the academy, it is that they never distinguished between my right to higher education and the desirability of my actually entering the academy—which is another way of saying again that they never recognized that there were things I could lose by becoming a scholarship boy.

Certainly, the academy changes those from alien cultures more than it is changed by them. While minority groups had an impact on higher education, largely because of their advantage in coming as a group, within the last few years students such as myself, who finally ended up certified as academics, also ended up sounding very much like the academics we found when we came to the campus. I do not enjoy making such admissions. But perhaps now the time has come when questions about the cultural costs of education ought to be delayed no longer. Those of us who have been scholarship boys know in our bones that our education has exacted a large price in exchange for the large benefits it has conferred upon us. And what is sadder to consider, after we have paid that price, we go home and casually change the cultures that nurtured us. My parents today understand how they are "Chicanos" in a large and impersonal sense. The gains from such knowledge are clear. But so, too, are the reasons for regret.

13 Counseling Puerto Ricans
Some Cultural Considerations
Christensen, Edward W.

Puerto Ricans comprise a significant percentage of potential clients for many counselors. The migration of Puerto Ricans to the mainland over the years has created cultural differences between Puerto Ricans raised in Puerto Rico and those raised in the U.S., but both groups are at a disadvantage in the dominant American culture. Migration back to the island in recent years is creating some problems for Puerto Rico, so Puerto Ricans often find prejudice both here and there. In this article the author, who married into a Puerto Rican family, discusses some values and traits that characterize Puerto Ricans and the behaviors that emerge from these traits. He offers practical suggestions for those counselors who have Puerto Rican clients.

In recent years the educational world has become increasingly concerned with students whose cultural backgrounds are different from those of the dominant culture in the U.S. This concern, though belated and still insufficient, has prompted other helping professions to follow the lead. Thus there has recently been increased publication on counseling members of minority groups, writers advocating giving more attention to the needs of clients who are culturally and ethnically different.

One of the outcomes of the increased attention given minority groups has been a tendency on the part of many to lump all minority individuals together. Thus, although early legislation and educational endeavors were designed to help blacks, American Indians, Mexican-Americans, and Puerto Ricans, they often served only to identify them all as having the same needs and disadvantages. Each group has protested this treatment, and all have insisted that their uniqueness be recognized and preserved. This need to understand the uniqueness of clients from specific cultural and ethnic backgrounds motivated the preparation of this article about counseling Puerto Ricans.

Some Facts about Puerto Rico

There is a great deal of ignorance among mainland Americans with regard to Puerto Rico. A few years ago, when I was in the U.S. on sabbatical leave from the University of Puerto Rico, I brought my automobile, which had Puerto Rican license plates. A number of people asked if the car had been driven from Puerto Rico! Other typical questions reveal a lack of knowledge concerning this significant group in our society. Mainland Americans have asked: "Aren't all Puerto Ricans dark-skinned?" "Does one need a passport to go there?" "You won't serve me that hot and spicy food, will you?"

Puerto Rico is an island in the Caribbean, about 1,050 miles from Miami and 1,650 miles from New York. The island is about 35 miles by 100 miles and has a population of over 2.8 million. Its population density is greater than that of China, Japan, or India. Puerto Ricans are all American citizens, proclaimed so by the Jones Act of 1917. The population is a mixture of Taino Indians, Africans, and Spaniards, although the Indian influence is much more cultural than biological, as conflicts with the Spaniards practically decimated that group. Skin colors range from as white as any Scandinavian to as black as the darkest African, with all shades and mixtures in between.

It is impossible in this article to clear up all the myths and misunderstandings about Puerto Rico and Puerto Ricans. Indeed, there is currently much study, debate, and conflict regarding many issues of Puerto Rico's culture, identity, and political future. (Readers will find relevant material cited in the list of suggested readings at the end of this article.) These larger issues will not be easily resolved, but the present reality concerning Puerto Ricans is crucial for today's educators and counselors. In order to perform in a helpful and ethical way in assisting clients to grow and make viable decisions, a counselor must recognize personal prejudices and erroneous assumptions.

The problem of understanding Puerto Ricans is confounded by the fact that today there are really two groups of Puerto Ricans. From a crowded island not overly endowed with natural resources beyond its people and its climate, thousands of Puerto Ricans have come to the mainland, especially in the period since World War II. Many have stayed. Scarcely a state is without any Puerto Ricans, and some places, such as New York City, Boston, Hartford (Connecticut), and several areas in New Jersey, have large numbers of Puerto Ricans. Many have raised families on the mainland, and these second- and third-generation Puerto Ricans are different in many significant ways from those who were raised on the island.

The mainland-raised Puerto Rican, sometimes called Neo-Rican, is generally English-dominant with respect to language. This Puerto Rican has adapted, as one might expect, to the unique environment of the urban setting but has retained a strong influence from and linkage to a primarily Latin American setting. Thus, having been brought up in another climate, with another language, with different fears and aspirations, and perhaps often with a different reference group, the mainland Puerto Rican is understandably different from the island Puerto Rican. Yet the culturally dominant group in the U.S. defines all Puerto Ricans in the same way, and the Neo-Rican often suffers from the same prejudices inflicted on the recent arrival from San Juan, Ponce, or Ciales.

In many ways, however, Puerto Ricans from the mainland and those from the island do share common cultural characteristics. As dangerous as generalizations can be, it is important for counselors to consider some of the qualities a Puerto Rican client might possess.

Cultural Characteristics

There are certain values and traits that are generally agreed on as being linked to the Puerto Rican ethos. Chief among these are *fatalismo, respeto, dignidad, machismo,* and *humanismo* (Hidalgo undated; Wagenheim 1970). Wells (1972) has added *afecto* to this list. (See the glossary at the end of this article for definitions of Spanish words used.) These cultural attributes are important to any group, and a wise counselor should have some understanding of them. The reader who has difficulty conceptualizing these terms may find it helpful to empathize with what the Puerto Rican experiences on entering an alien culture. The following explanations may help.

There is a certain amount of overlap in the words used above. *Dignidad* and *respeto,* which have to do with the dignity of an individual and respect for those deserving of it, are interrelated concepts. *Machismo,* generally connoting male superiority, is also part and parcel of the other cultural traits. Because these concepts are so central to the Puerto Rican as an individual and as a representative of a culture that is—at least politically—bound to this country, it is very important that the counselor understand how some of these attributes are translated into behaviors. The behaviors discussed apply in some degree to most Puerto Ricans, but in some instances they may be less typical of second-generation Puerto Ricans on the mainland.

Typically the Puerto Rican is highly individualistic, a person who is not used to working in concert with others, following in single file, and, in general, organizing in ways that Anglos would call "efficient." Whether in a traffic jam or a line of patrons in a bank, a Puerto Rican may break line and take a position ahead of others. But the Puerto Rican will also offer another person the same privilege, being much more tolerant than Anglos of this demonstration of individuality.

Another characteristic of Puerto Ricans is their demonstration of love and tolerance for children. It is rare that a baby or tot, taken down any street in Puerto Rico, is not exclaimed over, chucked under the chin, and generally complimented. This love for children is stronger than its stateside equivalent; generally speaking, in fact, the family unit is stronger among Puerto Ricans. Perhaps because of the love for children, illegitimacy is not frowned on or punished among Puerto Ricans. It is not unusual for families to add to their broods with nephews, nieces, godchildren, and even the children of husbands' alliances with mistresses. It is therefore difficult for the Puerto Rican arriving at a mainland school to understand all the fuss about different last names and shades of skin color and all the confusion about birth certificates among siblings.

The characteristic of gregariousness, a trait common to nearly all Puerto Ricans, often dismays many Americans, who view it as excessive when compared with their own culture. The existence of large families and extended families, the *compadrazgo* (godparent) relationship, and life on a crowded island are probably causes as well as effects of this gregariousness. Puerto Ricans love to talk, discuss, gossip, speculate, and relate. No one needs an excuse to have a fiesta. Music, food, and drink appear instantly if someone comes to visit. Group meetings, even those of the most serious nature, often take on some aspect of a social activity. I remember more than one dull and pedantic committee meeting at the University of Puerto Rico that was saved from being a total loss because refreshments and chatting were an inseparable part of the meetings. A colleague used to reinforce attendance at meetings in her office by furnishing lemon pie and coffee.

"Puerto Ricans are seldom found in professional or managerial jobs; they are usually working in low-paying, menial occupations, to an even greater degree than blacks."

Puerto Ricans' hospitality is related to their gregariousness. In the poorest home in a San Juan slum or in a remote mountain shack, a visitor will be offered what there is or what can be sent out for on the spot. And it is not good manners to refuse this hospitality; it is offered from the heart, and refusal is rejection. The visitor in this situation will give more by partaking of the hospitality than by bringing a gift.

As might be deduced from the preceding comments, Puerto Ricans are sensitive. Social intercourse has significant meaning, and Puerto Ricans typically are quite alert to responses they evoke in others and to others' behavior, even behavior of a casual nature. Often Puerto Ricans avoid a direct confrontation, and they do not like to give a straight-out no to anyone. Marqués (1967) is among those who have described Puerto Ricans as passively docile, and indeed docility is a noticeable Puerto Rican characteristic. Silén (1971), however, has interpreted this characteristic as actually having aggressive overtones, pointing out that historically this docility was simply a refusal to engage in battles that were impractical. Silén has also reminded us of some of the past and present revolutionary stirrings of the "docile" Puerto Rican. Whichever interpretation is accepted, there is evidence that there has been some change in this behavior, especially among younger Puerto Ricans on the island and those Puerto Ricans who have been raised on the mainland.

Puerto Ricans on the Mainland

For most readers of this article, the Puerto Rican living on the mainland is likely to be of greatest interest and relevance. There are approximately two million Puerto Ricans living in the U.S. They come to the mainland primarily for jobs. They generally do not intend to remain here and, as economic conditions for the family improve, increasingly return to the island. In recent years Puerto Rico has made some economic progress and some advances in creating jobs, and thus Puerto Ricans, who typically aspire to live in Puerto Rico, find it increasingly attractive to go back.

This return migration has created some economic, social, and educational problems for Puerto Rico. For example, when younger Puerto Ricans who have been raised in New York City or other areas return to the island, they face certain cultural assimilation problems not at all unlike those their parents faced when they came to the mainland. English-dominant young people must master Spanish for school, work, social life, and participation in family and civic affairs. These youngsters' modes of behavior are often in conflict with the attitudes and values of grandparents, uncles, and the general society. Some efforts are being made to deal with these conflicts, including the establishment of special classes given in English and even the employment of a bilingual counselor or two, but the island's resources are too limited to permit extensive help in this regard. It is fair to say, however, that the Puerto Rican returning to Puerto Rico is treated considerably better than the islander who comes to the U.S. mainland.

Puerto Ricans coming to the mainland often encounter prejudice. Part of this seems to be due to the fact that they are "foreign"; most Americans—even those whose parents were born in another country—are inclined to be cool, to say the least, toward people different from themselves.

"A person's name *is* that person, and a counselor's mispronouncing it—whether through carelessness or laziness—can easily be construed as the counselor's lack of interest in the client."

Certainly racism is another significant element in the prejudice against Puerto Ricans. Senior (1965) has reported:

> Census figures show that fewer non-white Puerto Ricans come to the States than whites, in comparison with their proportion of the population, and a special study indicates that a larger percentage of the non-whites return to their original homes after a sojourn on the mainland. (p. 46)

But problems for the Puerto Rican are not limited to prejudice. For those young people newly arrived in the States or born here of Puerto Rican parentage, the generation gap becomes compounded by what Senior has called "second-generationitis." These youngsters must contend not only with the expectancies and pressures of a different and dominant culture but also with conflicts of values representing two different cultures. Mainland Puerto Ricans may not be able to identify completely with the Puerto Rican culture, but neither are they a part of the dominant mainland culture. Social scientists often refer to this situation as the "identity crisis" of the Puerto Rican in the States.

As has been shown in the tragic treatment of blacks in the U.S., social and personal prejudice against a group is generally accompanied by a lack of economic opportunities for that group. Puerto Ricans are seldom found in professional or managerial jobs; they are usually working in low-paying, menial occupations, to an even greater degree than blacks. There are many causes for this. The low educational levels of Puerto Ricans on the mainland is undoubtedly a significant factor. Prejudice, suspicion, language difficulties, and the familiar self-fulfilling prophecy of low aspirations leading to lowly positions also play heavy roles in maintaining the Puerto Rican on the bottom rung of the economic and vocational ladder.

Practical Considerations for the Counselor

The following suggestions offered for counseling Puerto Ricans are based on my eleven years of experience as a counselor in Puerto Rico and on those human relations tenets to which all counselors presumably subscribe. The suggestions may seem simple and obvious to the reader; they are purposely so. They are intended as exhortations for those who are thoughtless, as reminders for those who forget, and as reinforcements for those who truly attempt to accept and understand their clients.

Examine your own prejudices. Counselors should consider their attitudes toward poor, rural, Spanish-speaking, racially mixed, culturally different clients. Knowledge alone cannot overcome prejudice, and an intellectual understanding expressed with emotional distaste will only serve to exacerbate the situation. If a counselor has negative stereotyped feelings about Puerto Ricans, it is not likely that his or her counseling relationships with them will be open and warm.

Call students by their right names. In Spanish, people are given two last names. The first last name is from the father's side of the family, the second from the mother's. The American custom is to look for the last word, and this becomes the last name. If this logic is followed with Latins, a student named Angel Rodríguez López gets called Angel López, thus dropping his father's family name. Not only might the father and son be understandably insulted by such cavalier treatment, but the boy's identity—in a real as well as a cultural sense—is in question. For those who fervently desire to maintain their cultural and personal identities without being antagonistic to the larger society, acknowledgment of the correct name can be critical.

Another element in this linguistic area is simply pronouncing names in reasonably accurate ways. Even though other students and staff may pronounce names inaccurately, it would seem that a counselor who espouses the establishment of good relationships might make a special effort in this area. A person's name *is* that person, and a counselor's mispronouncing it—whether through carelessness or laziness—can easily be construed as the counselor's lack of interest in the client. Counselors can check with a client about pronunciation. (Spanish, incidentally, is much more consistent in pronunciation than English, because each vowel is pronounced the same way in all words.)

Work with the family. For the Puerto Rican, the family is much more important than it is for the typical American. If possible, the counselor should deal not only with the young person but also with the family, getting to know them as well as the youngster. If this is not possible, the counselor can at least talk with the client about his or her family. Among Puerto Ricans, the family and extended family are often sought out for help more readily than is a counselor; research, in fact, indicates that the family is the source of greatest help (Christensen 1973). The counselor should realize that others are helping and should work with them, understanding that each person has something to offer. Ignoring this fact is equivalent to refusing to recognize that a client is also receiving help from another professional.

Refrain from using the child as an interpreter. In cases where a parent knows little English and the child is reasonably bilingual, it is a temptation to rely on the son or daughter to carry a message to the parent. This should be avoided whenever possible. Even though it might be a source of pride for the child, it might place the parent in a dependent position, preventing the parent from entering into the counseling relationship as a full partner. There is an additional concern: the possibility that the child might twist others' statements. Puerto Rican families are close, but a situation in which a parent continually communicates only through the child can alter relationships and create family strains.

Understand that to the Puerto Rican you are the foreigner. One cannot jump into instant relationships. The counselor must give the client time to know and trust him or her. To facilitate this, the counselor may need to meet the client outside of the school or the counselor's office. The counselor should share and be somewhat self-disclosing, revealing some things about his or her family, ideas, home, and so on, in order to give the client a chance to know the counselor as a person. Counselor self-disclosure can be a sign of trust for any client, but it is even more crucial where some feeling of "foreignness" is present in both counselor and client.

Understand the concept of "hijo de crianza." This term refers to someone other than the child's parents raising the child—either family members (such as an aunt or a grandmother), extended family members (such as a godparent), or even a friend or neighbor. It also may refer to a family's raising the father's children from another marriage or even from outside a legal union. Counselors must not apply their moral values in such situations. The child is the parents' child through love and acceptance, and exact relationships are not that important.

Be patient. This should be a given for all counselors with all clients, but it is especially true when counselors desire to establish any kind of relationship with clients from a different culture. Puerto Ricans have many obstacles to overcome, some of which are not of their own making. In the counseling relationship, counselors have to overcome some of these same hurdles. Counselors must demonstrate their credibility, honesty, and reliability, just as their Puerto Rican clients must do almost daily in an alien society. The difference is that the counselor is in a more advantageous position, and therefore the counselor's initiative is crucial. The Puerto Rican client may expect the counselor to be prejudiced, arrogant, and lacking in knowledge about Puerto Ricans. The burden is on the counselor to demonstrate that these expectations will not be fulfilled.

The Fruits of Labor

The counselor who works with Puerto Ricans of any age and in any setting may find some difficulty in doing so. But counselors who are willing to learn will find the effort rewarding. Puerto Rican clients need counselors as much as—or more than—other clients do. Moreover, in the final analysis, we Americans need them also. For they, along with all people of differing ethnic and cultural backgrounds, offer all of us a richness that even a wealthy country cannot afford to be without.

Glossary of Spanish Terms

afecto literally means "affect." Refers to the affective side of life—warmth and demonstrativeness.

compadrazgo refers to the relationship entered into when a person becomes a godfather (*padrino*) or godmother (*madrina*). This person then becomes a *compadre* or *comadre* with the parents of the child and traditionally not only takes on certain responsibilities for the child but also is closely related to the entire family of the other person. In some cases this may also involve even other *compadres,* and then the total relationships derived from this system of *compadrazgo* are complex and far-reaching and form the basis for what sociologists term the extended family, which is so characteristic of many societies.

dignidad dignity, but of special importance in Puerto Rico and closely related to *respeto.* One can oppose another person, but taking away a person's respect or dignity in front of others is about the worst thing one can do.

fatalismo fatalism.

humanismo humanism, especially as contrasted with the more pragmatic set of the typical Anglo.

machismo related to male superiority and, in its original form, implying the innate and biological inferiority of women. Characterized as an overcompensatory reaction to the dependence-aggression conflict, *machismo* is acted out through fighting and sexual conquest.

respeto signifies respect, especially respect for authority, family, and tradition.

References

Christensen, E.W. (Ed.) Report of the task force for the study of the guidance program of the Puerto Rican Department of Education, vocational and technical education area. San Juan, Puerto Rico: College Entrance Examination Board, 1973.

Hidalgo, H.A. The Puerto Rican. In National Rehabilitation Association (Ed.), *Ethnic differences influencing the delivery of rehabilitation services: The American Indian; the black American; the Mexican American; and the Puerto Rican.* Washington, D.C.: National Rehabilitation Association, undated.

Marqués, R. *Ensayos (1953-1966).* San Juan, Puerto Rico: Editorial Antillana, 1967.

Senior, C. *The Puerto Rican: Strangers—Then neighbors.* Chicago: Quadrangle Books, 1965.

Silén, J.A. *We, the Puerto Rican people: A story of oppression and resistance.* New York: Monthly Review Press, 1971.

Wagenheim, K. *Puerto Rico: A profile.* New York: Praeger, 1970.

Wells, H. *La modernización de Puerto Rico: Un analisis politico de valores e instituciones en proceso de cambio.* San Juan, Puerto Rico: Editorial Universitaria, 1972.

Suggested Readings

Adams, J.F. Population: A Puerto Rican catastrophe. Address delivered to the Puerto Rican League of Women Voters, Hato Rey, Puerto Rico, February 1972.

Cordasco, F., & Bucchions, E. *Puerto Rican children in mainland schools.* Metuchen, N.J.: The Scarecrow Press, 1968.

Espin, O.M., & Renner, R.R. Counseling: A new priority in Latin America. *Personnel and Guidance Journal,* 1974, *52*(5), 297-301.

Fernández Méndez, E. (Ed.) *Portrait of a society: Readings on Puerto Rican sociology.* San Juan, Puerto Rico: University of Puerto Rico Press, 1972.

Fitzpatrick, J.P. *Puerto Rican Americans: The meaning of migration to the mainland.* Englewood Cliffs, N.J.: Prentice-Hall, 1971.

14 Counseling Latinos

Ruiz, Rene A.
Padilla, Amado M.

Our purpose here is to provide background information and techniques that
will enable counselors to communicate more effectively and to counsel more
successfully with Latino clients. To achieve this, we have summarized
information that communicates the many ways in which Latino clients are
similar and dissimilar to other non-Latino clients. Deliberate effort is made to
identify resource documentation to provide interested counselors an
opportunity to explore contact areas in greater depth, if desired. This
summary material, which is designed to facilitate understanding of typical and
unique problems faced by Latinos, is organized around the following topical
outlines: (a) Demographic characteristics of the target population,
(b) Ethnohistory and culture, (c) Sources of psychological stress,
(d) Utilization of services, and (e) Factors reducing self-referral.

Following presentation of this introductory material, case histories of two
Latino clients appear. These were deliberately selected to illustrate points
made in preceding sections; but, in addition, they serve to facilitate the
presentation of specific recommendations for the counseling of Latino clients.
The case histories are followed by a concluding section presenting general
recommendations for counselors and the settings in which they function.

Demographic Characteristics of the Target Population

The term "Latino" is used in this article as a generic label including all
people of Spanish origin and descent. United States Bureau of the Census
reports (1971a, 1971b) indicate the existence of at least 9,000,000 Latino
residents in the United States. While this figure almost certainly
underestimates the current size of the Latino group, it appears adequate for
our purposes. Analyzing the Latino group by geographic area of origin, and
rounding by millions, population estimates as of 1972 are as follows: Central
and South America (0.5), Cuba (0.6), Mexico (5.0), Puerto Rico (1.5), and
other (1.5).

The census data further indicate that an absolute and relative majority of
Latinos are urban-dwellers; 82.5 percent compared with 67.8 percent for the

total population and 76 percent for Blacks. Furthermore, locus of residence and Latino subgroup membership are related. More specifically, Chicanos are heavily represented in the Southwest United States; 87 percent reside in Arizona, California, Colorado, New Mexico, and Texas. Most Puerto Ricans reside in either Connecticut, New Jersey, or New York (76%); while most immigrants from Cuba are situated in Florida.

In addition to being urban dwellers, disproportionately large numbers of Latinos are members of the lower income groups. The 1971 census reports that 2.4 million Latinos or 26.7 percent were classified as living ''in poverty.'' Closer examination of census data on personal and family income support the inference that the standard of living among Latinos is relatively lower than the general population. In 1970, for example, the median income for Latino males was $6,220 compared with $8,220 for non-Latino males. Examination of family income confirms the general trend; overrepresentation for Latinos in the lower income groups and underrepresentation in the higher income groups. More specifically, 23 percent of the families reported income of less than $5,000 a year compared with 14.7 percent of the general population; while only 18.4 percent had incomes greater than $15,000 compared with 35.5 percent of the general population. There is no reason to believe that this situation has improved from 1970 to 1976.

Difference in patterns of employment and unemployment between Latinos and the non-Latino population exist, and these are interpreted as representing additional stress for Latinos. With regard to status of employment, Latinos are overrepresented in occupations that are menial and low paying; for example, 76 percent are blue-collar workers. With regard to unemployment, a 1975 Bureau of Labor Statistics report indicates that during the third quarter of 1974 the unemployment rate among Latinos was 8 percent, which is intermediate between the national level (5%) and that among Blacks (10.5%). These data are somewhat deceptive, however, unless one considers the increase in unemployment during the preceding year was 29 percent among Latinos, compared with 22 percent among the general population and 8 percent among Blacks.

With respect to education the US census reports the following for Anglos, Black, and Latino males aged 25 years and older; median years of education: 12.2, 9.6, and 9.3 years; fewer than five years of schooling: 5.0, 13.5, and 19.5 percent; and, graduation from high school: 56.4, 34.7, and 32.6 percent. Thus, regardless of which of three educational criteria is examined, the inference remains unchanged. Latinos are provided the least education, compared with either the general population or to American blacks.

In conclusion, Latinos are, on the *average,* urban dwellers, poor and low paid, menially employed and fearful of layoffs, and undereducated relative to age peers who are not Latino. Factors such as these are unquestionably significant sources of stress in US society. It also follows that we would expect, because of increased stress, a relatively higher frequency of self-referrals for counseling and psychotherapy among Latinos. Keep this syllogism in mind while examining subsequent sections of this article.

Ethnohistory and Culture

Above, we presented demographic data that demonstrates how Latinos differ from the general population. Here we describe the Latino experience from a historical perspective as a means of documenting three major points. First, we maintain that Latinos may be thought of as members of a single cultural group in the sense they share historically similarities in language, values, and tradition. Second, we simultaneously maintain that this Latino culture group is highly heterogeneous, and that for some purposes, *should* be conceptualized as an aggregate of distinct subcultures, each possessing a recognizable pattern of unique traits. Third, we believe that information on ethnohistory and culture is important for non-Latino counselors who need to be able to differentiate between members of different Latino subcultures.

In terms of a commonsense example of relevance to our topic, we are arguing that a particular counseling program designed to deal with a specific type of problem might be highly successful with Chicanos, moderately successful with Cubans, and of only limited success with Puerto Ricans because of subcultural differences across groups.

The preceding argument is complex and subtle. What is involved is the identification of patterns of similarity among *individual* members of different subcultural groups, who are by definition unique in many aspects. The next step, of course, is to create "culturally relevant" programs of counseling and psychotherapy based on intragroup subculture similarities that achieve maximum success rates in constructive behavior change and personal growth. The interested reader is referred to Padilla and Ruiz (1973) and Padilla, Ruiz, and Alvarez (1975) for an analysis of culturally relevant counseling programs for Latinos.

Our ethnohistorical account begins with the Spanish explorers who arrived in the New World in the early 16th century, bringing with them a relatively homogeneous culture similar in language, values, tradition, and costume. In Mexico, they overthrew the Aztec empire, intermarried with the natives, and soon thereafter began to migrate north. The Rio Grande, or "Big River," current border between the United States and Mexico, was crossed in 1528. By the mid-16th century, settlements had been created in what today is Northern New Mexico. These original immigrants included Spaniards from Europe, native Americans from Mexico, and the *mestizo* or "mixed blood" progeny of these two groups.

These events contribute to our thesis in three ways. First, genetic merger resulted in the gradual creation of a new Indo-Hispanic culture. Second, Spaniards as well as the *mestizo* offspring sought new lands to explore and colonize. Third, the settlers who reached Northern New Mexico remained relatively isolated from Mexico and Spain, because of geographic distance and dilatory transportation. Later, they were outgrouped by the immigrants who came to call themselves the "Americans" of the United States. These Latinos came to refer to themselves as "Spanish-Americans," or Hispanos, and coincidentally were the first people of European or European-Indian stock to settle in what is present day United States.

This process of Spanish-Indian intermarriage and cultural fusion was occurring simultaneously in other parts of the New World. In some areas, native inhabitants were slain or driven off their land, and their cultures destroyed. Slaves from Africa were sometimes imported (Puerto Rico is a prime example) and the process of intermarriage and culture fusion continued for several hundred years. The net result, of course, was that a number of subculture groups were formed. The subgroups are commonly referred to as Latinos, or "the Latino culture," which blurs significant differences across groups. As our ethnohistorical analysis reveals, Latinos differ in genetic heritage as indicated by observable physical characteristics, and in cultural tradition (the relative extent to which a given subculture is based on influences from Europe, and the New World, or Africa.) Let's examine some of these differences more closely to learn how they can determine need for, and response to, counseling intervention.

Skin color is one obvious physical characteristic with a genetic link that differentiates Latino subgroups. The range in skin coloration is from "white," through *mestizo* and mulatto "brown," to African "black." Considering the long-standing prejudice in this country to people of color, it seems certain that darker Latinos experienced greater discrimination than lighter ones.

The types of subcultures formed were also influenced by original motivations for leaving their country of birth and migrating to a new country. Some Spaniards migrated for immediate personal gain with no thought of creating a new home. These people came to explore, colonize, exploit, and return. Others built new homes: they sought economic opportunity and personal liberty. Still others came because of interactions between complex social, political, economic, and personal factors. Today, Latinos have migrated to the United States in waves, to seek employment or to escape periods of civil strife in their country of origin.

Thus we can see that a large group of Latinos can be identified on the basis of shared characteristics: primarily, language, values, and tradition. Further, this large group includes a number of distinct subcultures that share these characteristics, but to varying degrees. This variation is attributable to the degree of acculturation among Latinos to the majority culture of the United States that is basically WASP and monolingual English. Here we will turn to an examination of acculturation because it bears directly upon the kinds of social stresses experienced by Latinos in the United States, which in turn is one factor that determines need for counseling.

One characteristic that determines rate of acculturation is fluency in English, yet the commitment to Spanish among Latinos is so strong that 50 percent report it as their "native tongue," and as their preferred "home language." What this means in effect is that unlike many other ethnic groups, Latinos overall have tenaciously held on to their Spanish language, despite the fact that English is the language of the school, work, and play.

Latinos also differ from mainstream Americans with regard to values (e.g., religious preference). The vast majority of Latinos profess Roman Catholicism, with only a relatively small percentage professing Protestant faiths. In contrast, the dominant religious preference of the majority culture is reversed; that is, more professed Protestants than Roman Catholics.

The characteristic of Latino tradition is extremely complex, and therefore more difficult to describe succinctly in terms of variation from the majority culture. The most prominent features, and those of greater significance for the counselor formulating programs based on cultural and subcultural differences, appear in the areas of family structure and attendant sex roles. The extended family structure is most common by far, but characteristically includes: (a) respect for the authority of a dominant father who rules the household; (b) unwavering love for the mother who serves a unifying function within the family; (c) formalized kinship relations such as the *compadrazgo* "godfather" system; and (d) loyalty to the family that takes precedence over other social institutions. In addition, sex roles are traditionally more rigid and demarcated more clearly, males are granted greater independence and at an earlier age than females, and there are greater expectations for achievement outside the home for males. Again, the reader is reminded these are summary statements; a more detailed analysis of family structure and sex-role behavior appears in Ruiz and Padilla (unpublished manuscript).

There exists an additional pattern of behavior, which seems to stem from family structure and sex role, which differentiates Latinos from non-Latinos. Latinos typically manifest *personalismo,* a term denoting a preference for personal contact and individualized attention in dealing with power structures, such as social institutions. Anglos, in contrast, seem to favor an organizational approach that follows impersonal regulations (the "chain of command"). Consistent with a preference for more personalized interaction is the observation of relatively more frequent physical contact among Latinos. For example, handshakes between acquaintances and *abrazos* (embraces) among friends are the norm upon meeting and leaving. The influence of *personalismo* appears early and is reflected in play. Mexican children are the most cooperative, Anglo the most competitive, and Mexican-American children are intermediate (Madsen & Shapira 1970). Of more immediate relevance to our thesis is the finding that Latino clients prefer to use first names rather than formal titles in centers dispensing counseling and psychotherapy services (Kline 1969).

Counselors interested in increasing their counseling skills by learning more about Latino culture will probably explore the social science literature.

This may prove to be hazardous, however, because this literature contains a certain degree of misinformation concerning the "true nature" of the Latino character. Unsupported "findings" based on single-study research, or subjective opinions presented in the context of unsubstantiated essays, seem to have been accepted by a segment of the scientific community. What may have occurred is that a certain degree of spurious "validity" has been created through constant repetition rather than through the gradual accumulation of validating research. Without casting aspersions on the motivation of persons creating or perpetuating such myths, it does seem as if the most widely disseminated and firmly held are pejorative in nature.

It has been alleged often, for example, that Latinos are fatalists (Heller 1967). The belief that Latinos adhere to predestination has been supported by a few studies showing, to use more technical language, higher "external reinforcement" scores on tests of "locus of control" (Lefcourt 1966; Rotter 1954, 1966). This finding disappears, however, when socioeconomic status is controlled (Stone & Ruiz 1974). Related to the myth of fatalism and belief in predestination is the idea that Latinos possess distorted attitudes toward time. Specifically, Latinos are presumably present time oriented, unduly emphasizing immediate gratification, and displaying underdeveloped skills in future planning. This tendency to enjoy the moment and to defer unpleasant responsibilities to some vague, indeterminate point in the future, seems widely accepted despite a dearth of supportive evidence. What may be occurring is that some non-Latinos translate common Latino responses such as mañana ("Tomorrow"), or *Lo que Dios desea* ("Whatever God wills"), into literal English equivalents. Any translation that ignores cultural and subcultural *values* runs the risk, of course, of communicating *meaning* inaccurately. It is at least conceivable that a Latino youngster who expends minimal effort in the pursuit of scholastic or academic goals is responding realistically to societal constraints based on discrimination and prejudice, rather than displaying any deficiency in "achievement motivation."

The last concept we explore to better acquaint counselors with the unique aspects of Latino clients is acculturation. Each Latino client, in addition to being a member of the greater Latino culture and some smaller Latino subculture, is simultaneously a member of the majority, Anglo culture to some degree. Degree of acculturation can be inferred from degree of commitment of cultural variables; that is, language values, tradition, diet, and costume. Thus, a Latino client who is monolingual Spanish or bilingual Spanish-English, with Spanish dominant: Roman Catholic; a member of an extended family; and who prefers ethnic food and dress is probably much less acculturated to the majority, Anglo culture of the United States than some other Latino client who is monolingual English, non-Catholic, from or in a nuclear family, and without preferences for the diet or clothing characteristic of his ethnic group. As we hope to show later, these variables of cultural preference and acculturation interact with the variable of *source of stress* to determine what type of counseling approach will be maximally successful with a given Latino client. It now seems appropriate to examine sources of stress for Latino clients.

Sources of Stress

In this section, we differentiate between *intrapsychic* and *extrapsychic* sources of stress. We use the former term (intrapsychic) to identify problems of a personal or individual nature that arise independent of ethnic minority group membership. We propose—although empirical evidence corroborating this supposition has not yet been collected—that Latino clients experiencing intrapsychic stress will respond similarly, if not exactly, as will non-Latino clients experiencing the same stress. For example, if a young person is graduating from high school, uncertain as to whether to attend college or which major to pursue, it probably makes relatively little difference whether this student is Latino or not. Regardless of ethnicity, a young person in such a dilemma would probably complain about feelings of uncertainty, indecision, insecurity, personal inadequacy, and general apprehension concerning his or her own, and familial expectations. Finally, ethnicity would probably have relatively little influence upon the type of counseling approach designed to help such a client formulate and achieve more compatible life goals with less personal discomfort.

We have reserved the term *extra psychic* to refer to sources of stress that stem from outside the person and that are basically societal or environmental rather than personal. Our interest, of course, lies with extrapsychic stress associated with ethnic minority group membership. Thus, we focus upon prejudices against Latinos and the effect of discriminatory practices upon character formation, personality function, and coping. We have already documented earlier, for example, that Latinos are victims of the "poverty cycle": depressed personal and family incomes, fewer years of education, overrepresentation in menial occupations, and elevated rates of unemployment. This cycle is self-perpetuating because the victims are less able to subsidize their own education, those of their children, or to qualify for better, higher paying employment. Furthermore, in comparison with other ethnic groups, Latino students possess fewer "role models" to imitate who have achieved success through continued education or training. Other stressful consequences of poverty include decreased social status, inadequate health care and nutrition, and a generally reduced quality of life.

This discussion suggests that the counselor may anticipate three "types" of Latino clients with regard to the sources of stress that motivate self-referral for counseling. Some will complain of intrapsychic stress and present problems similar to those of non-Latino clients. Others will be experiencing extrapsychic stress and will appear similar to other clients who are victims of prejudice and discrimination. But most Latino clients will probably seek counseling for problems stemming from both sources of stress. In any event, this analysis suggests that rates of self-referral for counseling and psychotherapy are expected to be elevated relative to the general population. Now let's examine relevant data to determine the accuracy of this prediction.

Utilization of Services

Available utilization data of public mental health service facilities indicates that Latinos, contrary to expectations, and despite *greater* stress, refer themselves *less* often for counseling and psychotherapy, relative to the general population (for review see Padilla & Ruiz 1973; Padilla et al. 1975; Ruiz, Padilla & Alvarez, in press). The most recent survey of utilization of state and county mental hospitals across the nation (Bachrach 1975) reveals the following: (a) the age-adjusted rate of admission for Latinos is 155 per 100,000 population, compared with 181 for other white and 334 for non-whites, (b) age-adjusted rate of admission rates are approximately double for Latino males compared with Latino females (212 to 103 per 100,000 population), and (c) adjusting for relative differences in the sizes of ethnic groups, Latino admissions are highest among the youngest (ages 14-25 years), and oldest (age 65 years and older).

Moving from the national scene and turning to geographic areas impacted with Mexican Americans, underutilization of counseling and psychotherapy continues. It has been estimated by Karno and Edgerton (1969) that Mexican Americans made up between 9 to 10 percent of California's population from 1962 to 1968. During this period, the percentages of Mexican Americans admitted for treatment in California facilities were as follows: 2.2 percent to the state hospital system, 3.4 percent to state mental hygiene clinics, 10.9 percent to the neuropsychiatric institute, and 2.3 percent to state and local facilities. The resident in-patient population was 3.8 percent. A similar pattern of underutilization of private and public mental hospitals by Mexican Americans has been found in Texas (Jaco 1960). Of even greater direct relevance are findings reported in an unpublished manuscript by Perez (1975) of significant underutilization of university counseling services by Chicano students.

Factors Reducing Self-Referral

Discouraging institutional policies may be largely responsible for the underutilization of counseling and psychotherapeutic services by Latinos. A sufficiently large body of literature describe counseling services as "inappropriate" or "irrelevant" in meeting the needs of the Latino community. All too frequently, services are provided in agencies or centers situated at unrealistic geographic distances from the residences of the target population. Further, it is obvious that monolingual Spanish, or bilingual Spanish-English clients, cannot be served adequately by monolingual English speaking professionals. Yet, this is precisely the situation at a number of treatment centers as described by Torrey (1972), Edgerton and Karno (1971), and Karno and Edgerton (1969). Other authors (Abad et al. 1974: Kline 1969; Torrey 1972; Yamamoto et al. 1968) have theorized that the process of counseling will be retarded when clients and counselors are members of different socioeconomic class groups or possess different sets of cultural values.

Elsewhere, (Padilla & Ruiz 1973; Padilla et al. 1975; Ruiz et al., in press), we have summarized arguments by others suggesting that Latinos refer themselves less often because of factors such as "pride" or some hypothetical characteristic of Latino culture that somehow functions to reduce the destructive effects of stress. Typical "stress resistant" factors have included the extended family, religious belief, and recourse to *curanderos* or "faith healers." In general, we have rejected these unsupported speculations, and have argued instead that Latinos have rejected traditional counseling services because of discouraging institutional practices, linguistic problems, and culture-class differences that retard communication. It now seems appropriate to review case histories—and to share our recommendations—as a means of showing how the sensitive counselor can create culturally relevant counseling programs that are specific to his Latino clients and that are more valid.

Case Histories

Here, we present case histories from Latino clients seeking counseling. We exercise our ethical responsibility to preserve confidentiality by minimizing identifying information. Nevertheless, these are "real," albeit disguised cases. Furthermore, we have fictionalized certain elements, as you shall see, to communicate theoretical points more lucidly. Even though both clients are "alike" because they are Latinos, we strongly advise the counselor to remain alert to individual differences based upon subculture group membership (such as Chicano versus Cuban), sources of stress (intrapsychic versus extrapsychic), and degree of acculturation (that is, relative degree of commitment to the majority group versus the subculture group). We propose that these are the variables of major significance in designing valid counseling programs for culturally different clients.

Case 1: Maria. This client identifies herself as "Spanish-American." Her ancestors have resided in Northern New Mexico under conditions of relative sociocultural isolation for generations. She is fluent in both Spanish and English, but her Spanish retains regional archaicisms unfamiliar to other Latinos and her English is slightly accented. Her politics are conservative, she was educated in a Roman Catholic school system, is committed to the dicta of her faith, and was reared in the large extended family structure that is traditional in that region.

Maria's life adjustment was uneventful until she left home for the first time and enrolled in a California college. There she was shocked by her encounters with Chicanos and Chicanas who were personally assertive, less inhibited in personal decorum, and more liberal politically. She could not deal with the rejection and disdain she experienced when she identified herself as "Spanish," rather than Chicana. This is her opening statement when she sought counseling.

> Moving away from home had a great psychological impact on me and my ideals. I had some difficulty adjusting myself to a completely new and independent form of life. Being Spanish-American, I was always closely bound to the family. When I tried to deviate from the norm, I was reprimanded and reminded of the obligation I had to the family. Living away from home taught me to appreciate them (family) and their conservative values more than I had before . . .but we sure are different from the people in California!

The brief history and presenting complaint identify Maria as a Latina whose subcultural identification is Hispano. Our comments on Latino ethnohistory, as well as the clients own opening comments, confirm the contention of differences across Latino subculture groups. Maria voices awareness that she is "different from the people (Chicanos) in California!" and we agree. Furthermore, we argue that Maria would become aware of other subculture group differences if her encounter had been with Puerto Ricans (or Cubans, or other Latinos), rather than California Chicanos.

With regard to degree of acculturation, Maria seems basically bicultural. Available history indicates she is a bilingual who is equally familiar with the values and traditions of both the majority culture and the Latino culture. Examining her personal value system stemming from identification with her Hispano subculture, she seems less assimilated into the Chicano subculture attending California colleges, than to the majority culture in some ways! This is an important point, expanded further in our discussion of sources of stress and recommendations for counseling.

Examining intrapsychic sources of stress first, Maria's major problem seems to be she is a college freshman away from home for the first time. Like other young people in a similar situation (regardless of ethnicity), Maria is almost certainly homesick and lonely. She probably misses friends, relatives, and familiar places. Her opening statement refers to problems in "adjusting." Her ability to tolerate and lessen distress is lowered because of her absence from familiar support systems (home, family, and church), while in a new, taxing, demanding, different, and frightening environment. At a less obvious level of analysis, there are hints that Maria is experiencing an identity crisis. She is clearly uncertain of subculture group identification as reflected by questions such as, "Am I Spanish as we call ourselves within the family, or Chicana as my new friends insist?" Maria has noted that fellow students are more assertive, striving, and goal-oriented; now she is beginning to wonder if perhaps she would get more of what she wanted out of life if she were less passive. For example, feminism and the Chicano movement intrigue Maria, but the people involved seem "pushy" to her in many ways. And at a more personal and intimate level, Maria is beginning to question her traditional conservatism and her decorous sexual mores.

With regard to extrapsychic sources of stress, Maria denies any major hassles with the dominant culture. While she is subjected to the same general level of prejudice and discrimination that other Latinos are, it seems neither personal or excessive at this time. Note, however, the anomalous situation with regard to her treatment by Chicanos and Chicanas. The Chicano student community rejects Maria because her self-designated "Spanishness" is misperceived as an attempt to deny her "Mexicanness."

How does the counselor respond to this complex of problems, and in what priority? We shall outline a culturally relevant treatment program but encourage the reader to anticipate our recommendations and to amplify upon them as he or she goes along. First, it seems to us the problem of priority is Maria's sense of personal isolation. We would recommend a supportive approach to minimize this intrapsychic source of stress. Although unstated, Maria is almost certainly experiencing dysphoric affect, probably depression ranging somewhere between mild to moderate degrees of severity. An initial approach that works well with problems of this sort is to minimize any tendencies toward apathy and social withdrawal by encouraging interpersonal interaction. Specifically, Maria, like any young person with depressive tendencies, should be encouraged to date, to go to parties, to mix with people her own age and so on. Simultaneously, Maria's major assets should be identified and reflected back to her, repeatedly, if necessary to enhance self-esteem. For example, if she is doing well academically she should be reminded of her intellectual assets: her bright mind, her good study habits, her perseverance, and so on. This supportive approach of confronting Maria with positive aspects of her life adjustment will tend to retard movement in the direction of increased depression.

A problem of second-order priority for Maria is her estrangement from the local Chicano student community. This is particularly lamentable for Maria because this group represents a "natural" but underutilized resource to combat what has been termed Maria's "first problem": her combined sense of low self-esteem, loneliness, mild depression, and isolation. Maria is a Chicana in more ways than she is not; and mutual realization of this aspect of her identity will facilitate Maria's admission into the Chicano group; in turn, it can provide her with much needed emotional support.

One reason Maria and the Chicano group have failed to achieve harmonious rapprochement may be a mutual misjudgment of how each perceives the other. It is conceivable that Maria is unaware that Chicanos perceive Mexican Americans who call themselves "Spanish" as denying their heritage; and some of the Chicanos may not know that Mexican Americans from Northern New Mexico refer to themselves in that manner with no connotation of deliberate efforts to "pass" from one ethnic group to another. Reconciliation may be achieved if both parties become more familiar with their own ethnohistory. While this goal could be attained by the counselor bringing this issue to the attention of the ethnic studies department, if one exists, and having them plan a course or lecture on ethnohistory, we propose an alternative course. We recommend Maria be informed of the possible source of the mutual misunderstanding discussed here, and that she be encouraged to confront those Chicanos who have been scornful. This approach has several advantages: Maria will be required to become more assertive; her approach behavior toward others will counteract her withdrawal tendencies; and everyone involved examines the problem from a fresh perspective.

The third problem for Maria is her blurred, changing, and developing sense of personal identity. She seems to be going through a psychological growth phase that involves questioning life values, but this process is evaluated by us as "normal" or "healthy" (Wrenn & Ruiz 1970). She is not exactly certain "who she is" as yet, but continued self-exploration should be encouraged by her counselor because enhanced self-awareness will minimize subjective discomfort and expedite self-actualization. The counselor maintains the responsibility, of course, for determining whether this third general recommendation is appropriate for Maria; and if so, of selecting the techniques and methods thought to be maximally growth-inducing for this client.

Case 2: Antonio. Like Maria, Antonio is bicultural and bilingual. Unlike Maria, however, he is a native Californian Chicano, he only attends college parttime, and he is a committed activist politically. In fact, Antonio attends so many Chicano meetings that his grades are suffering and his employers have chided him for his absenteeism and tardiness. Let's examine part of his opening statement during an initial interview to get a stronger sense of what he is like as a person.

> Because of Mexican American descent my parents wish to see their son attend a college or university and further the Chicano cause. We speak Spanish frequently at home and maintain the Mexican heritage. We are a proud family—of our home, community, and heritage...I wish to become something proud, an example to my thousands of little brothers and sisters in the barrios across the nation.

In a subsequent session, Antonio complained of oppression by local police due to their alleged prejudice against La Raza. When pressed for details, Antonio reported this pattern: he would visit one of the elementary school playgrounds in the neighborhood, introduce himself to small groups of children at play, and begin to instruct his "little brothers and sisters" in Chicano culture. Parents or school officials would contact the police, who would come to investigate "loitering" by a grown man in his late twenties. Antonio also complained of snide remarks made by various officers to the effect that he should shorten his hair length and stop wearing a decorated leather headband ("He looks like a damned Indian in a John Wayne movie.").

Here we present the same type of analysis as with Maria, but we can be more succinct because our theoretical approach is familiar by now. In terms of cultural group membership, Antonio is self-identified as "Chicano," and we concur with his opinion. He fails to recognize, however, the degree to which he is acculturated into the majority culture. Despite his Chicanismo, for example, his unaccented English is fluent and he is already far beyond the average Chicano in terms of number of years of education and potential employment and earning power.

The discrimination between intrapsychic and extrapsychic sources of stress becomes especially difficult when the two are conmingled, as with Antonio. Regardless of source of stress we can be fairly certain he is uncomfortable since he referred himself for counseling. His complaint that "people just don't understand" (elicited in a later part of the first meeting), can be interpreted in at least two ways. He may feel he may try harder to communicate more effectively. That is, he may believe major change must come from within. This is a classic example, of course, of motivation for personal change based on intrapsychic stress. On the other hand, Antonio may believe "he's O.K.," but that society is "not O.K." (Harris 1973). In such a case, he would experience stress as extrapsychic: that is, he would identify the source of his discomfort as environmental, rather than personal.

The first step in formulating a counseling program for Antonio is to render an opinion concerning the accuracy of his reporting and the quality of his judgment. To state the proposition as bluntly as possible, we are recommending that the counselor deal immediately with the question of whether or not Antonio is distorting reality. One needs to know, to use Antonio's polemic rhetoric, whether he is a hapless victim of "police oppression" as he claims, or, which is equally possible given the sparse information provided here, whether his relations with figures of authority are essentially "paranoid."

The answer to this question is important, because it tells us whether stress is mainly internal or external. This information can be used to create treatment programs of maximum relevance and efficacy. If it turns out that Antonio is psychotic and is imagining or exaggerating police intervention, then the counselor may respond with immediate support, seek psychiatric consultation concerning the need for ataractic medication or institutionalization, and begin preparing for whatever intervention model has the greatest probability for change in the direction of less inappropriate behavior. With regard to this latter point, we are referring to preferred modes of therapeutic theory and technique, such as, nondirective counseling versus psychoanalytic psychotherapy, reflection versus free association, and so on. If on the other hand, Antonio is not psychotic and is reporting accurately, then a much different approach is called for. Before describing a counseling program for Antonio based upon the opinion he is neither psychotic nor paranoid, but is reporting discrimination accurately, we discuss how such an opinion might be reached.

At the risk of appearing melodramatic, we ask the reader to examine his or her own biases concerning relations between ethnic minority group people and organized power structures such as civic agencies, government bureaucracies, or the police. This exercise in introspection bears upon points that follow and may be illuminating, particularly if the reader has given relatively little thought to the issue.

Our first point concerning this issue is that preconceptions and prejudices are dangerous since they obscure critical judgment. The skilled and responsible counselor responds to the needs of the client, not to idiosyncratic prejudgments. Regardless of whether your exercise in introspection revealed a "conservative" or "liberal" perception of relations between police and ethnics, it is a fact that some police, in some locales, at some times, do harass ethnics. It is equally true that some ethnics develop paranoid reactions of psychotic proportions and that imaginary police harassment is sometimes incorporated into a delusional system. Thus when ethnic clients report harassment, it is especially crucial that counselors avoid prejudgment and evaluate each report on its own merits.

In cases such as Antonio's, the accuracy of reporting of interaction with the police can be evaluated in several ways. If Antonio presents additional material for discussion that is unbelievable; for example, religious delusions, then it is more likely (but not absolutely certain) that his description of interactions with the police are equally distorted. His veracity can also be evaluated through the use of informants; for example, contacts with family members, friends, fellow employees, and so on. It goes without saying, of course, that evidence of previous delusional periods—whether reported by informants or documented by official records—tends to discredit current reporting. Psychological assessment devices, including tests and interviews, can help determine current personality functioning, but they may be of questionable validity when used by professionals with only superficial understanding of the client's culture (Padilla & Ruiz 1975).

The issue of Antonio's questionable judgment permeates the area of interpersonal relations. He appears relatively insensitive to the impact of certain aspects of his behavior and appearance upon others. Specifically, almost any stranger approaching unknown children on a playground will arouse suspicion. This seems especially true if the stranger is dressed in a manner that a more conservative school administrator or police would perceive as unusual or exotic. We are not recommending that counselors assume the function of sartorial consultants; but from what we know of Antonio, it appears he would benefit from some dispassionate and disinterested feedback concerning how he affects other people.

Little is known of Antonio's social life outside of his involvement with the Chicano movement. Regardless of ethnicity of client, many counselors would explore with a client his age-related peer interactions, his marital status, marriage plans, dating behavior, and heterosexual interest. Because Antonio is a member of a cultural group with a tradition of close family ties, and because he verbalizes the importance of family life, he would also recommend exploration of relevant experiences. Where does Antonio reside? Who does he live with? What is the extent of his interactions with related family members. Answers to questions about social and family life will help counselors determine whether or not Antonio experiences problems in these areas.

One final comment about Antonio. He states he wants a college degree, and even works part-time to subsidize his education, but his performance at school and on the job is marginal. We are *not* arguing that everyone must adhere to the so-called "Protestant ethic" by formulating life goals and by striving arduously to achieve them. Antonio has formulated life goals all right; he wants a college degree to further the cause of the Chicano movement. His goal-oriented behavior is so inefficient, however, that both goals are in jeopardy. Most people, Antonio included, would experience anxiety and frustration in such a life situation. Our recommendation for Antonio is that these aspects of his life be explored more closely with him. He may elect to reorder the priorities of his life, he may choose to modify his life schedule, or he may do both. But he must change something in order to reduce frustration, to achieve a more satisfying life adjustment, and to become more efficient in getting what he wants out of life.

Conclusion

Here we present general principles that can be applied in formulating more culturally relevant counseling programs for Latinos. For instance, the counselor knowledgeable of the importance of *personalismo* among Latinos may wish to greet Latino clients as soon as they arrive at the agency, even if it requires brief interruption of an ongoing session. A counselor sensitive to the Latino culture will immediately extend his hand and introduce himself, including first name rather than formal title. So-called small talk at this initial meeting, and at the beginning of subsequent sessions, is believed to be very important with Latino clients to establish and maintain rapport. Because of possible differences in the perception of time, we urge counselors to make an appointment to meet with the prospective client immediately, and to schedule that meeting as soon as possible, preferably that same morning, afternoon, or evening. As we have indicated earlier, cultural differences in temporal perspective are not perceived by us as pathological procrastination. We have argued elsewhere (Padilla et al. 1975) that Latinos *tend* to perceive psychological problems as more similar to physical problems than do non-Latinos. Thus nondirective approaches, requests for reviews of childhood history, or instructions to introspect should be used judiciously. In general, many Latino clients may have preconceptions of counseling interviews and sessions based on an analogue of a medical examination. Thus, they may anticipate a more active approach from the counselor; for example, inquiry that is goal-oriented and leading to concrete solutions for identified problems.

The higher frequency of extended family structure and the greater importance of family interaction in the daily lives of most Latinos indicate that family and other group approaches should be used more often.

Family-oriented therapies would probably yield higher success rates among Latinos than among non-Latinos regardless of whether the problem is intrapsychic or extrapsychic. It is important to keep in mind, however, that sex roles are more rigidly defined, sons have more and earlier independence, fathers have more prestige and authority, and the aged receive more respect. Such knowledge can be exploited to shape more valid counseling intervention. Thus the culturally sensitive counselor will not impute unconscious incestuous desire to a Latino father who expresses sharp interest in his daughter's suitors; nor would such a counselor misperceive the Latino daughter who tolerated such supervision as immature, unduly submissive, or pathologically compliant. Therapeutic responses based on an understanding, rather than a misinterpretation, of the meaning of certain behaviors within a given cultural context will obviously be more effective. Furthermore, familial interdependence, for example, married sons visiting their parents frequently, does not carry the connotation of pathological dependency such behavior might imply in other cultures.

These recommendations for culturally relevant counseling programs are meaningless unless Latinos can be motivated to refer themselves with greater frequency. To achieve this end, the centers and agencies that offer counseling services will have to be modified. Again, we summarize here recommendations presented in greater detail elsewhere (Padilla & Ruiz 1973; Padilla et al. 1975; Ruiz et al., in press).

First, we advocate that counseling centers emphasize a "business model" approach, and aggressively pursue clientele for their services. For example, one might begin with a local needs assessment program, simultaneously contacting and involving community people in planning, training, administration, and delivery of services. Once community needs have been identified and the relevant service programs established, it is time to advertise the availability of services. A multimedia approach in both English and Spanish would probably reach the largest number of Latinos. Second, new services are needed to deal with the Latino pattern of extrapsychic problems that make Latino clients different from non-Latino clients. Counseling centers could and should offer innovative services for Latinos such as these: written and oral translation contact with government agencies, building skill in obtaining employment and securing promotions, remedial education, and some type of course work teaching rights, responsibilities and privileges of a politico-legal nature. One example of the course work indicated in the final recommendation would be an educational experience teaching the structure of government, the effectiveness of political coalition, voting, and the impact of legislation on equal opportunity and affirmative action.

The third general recommendation for agency change concerns staffing. Our interpretation of the literature is that Latino clients will obtain maximum benefit from counselors knowledgeable with Latino ethnohistory and culture. To be effective, the counselors must "speak the language" of the client, both literally and figuratively. The number of Latino professionals already available is infinitesimally small (Ruiz 1970), and the disproportionately small number of Latinos enrolled in baccalaureate or doctoral programs (El-Khawas & Kinzer 1974) indicates underrepresentation of Latinos in the professions is going to continue in the foreseeable future. The short-range solution to this problem is two-fold; teach Spanish and Latino culture to non-Latino counselors, and teach counseling skills to Latinos at the paraprofessional level.

The fourth recommendation has been implied but is now made explicit. To become successful in delivering counseling services to the Latino community, agencies offering services must first gain the confidence and support of prospective clients. To accomplish this end, members of the community must infiltrate the agency at all levels of administration, be active in policy change and decision making, and be involved as teachers or students in the educational programs described earlier. To convince community people the agency is truly theirs, and therefore for their benefit, it would probably be wise to encourage the use of agency facilities for community events. In this context, the agency might celebrate Latino holidays in some appropriate way in addition to occasionally offering programs in the arts and humanities that would interest and attract potential users of available services. Consistent with our statements on the "business model," programs attracting participants represent excellent opportunities to inform people of agency activities. Latinos come to participate in a cultural program sponsored by the centers but simultaneously receive information via a brochure or brief announcement of the services offered by the agency.

(The preparation of this article was supported in part by Research Grant MH 24854 from the National Institute of Mental Health to the Spanish Speaking Mental Health Research Center at the University of California, Los Angeles.)

References

Abad, V.; Ramos, J.; and Boyce, E. A model for delivery of mental health services to Spanish-speaking minorities. *American Journal of Orthopsychiatry,* 1974, *44,* 584-595.

Bachrach, L.L. *Utilization of state and county mental hospitals by Spanish Americans in 1972.* Statistical Note 116. DHEW Publication No. (ADM), 1975, 75-158.

Edgerton, R.B., and Karno, M. Mexican American bilingualism and the perception of mental illness. *Archives of General Psychiatry,* 1971, *24,* 286-290.

El-Khawas, E.H. and Kinzer, J.L. Enrollment of minority graduate students at PhD granting institutions. *Higher Education Panel Reports.* Number 19, August, 1974.

Harris, T.A. *I'm OK—You're OK.* New York: Avon, 1973.

Heller, C. *Mexican-American Youth.* New York: Random House, 1967.

Jaco, E.G. *The social epidemiology of mental disorders: A psychiatric survey of Texas.* New York: Russell Sage Foundation, 1960.

Karno, M., and Edgerton, R.B. Perception of mental illness in a Mexican American community. *Archives of General Psychiatry*, 1969, *20*, 233-238.

Kline, L.Y. Some factors in the psychiatric treatment of Spanish Americans. *American Journal of Psychiatry*, 1969, *125*, 1674-1681.

Lefcourt, H.M. Internal versus external control of reinforcement. *Psychological Bulletin*, 1966, *65*, 206-220.

Madsen, M.C. and Shapira, A. Cooperative and competitive behavior of urban Afro-American, Anglo-American, Mexican-American, and Mexican village children. *Developmental Psychology*, 1970, *3*, 16-20.

Padilla, A.M. and Ruiz, R.A. *Latino Mental Health*. Washington, D.C.: U.S. Superintendent of Documents, 1973.

Padilla, A.M. and Ruiz, R.A. Personality assessment and test interpretation of Mexican Americans: A critique. *Journal of Personality Assessment*, 1975, *39*, 103-109.

Padilla, A.M.; Ruiz, R.A.; and Alvarez, R. Community mental health services for the Spanish-speaking/surnamed population. *American Psychologist*, 1975, *30*, 892-905.

Perez, M.S. Counseling services at UCSC: Attitudes and perspectives of Chicano students. Unpublished manuscript, 1975.

Rotter, J.B. *Social Learning and Clinical Psychology*. Englewood Cliffs, N.J.: Prentice-Hall, 1954.

Rotter, J.B. Generalized expectancies for internal versus external control of reinforcement. *Psychological Monographs*, 1966, *80*, 1-28.

Ruiz, R.A. Relative frequency of Americans with Spanish surnames in associations of psychology, psychiatry, and sociology. *American Psychologist*, 1971, *26*, 1022-1024.

Ruiz, R.A. and Padilla, A.M. Chicano psychology: The family and the *macho*. Unpublished manuscript, 1973.

Ruiz, R.A.; Padilla, A.M.; and Alvarez, R. Issues in the counseling of Spanish-speaking/surnamed clients: Recommendations for therapeutic services. In L. Benjamin (Ed.). *Counseling Minority Students*, in press.

Stone, P.C. and Ruiz, R.A. Race and class as differential determinants of underachievement and underaspiration among Mexican Americans. *Journal of Educational Research*, 1974, *68*, 99-101.

Torrey, E.F. *The mind game: Witchdoctors and psychiatrists*. New York: Emerson Hall, 1972.

U.S. Bureau of the Census. Persons of Spanish origin in the United States: November 1969. In *Current population reports* (Series P-20. No. 213). Washington, D.C.: U.S. Government Printing Office, 1971 (a).

U.S. Bureau of the Census. Selected characteristics of persons and families of Mexican, Puerto Rican, and other Spanish origin: March 1971. In *Current population reports* (Series P-20, No. 224). Washington, D.C.: U.S. Government Printing, 1971 (b).

Wrenn, R.L. and Ruiz, R.A. *The normal personality: Issues to insight*. Monterey, Calif.: Brooks/Cole, 1970.

Yamamoto, J.; James, Q.C.; and Palley, N. Cultural problems in psychiatric therapy. *Archives of General Psychiatry*, 1968, *19*, 45-49.

Selected Readings

Acosta, F.X. & Sheehan, J.G. Preferences toward Mexican American and Anglo American Psychotherapists. *Journal of Consulting and Clinical Psychology,* 1976, *44,* 272-279.

Christensen, E.W. When counseling Puerto Ricans...*Personnel and Guidance Journal,* 1977, *55,* 412-415.

Cross, W.C. & Maldonado, B. The counselor, the Mexican American, and the stereotype. *Elementary School Guidance and Counseling,* 1971, *6,* 27-31.

Edgerton, R.B. & Karno, M. Mexican-American bilingualism and the perception of mental illness. *Arch. Gen. Psychiat.,* 1971, *24,* 286-290.

Karno, M. & Edgerton, R. Perception of mental illness in a Mexican American community. *Archives of General Psychiatry,* 1969, *20,* 233-238.

Maes, W.R. & Rinaldi, J.R. Counseling the Chicano child. *Elementary School Guidance and Counseling,* 1974, *8,* 279-284.

Medina, C. & Reyes, M.R. Dilemmas of Chicano counselors. *Social Work,* 1976, *21,* 515-517.

Oragon, J.A. & Wibarri, S.R. Learn Amigo learn. *Personnel and Guidance Journal,* 1971, *50,* 87-89.

Padilla, A.M.; Ruiz, R.A.; & Alveraz, R. Community mental health services for the Spanish-speaking/surnamed population. *American Psychologist,* Sept., 1975, 892-905.

Palomares, U.H. Nuestros sentimientos son iguales, la diferencia es en la experiencia. *Personnel and Guidance Journal,* 1971, *50* (2), 137-144.

Ruiz, A.S. Chicano group catalysts. *Personnel and Guidance Journal,* 1975 *53,* 462-466.

The Latino Client
Cases and Questions

1. Assume you are a counselor at a large state university that has publicly stated support for all its federally mandated affirmative action programs. Recently, however, the Sociology Department's graduate admission procedure has been under fire by the campus newspaper for its practice of reserving twenty percent of its new admissions for Chicano students (the state in which the school is located is composed of 20% Chicanos).

   a. How do you feel about the selection procedure described?
   b. What action would you take in view of your feelings?
   c. What impact would you expect this to have on your ability to relate to Chicano students?

2. Assume you are a counselor in a state run rehabilitation agency. A Puerto Rican paraplegic enters your office looking very sullen and begins to question your ability to help her. She points out that you can not possibly understand her problems since you are not encumbered, as she is, by the forces of multiple oppression.

   a. How will you respond to her charges?
   b. What doubts do you have about your ability to work with this client?
   c. What are some of the cultural factors to which you need to be sensitive in working with this client?

3. Assume you are a counselor in an urban elementary school with a student enrollment that is 60% Anglo, 40% Chicano. Several physical confrontations have occurred in the school cafeteria recently, apparently the result of insult trading between Anglos and Chicanos over "Mex" and "Gringo" food. The school principal has asked you to work with some of the students involved.

   a. How do you plan to work (what is your role) with these students?
   b. Do you anticipate any difficulty in establishing a relationship with either the Anglo or Chicano students? How will you deal with the difficulty?
   c. What community resources might you want to tap in dealing with this problem?

Part 6 **Implica-
tions for
Minority
Group/
Cross-
Cultural
Counseling**

15 Proposed Minority Identity Development Model

It is clear from the readings provided in sections 2 through 5 that at least for the four racial/ethnic minorities discussed in this volume, each minority group has a unique cultural heritage which makes it distinct from other groups. Cultural distinction, however, has often been erroneously interpreted as evidence of cultural conformity and has frequently led to a monolithic view of minority group attitudes and behaviors. Clearly, uniformity of attitudes and behaviors is no more true for minority individuals than it is for members of the dominant culture. With regard to the very issue of cultural distinction, minority attitudes may vary from desire for total assimilation into the dominant culture to total rejection of the dominant culture and immersion in the minority culture (Parks, 1950).

In Chapter 8 Derald and Stanley Sue provide evidence of the disparate ways in which Chinese Americans respond to cultural conflict. Some reject their Chinese background entirely and try to assimilate into the dominant society. Others adhere to traditional cultural values and attempt to resist assimilation. Still others stress pride in their racial identity while refraining from the conformity inherent in both the traditional Chinese practices and assimilation into mainstream culture. In Chapter 12, Rodriguez refers to the conflict he and other minority academicians experience as they move away from the traditional culture of their forefathers, through (or around) the dominant culture, and toward a position of ethnic pride and independence, while establishing their own personal autonomy. Threads of similar transformational processes can be found in all the earlier readings.

The purpose of this chapter is to explicate a model of minority identity development that acknowledges coincidental identity transformational processes involving minority groups and utilizes these processes to help explain individual differences within minority groups. A number of earlier authors have also attempted to explain individual differences within racial/ethnic groups. Some of these early attempts took the form of simple typologies in which a particular minority group was divided into smaller sub-categories or types based on their degree of ethnic identification. As Hall, Cross, and Freedle (1972) point out, these sub-groups generally included both "conservative" and "militant" types, and one or two categories in between. Vontress (1971), for instance, theorized that Afro Americans conformed to three distinct sub-groups: (1) Colored, (2) Negro, and (3) Black. Briefly, these sub-categories represented decreasing levels of dependence upon White society and culture as the source of self-definition and worth, and an increasing degree of identification with Black society and culture. As another example, Mayovich (1973) typed Japanese Americans according to four separate categories: (1) Conformists, (2) Anomic, (3) Liberal, and (4) Militant. Mayovich (1973) hypothesized that as a result of their acceptance or rejection of traditional values and their involvement or detachment from social issues, all Japanese Americans (at least those of the Sansei generation) fell into one of these four types.

This method of "typing" minority individuals has come under heavy criticism in recent years, however. Banks (1972), for instance, contends that these theorists have mistakenly proposed labels that attribute certain fixed personality traits to people when, in fact, their behavior is a function of a specific situation. Others (Cross, 1970; Hall, Cross, & Freedle, 1972; Jackson, 1975) have suggested that any attempt to define minority "types" must acknowledge movement of individuals across categories. In spite of such criticisms, it is important to recognize the early typologies as pioneering attempts that paved the way for more sophisticated models of identity development.

A second major approach has viewed minority attitudes and behavior as a product of an identity development continuum. This approach differs from earlier typologies in that minority attitudes and behaviors are viewed as flexible and a function of the individual's stage of identity development. Rather than type the individual, stages of development through which any minority person may pass are described. Attitudinal and behavioral attributes are, therefore, not viewed as fixed characteristics, but as related to identity development.

These early attempts to define a process of minority identity development were almost exclusively the work of Black intellectuals who were obviously influenced in their thinking by the impact of social, psychological and cultural events in the 60's. Hall, Cross, and Freedle (1972) describe how these events highlighted the process of Black identity transformation:

> We have seen a change in the nature of black-white relations in America. To be sure, this change has produced many consequences, one of which has been an identity transformation among American blacks. The transformation has been from an older orientation whereby most blacks viewed themselves as inadequate, inferior, incapable of self-determination, and unable to cope with the intricacies of life in a complex society, to one of feeling adequate, self-reliant, assertive and self-determinative (p. 156).

The most highly developed models of Black identity transformation have been offered by Cross (1970, 1971) and Jackson (1975). Each of these men, independent of the other, developed a four-stage identity development process, although each acknowledges the influence of earlier writers (Crawford & Naditch, 1970; Sherif & Sherif, 1970; Thomas, 1971; Wallace, 1964). Cross (1971) described his model as a "Negro-to-Black Conversion Experience" consisting of pre-encounter, encounter, immersion, and internalization stages, and an exploratory study by Cross and two colleagues (Hall, Cross, & Freedle, 1972) provides some tentative support for these stages of development. According to the model, Blacks at the pre-encounter stage are "programmed to view and think of the world as being non-black, anti-black, or the opposite of Black" (Hall, Cross, & Freedle, 1972, p. 159). At the next stage, the encounter stage, the Black individual becomes aware of what being Black means and begins to validate him/herself as a Black person. During the immersion stage, the Black person rejects all non-black values and totally immerses him/herself in Black culture. Finally, in the internalization stage, the Black person gains a sense of inner security and begins to focus on "...things other than himself and his own ethnic or racial group" (Hall, Cross, & Freedle, 1972, p. 160).

Jackson (1975) identifies a similar four-stage process as the Black Identity Development Model. In stage one—Passive Acceptance—the Black person accepts and conforms to White social, cultural, and institutional standards (p. 21). In stage two—Active Resistance—the Black person rejects all that is White and attempts to remove all White influences upon his/her life (p. 22). In stage three—Redirection—the Black individual no longer admires or despises what is White, but rather considers it irrelevant to Black Culture (p. 23). Finally, in stage four—Internalization—the Black person acknowledges and appreciates the uniqueness of the Black culture, and comes to accept and reject various aspects of American culture based on their own merits.

Although these identity development models pertain specifically to the Black experience, the editors of the present text believe that some of the basic tenets of these theories can be generalized and applied to other minority groups, due to their shared experience of oppression. Several earlier writers (Stonequist, 1937; Berry, 1965) have also observed that minority groups share the same patterns of adjustment to cultural oppression. Parallels are most easily drawn between Blacks and other racial/ethnic groups. During the past two decades, for instance, the social and political activity of Latinos, Asian Americans, and Native Americans has resulted in an identity transformation for persons within these groups, similar to that experienced by Black Americans. A Third World Consciousness has emerged, with the common experience of oppression clearly serving as the unifying force.

Parallels between the Black experience and that of women (Myrdal, 1944; Cox, 1976) and gays (Murphy, 1974) have also been suggested. Women, "gays," the aged, the handicapped, and other oppressed groups have become increasingly conscious of themselves as objects of oppression, and this has resulted in changed attitudes toward themselves, their own minority groups, other minority groups, and members of the dominant culture. Based on views expressed by earlier writers and our own clinical observation that these changes in attitudes and subsequent behavior follow a predictable sequence, we propose a five-stage, Minority Identity Development (MID) model.

The MID model we propose is not presented as a comprehensive theory of personality development, but rather as a schema to help counselors understand minority client attitudes and behaviors within existing personality theories. The model defines five stages of development that oppressed people may experience as they struggle to understand themselves in terms of their own minority culture, the dominant culture, and the oppressive relationship between the two cultures. Although five distinct stages are presented in the model, the MID is more accurately conceptualized as a continuous process in which one stage blends with another and boundaries between stages are not clear.

It is our observation that not all minority individuals experience the entire range of these stages in their lifetimes. Prior to the turbulent 1960's, a decade in which the transition of many individuals through this process was accelerated and, therefore, made more evident, many people were raised and lived out their lives in the first stage. Nor is the developmental process to be interpreted as irreversible. It is our opinion that many minority individuals are raised by parents functioning at level five, but in coming to grips with their own identity, offsprings often move from level five to one of the lower levels. On the other hand, it does not appear that lower levels of development are prerequisite to functioning at higher levels. Some people born and raised in a family functioning at level five appear never to experience a level one sense of identity.

At each level we provide examples of four corresponding attitudes that may assist the counselor to understand behaviors displayed by individuals operating at or near these levels. (It is our contention that minority behavior, like all human behavior, can only be fully understood within the context of the attitudes that motivate it.) Each attitude is believed to be an integral part of any minority person's identity; how he/she views: (a) self, (b) others of the same minority, (c) others of another minority, and (d) majority individuals. It was not our intention to define a hierarchy with more valued attitudes at higher levels of development. Rather, the model is intended to reflect a process that we have observed in our work with minority clients over the past two decades.

Minority Identity Development Model

Stage One—Conformity Stage
Minority individuals in this stage of development are distinguished by their unequivocal preference for dominant cultural values over those of their own culture. Their choice of role models, life styles, value system, etc., all follow the lead of the dominant group. Those physical and/or cultural characteristics which single them out as minority persons are a source of pain, and are either viewed with disdain or are repressed from consciousness. Their views of self, fellow group members, and other minorities in general are clouded by their identification with the dominant culture.

A. *Attitude toward self: Self-depreciating attitude.* Individuals who acknowledge their distinguishing physical and/or cultural characteristics consciously view them as a source of shame. Individuals who repress awareness of their distinguishing physical and/or cultural characteristics depreciate themselves at a subconscious level.
B. *Attitude toward members of the same minority: Group-depreciating attitude.* Fellow minority group members are viewed according to dominant held beliefs of minority strengths and weaknesses.
C. *Attitude toward members of different minority: Discriminatory attitude.* Other minorities are viewed according to the dominant group's system of minority stratification (i.e., those minority groups that most closely resemble the dominant group in physical and cultural characteristics are viewed more favorably than those less similar).
D. *Attitude toward members of dominant group: Group appreciating attitude.* Members of the dominant group are admired, respected, and often viewed as ideal models. Cultural values of the dominant society are accepted without question.

Stage Two—Dissonance Stage
In the Dissonance stage of identity development, which is typified by cultural confusion and conflict, the minority individual encounters information and/or experiences that are inconsistent with previously accepted values and beliefs, and consequently is led to question and to some degree challenge, attitudes acquired in the Conformity stage.

A. *Attitude toward self: Conflict between self-depreciating and self-appreciating attitudes.* With a growing awareness of minority cultural strengths comes a faltering sense of pride in self. The individual's attitude toward distinguishing physical and/or cultural characteristics is typified by alternating feelings of shame and pride in self.
B. *Attitude toward members of same minority: Conflict between group-depreciating and group-appreciating attitudes.* Dominant-held views of minority strengths and weaknesses begin to be questioned, as new, contradictory information is received. Cultural values of the minority group begin to have appeal.
C. *Attitude toward members of a different minority: Conflict between dominant-held views of minority hierarchy and feelings of shared experience.* The individual begins to question the dominant-held system of minority stratification, and experiences a growing sense of comradeship with other oppressed people. Most of the individual's psychic energy at this level, however, is devoted to resolving conflicting attitudes toward self, the same minority, and the dominant group.
D. *Attitude toward members of dominant group: Conflict between group appreciating and group depreciating attitude.* The individual experiences a growing awareness that not all cultural values of the dominant group are beneficial to him/her. Members of the dominant group are viewed with growing suspicion.

Stage Three—Resistance and Immersion Stage

In this stage of development, the minority individual completely endorses minority-held views and rejects the dominant society and culture. Desire to eliminate oppression of the individual's minority group becomes an important motivation of the individual's behavior.

A. *Attitude toward self: Self-appreciating attitude.* The minority individual at this stage acts as an explorer and discoverer of his/her history and culture, seeking out information and artifacts which enhance his/her sense of identity and worth. Cultural and physical characteristics which once illicited feelings of shame and disgust at this stage become symbols of pride and honor.

B. *Attitude toward members of the same minority: Group-appreciating attitude.* The individual experiences a strong sense of identification with and commitment to his/her minority group, as enhancing information about the group is acquired. Members of the group are admired, respected, and often viewed as ideal models. Cultural values of the minority group are accepted without question.

C. *Attitude toward members of a different minority: Conflict between feelings of empathy for other minority experiences and feelings of culturocentrism.* The individual experiences a growing sense of camarderie with persons from other minority groups, to the degree to which they are viewed as sharing similar forms of oppression. Alliances with other groups tend to be short-lived, however, when their values come in conflict with those of the individual's minority group. The dominant group's system of minority stratification is replaced by a system which values most those minority groups that are culturally similar to the individual's own group.

D. *Attitude toward members of dominant group: Group-depreciating attitude.* The individual totally rejects the dominant society and culture, and experiences a sense of distrust and dislike for all members of the dominant group.

Stage Four—Introspection Stage

In this stage of development, the minority individual experiences feelings of discontent and discomfort with group views rigidly held in the Resistance and Immersion stage, and diverts attention to notions of greater individual autonomy.

A. *Attitude toward self: Concern with basis of self-appreciating attitude.* The individual experiences conflict between notions of responsibility and allegiance to minority group and notions of personal autonomy.

B. *Attitude toward members of same minority: Concern with unequivocal nature of group appreciation.* While attitudes of identification are continued from the preceding Resistance and Immersion stage, concern begins to build up regarding the issue of group-usurped individuality.

C. *Attitude toward members of a different minority: Concern with ethnocentric basis for judging others.* The individual experiences a growing uneasiness with minority stratification that results from culturocentrism and the greater value placed on groups experiencing the same oppression than those experiencing a different oppression.

D. *Attitude toward members of dominant group: Concern with the basis of group depreciation.* The individual experiences conflict between attitude of complete distrust for the dominant society and culture, and attitude of selective trust and distrust according to dominant individuals' demonstrated behaviors and attitudes. The individual also recognizes the utility of many dominant cultural elements, yet is confused as to whether to incorporate such elements into his/her minority culture.

Stage Five—Synergetic Articulation and Awareness Stage

Minority individuals in this stage experience a sense of self-fulfillment with regard to cultural identity. Conflicts and discomforts experienced in the introspection stage have been resolved, allowing greater individual control and flexibility. Cultural values of other minorities as well as those of the dominant group are objectively examined and accepted or rejected on the basis of prior experience gained in earlier stages of identity development. Desire to eliminate *all* forms of oppression becomes an important motivation of the individual's behavior.

A. *Attitude toward self: Self-appreciating attitude.* The individual experiences a strong sense of self-worth, self-confidence, and autonomy as the result of having established his/her identity as an individual, a member of a minority group, and/or a member of the dominant culture.

B. *Attitude toward members of the same minority: Group appreciating attitude.* The individual experiences a strong sense of pride in the group without having to accept group values unequivocally. Strong feelings of empathy with the group experience are coupled with an awareness that each member of the group is an individual.

C. *Attitude toward members of a different minority: Group appreciating attitude.* The individual experiences a strong sense of respect for the group's cultural values coupled with an awareness that each member of the group is an individual. The individual also experiences a greater understanding and support for all oppressed people, regardless of their similarity to the individual's minority group.

D. *Attitude toward members of the dominant group: Attitude of selective appreciation.* The individual experiences selective trust and liking for members of the dominant group who seek to eliminate repressive activities of the group. The individual also experiences an openness to the constructive elements of the dominant culture.

Implications of the MID Model for Counseling

As suggested earlier, the MID model is not intended as a comprehensive theory of personality, but rather as a paradigm to help counselors understand minority client attitudes and behaviors. In this respect, the model is intended to sensitize counselors to: (1) the role oppression plays in a minority individual's identity development, (2) the differences that can exist between members of the same minority group with respect to their cultural identity, and (3) the potential which each individual minority person has for changing his/her sense of identity. Beyond helping to understand minority client behavior, the model has implications for the counseling process itself.

Table 1
Summary of Minority Identity Development Model

Stages of Minority Development Model	Attitude toward self	Attitude toward others of the same minority	Attitude toward others of different minority	Attitude toward dominant group
Stage 1— Conformity	self-depreciating	group-depreciating	discriminatory	group-appreciating
Stage 2— Dissonance	conflict between self-depreciating and appreciating	conflict between group-depreciating and group-appreciating	conflict between dominant held views of minority hierarchy and feelings of shared experience	conflict between group-appreciating and group-depreciating
Stage 3— Resistance and Immersion	self-appreciating	group-appreciating	conflict between feelings of empathy for other minority experiences and feelings of culturocentrism	group-depreciating
Stage 4— Introspection	concern with basis of self-appreciation	concern with nature of unequivocal appreciation	concern with ethnocentric basis for judging others	concern with the basis of group depreciation
Stage 5— Synergetic Articulation and Awareness	self-appreciating	group-appreciating	group-appreciating	selective appreciation

The general attitudes and behaviors which describe minority individuals at the Conformity stage (e.g., denial of minority problems, strong dependence and identification with dominant group, etc.) suggest that clients from this stage are unlikely to seek counseling related to their cultural identity. It is more likely that they will perceive problems of cultural identity as problems related to their personal identity. Clients at this stage are more inclined to visit and be influenced by counselors of the dominant group than those of the same minority. Because of the client's strong identification with dominant group members, counselors from the dominant group may find the conformist client's need to please and appease a powerful force in the counseling relationship. Clients at the Conformity stage are likely to present problems that are most amenable to problem solving and goal-oriented counseling approaches.

Minority individuals at the Dissonance stage of development are preoccupied by questions concerning their concept of self, identity, and self-esteem; they are likely to perceive personal problems as related to their cultural identity. Emotional problems develop when these individuals are unable to resolve conflicts which occur between dominant-held views and those of their minority group. Clients in the Dissonance stage are more culturally aware than Conformity clients and are likely to prefer to work with counselors who possess a good knowledge of the client's cultural group. Counseling approaches that involve considerable self-exploration appear to be best suited for clients at this stage of development.

Minority individuals at the Resistance and Immersion stage are inclined to view all psychological problems (whether personal or social in nature) as a product of their oppression. The likelihood that these clients will seek formal counseling regarding their cultural identity is very slim. In those cases when counseling is sought, it will tend to be only between members of the same minority group, and generally in response to a crisis situation. Therapy for Stage Three clients often takes the form of exposure to, and practice of, the ways and artifacts of their culture. An example of this might be a woman who experiences a release of tension and anxiety because of her involvement in a class on women's liberation. Clients at this stage who do seek counseling are likely to prefer group process and/or alloplastic approaches to counseling.

Clients at the Introspection stage are torn between their preponderant identification with their minority group and their need to exercise greater personal freedom. When these individuals are unable to resolve mounting conflict between these two forces, they often seek counseling. While Introspective clients still prefer to see a counselor from their own cultural group, counselors from other cultures may be viewed as credible sources of help if they share world views similar to those of their clientele and appreciate their cultural dilemma. Counselors who use a self-exploration and decision-making approach can be most effective with these clients.

Clients at the fifth stage of identity development have acquired the internal skills and knowledge necessary to exercise a desired level of personal freedom. Their sense of minority identity is well balanced by an appreciation of other cultures. And, while discrimination and oppression remain a painful part of their lives, greater psychological resources are at their disposal in actively engaging the problem. Attitudinal similarity between counselor and client becomes a more important determinant of counseling success than membership-group similarity.

Discussion of the MID model's implications for counseling is admittedly highly speculative at this point, and the model itself requires empirical verification before more definitive inferences are drawn. We hope the model will stimulate much needed research with regard to minority identity development and that it will serve to make counselors more sensitive to the needs of the minority client. In the final chapter we suggest other areas where research is needed, and offer recommendations for counseling practice and counselor education related to minority group/cross-cultural counseling.

References

Banks, W. The Black client and the helping professionals. In R.I. Jones (Ed.) *Black Psychology*. New York: Harper & Row, 1972.

Berry, B. *Ethnic and race relations*. Boston: Houghton Mifflin, 1965.

Cox, S. *Female psychology: The emerging self*. Chicago: Science Research Associates, 1976.

Crawford, T.J., & Naditch, M. Relative deprivation, powerlessness, and militancy: The psychology of social protest. *Psychiatry, 1970, 33,* 208-223.

Cross, W.E. The black experience viewed as a process: A crude model for black self-actualization. Paper presented at the Thirty-fourth Annual Meeting of the Association of Social and Behavioral Scientists, April 23-24, 1970, Tallahassee, Florida.

Cross, W.E. The Negro-to-Black conversion experience. *Black World,* 1971, *20,* 13-27.

Hall, W.S.; Cross, W.E.; & Freedle, R. Stages in the development of Black awareness: An exploratory investigation. In Reginald L. Jones' (Ed.) *Black Psychology,* New York: Harper & Row, 1972, 156-165.

Jackson, B. Black identity development. *MEFORM: Journal of Educational Diversity & Innovation,* 1975, *2,* 19-25.

Maykovich, M.K. Political activation of Japanese American youth. *Journal of Social Issues,* 1973, *29* (2), 167-185.

Murphy, J. *Homosexual Liberation*. New York: Praeger Publishers, 1971.

Myrdal, G. An American dilemma: The Negro problem and modern democracy. New York: Harper and Row, 1944.

Parks, R.E. *Race and culture*. Glencoe, Ill.: The Free Press, 1950.

Sherif, M., & Sherif, C. Black unrest as a social movement toward an emerging self identity. *Journal of Social and Behavioral Sciences,* 1970, *15,* 41-52.

Stonequist, E.V. *The marginal man*. New York: Charles Scubner's Sons, 1937.

Thomas, C.W. *Boys no more*. Beverly Hills, Ca.: Glencoe Press, 1971.

Vontress, C.E. Racial differences: Impediments to rapport. *Journal of Counseling Psychology,* 1971, *18* (1), 7-13.

Wallace, A.F.C. *Culture and personality*. New York: Random House, 1964.

16 Future Directions in Minority Group/Cross-Cultural Counseling

Counseling Practice

In Chapter 2 it was noted that a great deal of criticism by minority individuals has been directed at the traditional counseling role. Timebound, space-bound, cathartic counseling is rejected by these critics as largely irrelevant to minority life experiences and needs. The counselor, they argue, needs to get out of the office and meet the client on the client's ground. Rather than demanding that the client adapt to the counselor's culture, the counselor should adjust to and work within the client's culture. Furthermore, minority individuals are by definition oppressed, and it is highly unlikely that any minority client problem is ever totally free of this oppression. Providing an empathic ear so that the client can reassess past experiences, or even changing the client's behavior so that he or she can cope better with the environment, does not eliminate the oppression.

Several roles that overcome at least some of the criticisms leveled by minority critics, have been proposed as alternatives to the traditional counseling role. For the most part, these roles are not really new, since they have been proposed and to some degree implemented in the past (Pine, in his 1972 article, refers to them as "old wine in new bottles"). They are "new," however, in that they have not gained widespread acceptance by the counseling profession, and the traditional counseling role remains solidly entrenched as the counselor's primary modus operandi.

In general it can be said these alternative roles involve the counselor more actively in the client's life experiences than does the traditional role, and the former often require the counselor to move out of his/her office into the client's environment. They also share a preventative thrust rather than the more traditional remedial focus. Because of this there is considerable overlapping of the role functions, but each includes some aspects which are unique to the role. The alternative roles to be discussed are: (1) outreach role, (2) consultant role, (3) ombudsmun role, (4) change agent role, and (5) role as facilitator of indigenous support systems.

Outreach role

The outreach role requires that counselors move out of their offices and into their clients' communities (Weinrach, 1973; Mitchell, 1971a). Minority clients in educational settings are often hesitant to contact counselors (Calia, 1966); and Haettenschwiller (1971) urges counselors to make the initial contact with minority students on the students' home ground, thus establishing the counselor as a person, "...to whom the student can turn when confronted by the uncertainty and ambiguity of institutional demands" (p. 31). Meeting clients in this manner allows the counselor to divest him/herself of the Establishment association that an office visit can generate. Woods (1977) describes a counseling services program that relies heavily on group counseling and group activities rather than on traditional one-to-one counseling and, in keeping with an outreach philosophy, the group sessions are often, "...conducted at students' apartments for potluck dinners, and at local beaches and parks for picnics and games" (p. 417).

By making him/herself available in the client's environment, the counselor is in a better position to respond to client needs at the time they are experienced. Exposure to the client's world may also help the counselor understand the cultural experience of the client and may enhance the counselor-client relationship. Furthermore, the counselor as an outreach worker may be in a position to observe directly the environmental factors that are contributing to the client's problems, and the counselor is less likely to attribute deviations from majority norms to pathology. In addition to direct exposure to the environment of minority clients, counselors should become actively involved in community and social programs and activities in their minority clients' communities (Wilson & Calhoun, 1974).

Consultant Role

The goal of consultation is the development of a nurturing ecological system designed to optimize each client's self-growth (Blocker & Rapoza, 1972). In this role the counselor works with teachers, parents, peers, and others who have an impact on the minority client (Maes & Rinaldi, 1974).

Perhaps the most effective way a counselor can function as a consultant vis a vis minorities is by designing and implementing a peer counseling program. Minority client populations frequently find it easier to trust a peer than a professional, regardless of the professional's membership-group status. Gravitz and Woods (1976) describe a peer counseling program in which Third World students function as liaison between the University and minority students. Peer counselors focus their efforts on the "...clinically asymptomatic student who has problems of living in a complex university community" (p. 231). The primary philosophy of this peer counseling program is to serve a preventative function; to anticipate minority student difficulties and to alleviate them before they become aggravated. In order to do this, peer counselors often spend much of their time outside the counseling center, meeting minority students in residence halls, student centers, and minority centers. In addition to providing direct services to minority students, one result of the peer counseling program reported by Gravitz and Woods is that an increased number of minority students make contact with the counseling center's professional staff.

The training of minority peers is an important aspect of any minority peer or paraprofessional program. D.W. Sue (1973) has described a training program for Third World student counselors; this includes a course on peer counseling of minority students offered for credit. The course stresses six content areas: (1) the cultural backgrounds of the minorities to be served, (2) techniques of counseling, (3) crisis intervention, (4) ethical issues, (5) behavior pathology, and (6) referral sources. In addition, trainees spend 1½ hours a week role-playing counselor-counselee interactions in small groups supervised by a professional counselor. In general, the role-playing sessions are aimed at helping trainees develop skills associated with facilitative and action conditions (Carkhuff, 1971) of the helping relationship. Sue reports that an important aspect of the training procedure is the feedback provided by fellow trainees.

Lewis and Lewis (1977) have pointed out that counselors can also serve as consultants with groups of minority people who want to organize in order to improve the conditions under which they live. They describe four ways the counselor can serve in this capacity: the counselor can assess community needs, coordinate activities and resources, provide training in skill building, and advocate change.

Ombudsmun and Change Agent Roles

In both the ombudsmun role and the change agent role the counselor discards entirely the intrapsychic counseling model, and views clearly the problem as existing outside the minority client. Economic, political, social, emotional, and other forms of oppression are viewed as the underlying causes of minority client problems, and the counselor's role is to combat oppression. The two roles differ slightly, however, in terms of focus.

Ombudsmun. The ombudsmun role (spelled with a *u* to avoid a sexist connotation) originated in Europe where it functions as a protector of citizens against bureaucratic mazes and procedures (Bexelius, 1968). A number of colleges and universities in this country have instituted the ombudsmun role, and recently school counselors have been urged to serve as student advocates (Ciavarella & Doolittle, 1970). In this role the counselor represents a client or group of clients who have brought a particular form of oppression to the counselor's attention. Being an empathic counselor who suggests alternative ways of coping with a particular problem is not enough; the counselor must be willing to pursue actively alternative courses with or for the client, including making "a personal contact for the student who is overwhelmed by the bureaucracy" (Mitchell, 1971, p. 36). Not infrequently the injustice involves the institution employing the counselor, either directly or indirectly, making the counselor somewhat unpopular at times with institutional administrators. If the client's goals are in conflict with those of the institution, "the counselor must decide to represent the student and not the institution or the system" (Williams & Kirkland, 1971, p. 114), presumably within ethical restrictions imposed by the profession. When a minority client is involved, the ombudsmun has the added responsibility for making certain that the minority person can benefit fully from the social and economic resources of the majority culture without losing what is unique and valued in his/her own culture (Maes & Rinaldi, 1974).

Change Agent role. In the change agent role the counselor assumes an alloplastic counseling position, devoting considerable time and energy to changing the social environment of his/her minority clientele (Banks, 1972). By necessity, this often means changing the social environment of majority peers and superiors in the offending environment. Like the ombudsmun role, counselors in this role must often identify the problem as residing with the very institution that employs them and must be willing to confront their employers (Williams & Kirkland, 1971).

As a change agent the counselor need not represent a particular client or group of clients known to the outsider. Rather, the entire minority culture experiencing an injustice functions as the client. Furthermore, the counselor serving as a change agent frequently assumes a low visibility stature, often finding it useful to mobilize other influential persons in the offending institution so as to bring about change (Waltz & Benjamin, 1977).

Anderson & Love (1973) exhort counselors to, ''. . .assume responsibility for making efforts to increase positive human relations and fostering development of a multicultural view of the world'' (p. 667), and suggest psychological education as a vehicle to aid this process. The Division 17 Professional Affairs Committee of the American Psychological Association agrees that special measures are needed to combat institutional oppression of minority people in this country.

> Problems of institutional racism are paramount on a university campus. Counseling alone on discrimination issues will be ineffective. Counseling psychologists must involve themselves in affirmative action programs, sponsor symposia and workshops on racism in society, and actively involve themselves in programs of cultural awareness. (Ivey, 1976, p. 10-11).

As a change agent, however, the counselor need not necessarily spend his/her time confronting institutional bureaucracy. The counselor can work directly with majority clients in an attempt to move them toward the goal of reducing racism, sexism, and other discriminatory attitudes toward minorities. Katz and Ivey (1977) describe a racism awareness training program that could easily be adapted to majority attitudes toward non-racial minorities. The program involves a re-education process designed, ''. . .to raise consciousness of White people, help them identify racism in their life experience from which their racist attitudes and behaviors have developed, and move them to take action against institutional and individual racism'' (p. 487). The six phases of the program are designed to help participants to:

1. Increase their understanding of racism in society and themselves.
2. Confront discrepancies existing between the myths and reality of American ideology and behavior.

3. Sort through some of their feelings and reactions that were triggered by phases 1 and 2.
4. Confront the racism in the white culture that their own actions support.
5. Understand and accept their whiteness.
6. Develop specific action strategies to combat personal and institutional racism (p. 487).

The authors' suggestion that racism is a White problem and White counselors should assume a major role in dealing with it, is plausible. Majority counselors are, in some respects, in the best position to confront the majority population with their own stereotypic attitudes and behaviors.

Role as Facilitator of Indigenous Support Systems

Pedersen (1976) has discussed the need for counselors who are engaged in international cross-cultural counseling to be aware of the culture's indigenous mental health care systems. Within most United States minority group cultures, certain procedures have also evolved to assist the individual who is experiencing a psychological problem. Frequently counselors are unaware of or are disdainful of these procedures, preferring to engage the client in the very counseling process so heavily criticized by minority representatives. The inevitable result is a mismatch of treatment and need, loss of credibility in the counselor, and the client's disengagement from counseling. We would like to suggest that counselors may be able best to serve their minority clientele by attempting to facilitate rather than discourage use of indigenous support systems.

The counselor working with a minority client might begin the facilitative process by exploring with the client how he/she has dealt with similar problems in the past. Familiarity with the client's culture will help the counselor understand culturally relevant support systems that may assist the client. For instance, among some Mexicano groups *curanderos* perform many of the functions of a counselor. In numerous minority cultures the extended family plays an important supportive role. In others (e.g. women, gays), the family may provide little support, but peers provide the reinforcement needed to survive and overcome crises. The counselor can facilitate problem resolution by encouraging the client to use these support systems where appropriate.

In many cases minority client problems can be linked directly to oppression. Depression, for instance, may result from years and years of futile attempts to achieve some measure of social equality. A facilitative counselor might encourage a client experiencing depression of this nature to participate in an organization within the client's culture that fosters minority community pride.

Not all cultural adaptations to psychological problems engender growth, and in some instances the client may be too acculturated to benefit from procedures developed by the minority culture. In these instances the facilitative process begins with an exploration of processes with which the client feels comfortable. A key distinction in these cases, however, is that the exploration serves to discover a process for resolving the client's difficulty, not as a process for resolving a problem in and of itself.

Counselor Education

In response to the negative view minorities have of counseling, some authors have suggested that indigenous and paraprofessional counselors should be trained for minority group counseling, since it is doubtful whether majority counselors can become truly sensitive to minority needs (Ward, 1970). Yet, in view of the multicultural makeup of American society, it seems highly unlikely that counselors being trained today (especially those being trained for educational settings) will escape contact with culturally different clients. It seems imperative, therefore, that counselors of all cultural backgrounds be at least minimally prepared to work with clients who differ culturally from themselves.

Need for Cross-Cultural Counseling Emphasis

To date, however, very few counselor training programs have developed and offered systematic training in multicultural counseling (Bryson & Bardo, 1975). Even in the much discussed area of cross-racial counseling, very few training centers have "...given necessary attention to assisting developing professionals in recognizing, understanding, and resolving the more subtle forms that undesirable attitudes concerning race may take in therapeutic relationships where skin color becomes an important variable" (Gardner, 1971, p. 86).

Where courses in minority counseling have been developed, they have often been instituted at the insistence of a single, vocal, minority group and have tended to focus on a limited clientele. The rationale for such courses is that majority counselors must receive intensive training from a minority perspective (Cross & Maldonado, 1971; Williams & Kirkland, 1971). Since each minority group within the United States is deserving of this sort of professional attention, this approach to course development presumably could result in the proliferation of a large number of courses. Each program would be designed to sensitize majority counselors to the life experiences and special needs of a single minority group. While each of these groups is deserving of such attention, it seems unlikely that counselor education programs will offer more than one or two minority counseling courses (often some version of "counseling Blacks" and "counseling women"). The predictable outcome is that little attention will be focused on the numerous other minority groups that counselors may come in contact with.

Several additional problems present themselves when classes are developed that focus on counseling one or two minority groups to the exclusion of others. Students and instructors often mistakenly assume that a dynamic applicable to one minority group can be generalized to others. Also, since the professional literature pays little attention to minority counselor-majority client and minority counselor-minority client interaction (Gardner, 1971; Sattler, 1970), these courses seldom focus on the minority counselor condition. This occurs in spite of the fact that minority counseling courses are frequently instituted at the insistence of and are primarily patronized by minority counselors-in-training.

We are not suggesting that specialized courses in counseling particular minority groups should not be developed. Nor are we suggesting that minority group students should not be involved in the design and implementation of training programs. We agree with Bell (1971) who provides a convincing argument in favor of their involvement. The point we are making is that courses are needed in cross-cultural counseling, courses which sensitize counselors to a variety of minority cultures, and examine the common experiences of various minority groups as well as their differences. Such courses should give attention to the minority counselor as well as to the majority counselor role in cross-cultural counseling.

One of the major objectives of a cross-cultural counseling class should be to acquaint the student with etic and emic qualities of favored counseling approaches. For instance, it seems clear that rapport is a culturally generalizable element basic to all counseling interaction (Vontress, 1971, 1973, 1974). Techniques to establish rapport, however, may be culturally specific and not capable of generalization. Nondirective techniques presently taught in many training programs as rapport building responses may actually antagonize some minorities or seem meaningless to others (Sue & Sue, 1972a). As Bryson and Bardo (1975) point out, "...it can no longer be assumed that techniques and strategies that are successful with one group of clients will work effectively with another group" (p. 14). Yet it would be a serious error to assume that all concepts associated with counseling theory developed to date must be discarded when working with a minority client. For instance, the learning theory principles upon which behavioral counseling is predicated presumably hold true in any culture. It seems axiomatic that operant conditioning, classical conditioning, and vicarious learning concepts apply to one culture as well as another. The ways in which these principles may manifest themselves in a variety of cultures may differ, however, and what may be a reinforcing stimulus in one culture may prove to be adverse in another.

In addition to courses specifically designated as cross-cultural counseling or multicultural counseling courses, all counselor education offerings should be revised to include minority-relevant topics. Mitchell (1971) offers a model of such a program. (See Chapter 11 of the present text).

Literature Related to Training Counselors of Minority Group Clients

Vontress (1974) has suggested that, "although a course in counseling racial and ethnic minorities may be another exciting and rewarding cognitive exposure, needed most are affective experiences designed to humanize counselors'' (p. 164). The experiences which he and other authors suggest are needed are those designed to increase counselor understanding in two areas: first, to understand themselves and their previously unrecognized biases; second, to gain appreciation for the experiences of someone who is culturally different and to become open to divergent life styles (Calia, 1966). In order to achieve these goals, ''sensitivity training'', in which the counselor lives and works in the minority community to experience it first hand, is recommended (Vontress, 1971).

Several authors have proposed that prior to direct experience in a cross-cultural setting, counselors in training should be exposed to simulated cross-cultural encounters. Bryson, Renzaglia, & Danish (1974) describe a simulation training procedure designed ''. . .to assist counselors in training and other human service workers to function successfully with Black citizens'' (p. 219), which might be adapted to other cross-cultural situations. A counselor trainee group is shown a number of videotaped or filmed vignettes in which actors portray the emotions associated with rejection, fear of rejection, intimacy given, and fear of intimacy (p. 219). The trainees are asked to think of the role player as a client, and to respond affectively and empathically. The trainees as a group then discuss their reactions to the simulated situation. During the discussion, trainees are asked to (a) identify the role-played emotion, (b) identify their own emotional reaction, and (c) suggest alternative responses to the role-played emotion.

An intriguing simulation procedure has been described by Pedersen (1977), who views counseling as a power struggle between client and counselor and the problem. Counselor trainees are divided into teams of three in which one trainee portrays the counselor, one the client, and one the ''anticounselor.'' The client and ''anticounselor'' are matched with respect to cultural factors as closely as possible and the ''anticounselor's'' role is to use ''. . .cultural similarity with the client in order to disrupt the counselor-client cross-cultural coalition'' (p. 95). The ''anticounselor'' may attempt to build a coalition with the client by privately supplying negative feedback to the client about the counselor, or may attempt to destroy a client-counselor coalition by joining the counseling interaction and attacking the counselor openly. Pedersen reports that this procedure has been successfully employed with both prepracticum training and as part of an in-service workshop. A one-hour videotape consisting of four triad interviews and a training manual have been developed for use in any counselor training program.

Lewis and Lewis (1970) propose a training model in which beginning counselors-in-training are paired with experienced counselors and placed as teams in inner-city schools to work as full-time counselors. While on-the-job experience working with disadvantaged youth would serve as the basic core of this program, didactic course work taught in participating public schools would bridge theory and practice requirements. A major objective of this training model would be to develop counselors ''. . .skilled in the processes of consultation and change and group and individual counseling'' (Lewis & Lewis, 1970, p. 37).

Mitchell (1971) describes a counselor training model which is similar to the Lewis-Lewis (1970) model but has the advantage of having already been implemented. The program is designed to provide for a Black perspective, but includes several features that could be generalized to cross-cultural situations. For instance, in implementing the new program, internships were developed in predominately minority-attended schools. Also, in addition to developing new courses aimed at understanding the Black experience, core guidance and counseling courses were designed to include minority-relevant materials. This could conceivably be done in any counselor education program. Most programs, for instance, include the equivalent of such courses as Introduction to Guidance/Counseling, Test and Measurements, and Vocational and Educational Information. The Introduction course could include a discussion of how the promise of guidance has fallen short for minority students (Russell, 1970). The testing class could devote considerable attention to cultural test biases as well as to problems of validity and reliability (Barnes, 1972). And the Vocational class could focus on the special problems of minorities in obtaining and retaining jobs (Miller & Oetting, 1977). For a more detailed explanation of this model, see Chapter 11 of the present text.

While not proposed as a training technique for counselors, the Racism Awareness training procedure described by Katz and Ivey (1977) might easily be adapted to counselor education programs. This training procedure, described in some detail in the earlier section on the change agent role, could easily be expanded to deal with other stereotypic attitudes and behavior.

Training for Activist Roles Needed

The major challenge in the future to counselor education vis a vis minority group/cross-cultural counseling is the establishment within the profession of activist alternatives to the traditional counseling role. Until such time as counselor education programs define outreach, consultation, ombudsmun, change agent, and facilitator of indigenous support systems roles as viable alternatives to time-bound, space-bound, personal-social counseling, it seems unlikely these roles will be accepted and implemented by the profession in general (Atkinson, Froman, Romo, & Mayton, 1977). Counselor education's long-standing love affair with the intrapsychic model of client problems must cool, and the effects of an oppressive society be acknowledged, before counseling as a profession will achieve credibility with a large portion of the minority populations.

Counseling Research

Sattler (1970) reviewed the research concerned with the effect of *experimenter* race on experimentation, testing, interviewing, and psychology, and found only three studies related to counselor-client interaction. While a number of studies have been carried out since Sattler completed his review, empirical research in this area is still generally lacking. Several reasons for the relative paucity of research concerned with minority group/cross-cultural counseling present themselves. One possibility is that a majority-controlled counseling research establishment has simply not viewed minority status as an important factor in counseling. Counselor educators and researchers who espouse an etic counseling approach may feel cultural factors in counseling play a subordinate role to counseling techniques in affecting counseling outcome.

Another reason may be that majority researchers believe that the topic is a highly controversial issue and prefer to conduct research on less controversial subjects. As Gardner (1971) points out, "...many blacks have called for a moratorium on all further efforts by white investigators to study and explain the psychological and social characteristics of blacks" (p. 78). Similar requests have been made by other minority professionals who believe that forays by majority researchers into minority cultures have resulted in reinforced stereotypes rather than enlightened understanding. While aimed primarily at researchers in sociology and psychology who have attempted to explain minority behavior in terms of deviance from majority norms, the attitude that the majority researcher-minority subject combination is destined to produce distorted, biased results has obviously become generalized to counseling psychology.

Furthermore, individual members of various minority groups have grown increasingly resistant to research and refuse to serve as subjects (Sue & Sue, 1972b). Black males are understandably reluctant to participate in any activity that smacks of experimentation. Perhaps the most tragic abuse of research with human subjects in this country occurred when 400 Black men identified during the 1930's as having syphilis were allowed to suffer its effects without treatment (infamously known as the Tuskegee experiment). At least 48 of these men died and numerous others were permanently maimed as a direct result of the disease. A number of other studies with potentially harmful effects have been conducted on inmates (a majority of whom are members of racial/ethnic minorities) in federal and state prisons either without the subjects' knowledge or with direct or indirect coercion.

Proposed Research Model for Minority Group/Cross-Cultural Research

The suggestion has been made that the impacts of the preconceptions or prejudices of the experimenter on cross-cultural counseling research can be minimized when the researcher feels "comfortably polycultural" (Vontress, 1976, p. 2). We feel that the danger of cultural bias on the part of a single researcher, no matter what his/her race, socioeconomic background, sex, sexual orientation, etc., is unavoidable. It seems unlikely that any researcher has totally escaped the impact of cultural stereotyping that may be present as unrecognized bias in the design, implementation, and/or data analysis of a research project.

The possibility of unrecognized bias can be reduced, however, when research teams are composed of at least one representative from each cultural group included in the study. We are proposing, in effect, whenever two or more cultural groups are represented in a research design, that each group have an advocate on the research team, who is likely to be sensitive to cultural bias. Objectivity might also be enhanced if the research team included a person whose cultural background was not directly related to the variables under study. Thus, a research team examining the effectiveness of Black or White counselors with Black or White clients might include an Asian American researcher as well as Black and White investigators.

The American Psychological Association hosted a conference on professional training at Vail, Colorado, in 1973; on that occasion one recommendation developed was that "...counseling of persons of culturally diverse backgrounds by persons who are not trained or competent to work with such groups should be regarded as unethical" (Pedersen, 1976, p. 35). We would like to recommend that a similar ethical restriction be placed on minority group/cross-cultural researchers.

Areas Where Research Is Needed

Some barriers and benefits resulting from cross-cultural counseling were presented in the first chapter. For the most part, these variables have been identified through clinical observation, with little solid research evidence to support their effect on the counseling relationship. Research is needed to establish this effect, then to determine how benefits can be maximized and obstacles minimized. Also, since much of the writing in this area has been done by Black theorists, research is needed to determine if these factors can be generalized and applied to other cultures.

Research is also needed to determine the etic quality of current counseling approaches. What are the underlying assumptions of behavioral counseling, transactional analysis, gestalt therapy, rational emotive therapy, reality therapy, existential approaches to counseling, which apply to all cultures? Which techniques based on these assumptions are equally applicable to all cultures? What assumptions are obviously not applicable to all cultures, and what implications does this have for associated techniques? What are the emic solutions to psychological problems that have been developed within the various cultures in American society? How can counseling be used to increase the effectiveness of these procedures? Draguns (1976) argues that both etic and emic counseling approaches are needed and that both "...are equally valid and complimentary....The crucial thing is to recognize these orientations for what they are; practical and conceptual pitfalls appear only when the etic orientation is mistaken for the emic or vise versa" (p. 3). Research is sorely needed that identifies etic and emic qualities of current counseling procedures.

In Chapter 15 we proposed a Minority Identity Development model that we hope will stimulate research in minority group/cross-cultural counseling. The Minority Identity Development model itself needs empirical verification. Hall, Cross, & Freedle (1972) found experimental support for a Black Identity Development model, and their study could serve as a prototype for research on Minority Identity Development.

Research which examines the effect of group membership and attitude similarity on counseling process and outcome also appears promising. The relationship of racial, sexual, socioeconomic, religious, and sexual orientation similarities to counseling effectiveness is yet to be determined. The relationship of group membership and attitudinal similarities to the nature of the client's problems in a variety of dimensions (related or unrelated to client minority status, personal-social-educational-vocational, internal-external locus of problem) needs to be assessed. Given group membership dissimilarity, how can attitudinal similarity be communicated by the counselor? One interesting hypothesis which needs testing is that when the counselor responds with empathy, he/she is perceived by the client as holding similar values. If so, are there more effective ways of communicating attitudinal similarity?

Finally, research is needed to assess the effectiveness of activist counseling roles when dealing with minority clientele. Are counselors who serve as ombudsmuns, change agents, etc., actually perceived by minority clients as more helpful than counselors who function in a more traditional role? More important, what is the actual impact of counselors functioning in these roles?

If this book helps to stimulate research activity in these and other areas related to minority group/cross-cultural counseling, it will have served an important purpose. We are optimistic that the barriers to cross-cultural counseling can be bridged.

References

Anderson, N.J., & Love, B. Psychological education for racial awareness. *Personnel and Guidance Journal*, 1973, *51*, 666-670.

Atkinson, D.R.; Froman, T.; Romo, J.; Mayton, D.M., II. The role of the counselor as a social activist: Who supports it? *The School Counselor*, 1977, *25*, 85-91.

Banks, W. The Black client and the helping professionals. In R.I. Jones (Ed.) *Black Psychology*. New York: Harper & Row, 1972.

Barnes, E.J. Cultural retardation or shortcomings of assessment techniques? In R.L. Jones (Ed.) *Black Psychology*. New York: Harper & Row, 1972.

Bell, Robert L., Jr. The culturally deprived psychologist, *The Counseling Psychologist*, 1971, *2*, 104-106.

Bexelius, A. The ombudsman for civil affairs. In D.C. Rowat (Ed.), *The ombudsman: Citizen's defender*. Toronto: University of Toronto Press, 1968.

Blocker, D.H., & Rapoza, R. A systematic eclectic model in counseling-consulting. *Elementary School Guidance and Counseling*, 1972, *7*, 106-112.

Bryson, S.; & Bardo, H. Race and the counseling process: An overview. *Journal of Non-White Concerns in Personnel and Guidance*, 1975, *4*, 5-15.

Bryson, S.; Renzaglia, G.A., & Danish, S. Training counselors through simulated racial encounters. *Journal of Non-White Concerns in Personnel and Guidance*, 1974, *3*, 218-223.

Calia, V.F. The culturally deprived client: A re-formulation of the counselor's role. *Journal of Counseling Psychology*, 1966, *13*, 100-105.

Carkhuff, R.R. *The development of human resources*. San Francisco: Holt, Rinehart, & Winston, 1971.

Ciavarella, M.A. & Doolittle, L.W. The Ombudsman: Relevant role model for the counselor. *The School Counselor*, 1970, *17*, 331-336.

Cross, W.C., & Maldonado, B. The counselor, the Mexican American, and the stereotype. *Elementary School Guidance and Counseling*, 1971, *6*, 27-31.

Draguns, J.G. Counseling across cultures: Common themes and distinct approaches. In P.B. Pedersen, W.J. Lonner, & J.G. Draguns (Eds.), *Counseling across cultures*. Honolulu: The University of Hawaii Press, 1976.

Gardner, L.H. The therapeutic relationship under varying conditions of race. *Psychotherapy: Theory, Research and Practice*, 1971, *8* (1), 78-87.

Gravitz, H.L., & Woods, E. A multiethnic approach to peer counseling. *Professional Psychology*, 1976, *8*, 229-235.

Haettenschwiller, D.L. Counseling black college students in special programs. *Personnel & Guidance Journal*, 1971, *50*, 29-35.

Hall, W.S.; Cross, W.E., & Freedle, R. Stages in the development of Black awareness: An exploratory investigation. In Reginald L. Jones' (Ed.) *Black Psychology*, New York: Harper & Row, 1972, 156-165.

Ivey, A.E. *Counseling psychology, the psychoeducator model and the future*. Paper prepared for APA Division 17 Professional Affairs Committee, 1976.

Katz, J.H., & Ivey, A. White awareness: The frontier of racism awareness training. *Personnel and Guidance Journal*, 1977, *55*, 485-489.

Lewis, M.D. & Lewis, J.A. Relevant training for relevant roles: A model for educating inner-city counselors. *Counselor Education and Supervision*, 1970, *10* (1), 31-38.

Lewis, M.D., & Lewis, J.A. The counselor's impact on community environments. *Personnel and Guidance Journal*, 1977, *55*, 356-358.

Maes, W.R., & Rinaldi, J.R. Counseling the Chicano child. *Elementary School Guidance and Counseling*, 1974, *9*, 279-284.

Miller, C.D., & Oetting, G. Barriers to employment and the disadvantaged. *Personnel and Guidance Journal*, 1977, *56*, 89-93.

Mitchell, H. Counseling black students: A model in response to the need for relevant counselor training programs. *The Counseling Psychologist*, 1971, *2* (4), 117-122. (a)

Mitchell, H. The black experience in higher education. *The Counseling Psychologist*, 1971, *2* (1), 30-36. (b)

Pedersen, P.B. The field of intercultural counseling. In P. Pedersen, W.J. Lonner, & J.G. Draguns (Eds.) *Counseling across cultures*.

Pedersen, P.B. The triad model of cross-cultural counselor training. *Personnel and Guidance Journal*, 1977, *56*, 94-100.

Pine, G.J. Counseling minority groups: A review of the literature. *Counseling and Values*, 1972, *17*, 35-44.

Russell, R.D. Black perception of guidance. *Personnel and Guidance Journal*, 1970, *48*, 721-728.

Sattler, J.M. Racial Experimenter Effects in experimentation, testing, interviewing and psychotherapy. *Psychological Bulletin*, 1970, *73*, 137-160.

Sue, D.W. Ethnic identity: The impact of two cultures on the psychological development of Asians in America. In D.W. Sue & Wagner (Eds.) *Asian Americans: Psychological perspectives*. Ben Lomand, California: Science and Behavior Books, Inc., 1973, 140-149.

Sue, D.W., & Sue, S. Counseling Chinese-Americans. *Personnel and Guidance Journal*, 1972, *50*, 637-644. (a)

Sue, D.W., & Sue, S. Ethnic minorities: Resistance to being researched. *Professional Psychology*, 1972, *3*, 11-17. (b)

Vontress, C.E. Racial differences: Impediments to rapport. *Journal of Counseling Psychology*, 1971, *18* (1), 7-13.

Vontress, C.E. Counseling: Racial and ethnic factors. *Focus on Guidance*, 1973, *5*, 1-10.

Vontress, C.E. Barriers in cross-cultural counseling. *Counseling and Value*, 1974, *18* (3), 160-165.

Vontress, C.E. Racial and ethnic barriers in counseling. In P.B. Pedersen, W.J. Lonner, & J.G. Draguns (Eds.) *Counseling across cultures*. Honolulu: The University of Hawaii Press, 1976.

Waltz, G.R., & Benjamin, L. *On becoming a change agent*. Ann Arbor: Eric Counseling and Personnel Services Information Center, 1977.

Ward, E.J. A gift from the ghetto. *Personnel and Guidance Journal*, 1970, *48*, 753-756.

Weinrach, S. Integration is more than just busing. *The School Counselor*, 1973, *20*, 276-279.

Williams, R.L., & Kirkland, J. The white counselor and the black client. *The Counseling Psychologist*, 1971, *2*, 114-116.

Wilson, W., & Calhoun, J.F. Behavior therapy and the minority client. *Psychotherapy: Theory, Research and Practice*, 1974, *11* (4), 317-325.

Woods, E. Counseling minority students: A program model. *Personnel and Guidance Journal*, 1977, *55*, 416-418.

Author Index

Subject Index

abrazos, 173
afecto, 161, 166
Alien Land Law of 1913, 71
alloplastic, 12, 199
alternatives to the traditional counseling role, 201–206
Amendments to the Constitution (13th, 14th, & 15th), 109
American Indian Historical Society, 44
anticounselor, 208
autoplastic, 12

barriers to cross-cultural counseling, 14–20
benefits to cross-cultural counseling, 21, 22
Black American typologies, 192
Black identity transformation, 192, 193
Brown Vs Board of Education, 110
Bureau of Indian Affairs (BIA), 31

Chinese Exclusion Act of 1882, 71
class bound values, 15, 16
Coalition of American Indian Citizens, 44
color or culture blindness, 18
compadrazo, 162, 166, 173
Conformity Stage, 194, 199
counselor-client coalition, 208
countertransference, 18, 19, 22
cross-cultural counseling, 7
cultural bound values, 14, 16–18
culturally deprived, 5, 17
culturally disadvantaged, 5
culturally distinct, 6
culture, 3, 5, 14, 16, 147
culture conflict, 86–89, 96, 100, 103
curanderos, 177, 205

dignidad, 161, 166
Dissonance Stage, 195, 198, 199

emic-etic dichotomy, 13
ethnicity, 4, 23
extra psychic, 147, 175, 177, 179, 181, 184

fatalismo, 161, 166
Federal Chinese Exclusion Act, 86
First World, 7

Gentleman's Agreement of 1907, 71

hijo de crianza, 165
humanismo, 161, 166

Indian Reorganization Act, 40, 43
inter-minority group counseling, 20, 21
intra-minority group counseling, 20
intrapsychic model, 12, 23, 175, 177, 179, 181, 184
Introspection Stage, 196, 197, 198, 199

Japanese-American Citizens' League, 92
Jones Act of 1917, 160

La Raza, 180
League of Nations, 44

machismo, 160, 166
marginal man, 87, 103
mestizo, 171
minority, 6
minority group/cross-cultural counseling, 3, 7
model minority, 67, 69–80, 86, 95
mulatto, 172

National Association for the Advancement of Colored People, 110
National Congress of American Indians, 44, 46, 48
National Youth Council, 44
Nisei Japanese Americans, 71

Pan American Indians, 44
personalismo, 173, 183

race, 3, 4
resistance, 19